KNITTING LACE

The 19th-century knitted-lace sampler above, upon which this book is based, is part of the collection of The Brooklyn Museum (accession number 74.12.1; gift of Mr. Joseph McCrindle). Worked in a natural color, 3-ply cotton thread, this sampler is 15 ft. (457cm) long and contains 91 patterns. It averages 3½ in. (9cm) wide, with 45 to 50 stitches in each pattern, including selvedges.

KNITTING LACE

A Workshop with Patterns and Projects

SUSANNA E. LEWIS

Based on a sampler from The Brooklyn Museum

Taunton
BOOKS & VIDEOS

for fellow enthusiasts

First printing: July 1992
Second printing: February 1996
Printed in the United States of America

A THREADS Book

THREADS® is a trademark of The Taunton Press, Inc., registered
in the U.S. Patent and Trademark Office.

The Taunton Press, 63 South Main Street, Box 5506, Newtown,
CT 06470-5506

Library of Congress Cataloging-in-Publication Data

Lewis, Susanna E.
        Knitting lace : a workshop with patterns and projects / Susanna E.
Lewis ; based on a sampler from the Brooklyn Museum.
            p.   cm.
        "A Threads book."
        Includes bibliographical references and index.
        ISBN 0-942391-52-7
        1. Knitted lace–Patterns. I. Brooklyn Museum. II. Title.
TT805.K54L48   1992   92-7457
746.2'26041–dc20   CIP

To Ann Coleman, with grateful thanks for giving me the opportunity to learn about lace knitting from this sampler and to share it with others through this book.

The royalties earned from the sale of this book are being put into a special fund at The Brooklyn Museum toward the purchase of future acquisitions for the Collection of Costumes and Textiles.

CONTENTS

FOREWORD

Museum collections can serve many purposes at the same time. Although the first and foremost reason for a work to be in an art museum is its aesthetic quality and artistic importance, an object can serve as a document of an artist's method and also as a teaching tool. These documents provide not only an insight into the thinking of an artist in the past, but also an inspiration for artists and craftspeople in the present. Such is the case with the knitted-lace sampler that is the subject of this book.

The Brooklyn Museum has a long tradition of providing a link between collections and designers of costumes and textiles. During World War I, when American designers were denied access to European sources, The Brooklyn Museum, under the guidance of Stewart Culin, the Museum's first Curator of Ethnology, and Morris D. C. Crawford of Fairchild Publications, made its textile collections available to the design world. The relationship between the Museum and the design world became a formal one in 1948 with the establishment of the Edward C. Blum Design Laboratory, which operated at the Museum until 1972. Since that time, the curatorial departments at The Brooklyn Museum have continued to work closely with scholars and designers to make the Museum's superb collections available for inspiration to a broad audience.

This book, which focuses on a single fascinating object from The Brooklyn Museum's collection and makes its lessons available to the public, is evidence of just how much can be gleaned from the works of art preserved here.

—Robert T. Buck
Director, The Brooklyn Museum

PREFACE

Understanding something that may seem almost too ordinary is the challenge offered by many a knitted object. Usually we know what the piece is intended for but lack any concept of how it might have been developed. Today, many people unfamiliar with knitting techniques generalize that no fewer than two sticks (needles or pins) are manually or mechanically employed to catch and loop a continuous thread. The process sounds easy; it appears that the product will be basic, if not boring. But if skill, imagination and dexterity are melded with the tools, then the product is one of wonder for its remarkable diversity. The knitter has within his or her control the ability to create simultaneously not only fantastically patterned fabric but also a garment. In most other garment-making processes, the fabric must be created first, then separately manipulated into a garment.

The complexities of knitting extend even to its history and development. Most authorities agree on a number of basic points: That the origin of knitting techniques is obscure; that its evolution may be convoluted (which came first, the knitting frame or pins?); that ancient civilizations around the Mediterranean practiced the skill; that high degrees of professionalism were exhibited by the members (usually male) of British and Continental knitting guilds; that both men and women in outlying regions produced knitted goods of characteristic form and design, as in Fair Isle and Shetland products; and that too many terms —*tricot, jersey, stockinette, knit* —describe indistinguishably made products.

Whatever their stitch name, hand-knitting techniques have been much curtailed in this country in the last 90 years compared to prior times and other countries. Our stitch vocabulary is nowadays limited, and the call for fashionable hand-knitted garments tends to be confined to sweaters, men's socks, mufflers, baby garments, a smattering of headwear, wraps, gloves or mittens, and women's dress outfits. Machine-knitted pieces incorporate all the above plus undergarments and hosiery. By contrast, in the 18th and 19th centuries there were sleeves, collars, purses, handbags, day and night caps, slippers and stockings; for men, shawls, breeches and pantaloons; for children, dresses, jackets and coats; and for all, leggings and elbow, knee and chest warmers. Examples of historic knitting also encompass bed and table covers, doilies, rugs and decorative borders. The latter, usually of knitted lace, embellish handkerchiefs, nightgowns, lingerie, household linens and many of the previously mentioned artifacts.

By the second half of the 19th century, those literate and interested in knitting could find printed instructions in specialized needlework publications or in monthly journals like *Godey's Ladies Magazine* and *Harper's Bazaar.* But because the instructions were often plagiarized from one publication to another and/or were freshly translated from an original German-language source, they were not always accurate. As an ongoing form of reference, just as in the heyday of the guilds when the majority could not read, motifs continued to be documented within the structure of a sampler offering visual rather than written instructions.

The intention of this book, which is based on a 19th-century sampler of knitted designs, is not only to provide a multitude of patterns for knitting lace, but also to tease the adventuresome designer and needleworker into applying the motifs to other techniques. Imagination need be the only restraint. To stir thinking, a variety of proposals are put forth by well-known designer and fiber artist, writer, teacher and knitter, Susanna E. Lewis. This book is a reflection of her skill and knowledge, and of her desire to share with and inspire others. A dedicated volunteer who has worked with laces and knitted artifacts at The Brooklyn Museum, she has reaffirmed that elements from the past can be as creatively stimulating now as then. Her translation of the sampler has extended the boundaries of its original purpose. We hope that by sharing the sampler, many creative moments emerge as ideas grow, drawn from a structure built of these 91 patterns and then some.

—*Elizabeth Ann Coleman*
Curator of Costumes and Textiles,
The Brooklyn Museum, 1969-1990

INTRODUCTION

Lace—that wonderful fabric made with light, air and space. Soft, floating shawls, delicate trims and borders, wedding veils—all have a touch of the fantastic. *Punto in aria* (points in the air), the name given to an early Venetian lace, beautifully describes all laces, for the chief element of lace *is* space. The space is framed by threads, which give it shape; the threads in turn create their own shapes to complement the spaces.

The forerunners of all laces are embroidery, netmaking and weaving, all of which have been practiced since ancient times. During the late Middle Ages, these techniques developed into the needle and bobbin laces, which are the oldest and most highly diversified in style of all laces. They reached a peak of popularity in the courts of Europe during the 17th and 18th centuries, creating a demand for fabrics of technical perfection and artistic beauty that only a privileged few could afford. The hundreds of lace makers all over Europe who created these gossamer fabrics were never permitted to wear or own them.

According to legend, lace knitting had its own first spurt of popularity in the courts of Europe. A popular story is that of a Mrs. Montague's gift to Queen Elizabeth around 1565 of silk stockings patterned with eyelet diamonds. How much of the story is true is open to speculation; but during this period the knitting of caps, hosiery and gloves was a thriving industry that used wool for the commoner and silk for the nobility. It's not unlikely that during this period the desire for the luxury of knitted silk patterned with openwork might have manifested itself in the outfitting of one's legs.

The frame-knitting industry, which was well developed by the end of the 18th century, is largely responsible for making cotton and silk hosiery, in patterns and lace, available to a wider range of economic classes of people. Lace knitted by hand appeared in folk costume—in stockings, trimmings for aprons and petticoats, elaborate caps and young children's dresses. Local areas often developed their own highly stylized patterns, which were given local names. As the popularity of lace knitting spread, so did the patterns, but frequently with a variation and a change in name from one locale to another. Patterns were rarely published or even written down, particularly in remote communities, because illiteracy

was widespread and paper was scarce and expensive. Instead, knitters customarily made samplers to record patterns. A knitter could later choose a design from a sampler to pattern a knitted garment or to decorate another article.

The sampler

The knitted lace sampler in this book was probably made in southern Germany or Austria sometime in the early to the mid-19th century. The exact location and date of its origin are unknown. Of the sampler's 91 patterns, 83 can be classified as lace; the remaining eight are more or less solid, textured patterns.

Many of the patterns are what we would call traditional or are variants of well-known patterns. Very similar patterns can be found in the 19th-century samplers and knitted articles of many regions across Europe. Several patterns are close to ones nowadays termed "Shetland" (from Scotland's Shetland Islands), even though, as this sampler shows, the knitters of both Unst and Bavaria can claim the same patterns as part of their respective traditions. Intricate figurative designs, either those that were the work of professional knitters in earlier centuries or those worked by the gentlewomen of the Victorian era, are not included in this sampler. What this sampler contains are the kinds of patterns used by the average family in the early to mid-1800s, patterns handed down from one generation to the next that became ingrained in the traditions and lore of the local area.

It isn't hard to find pictures of knitted-lace samplers. For example, *Mary Thomas's Book of Knitting Patterns* (see the Bibliography on p. 205) has photographs of eight samplers containing lace stitches. Many museum collections in the United States have at least one knitted sampler, and most of them are truly works of art. A typical sampler in a museum collection would be knitted of fine cotton thread on wire needles, with the pattern blocks closely related in size, the selvedges straight and even, and the whole strip surrounded by a beautiful edging—in short, it would likely be almost perfect in execution.

In contrast, the sampler in this book, although beautiful and delicate, isn't perfect. It has broken threads, brown spots from age and crooked selvedges from patterns that bias and skew the strip. There are little mistakes everywhere, loose rows and loose stitches, and some sections are only partially patterned. And the sampler has no beautiful edging around its perimeter.

But I don't think this sampler was meant to be a show piece. I think it was meant for recording what the knitter had learned. It's heartwarming to see by the progression of the patterns how this knitter learned about the principles of lace knitting and how a series of patterns evolved from the simple to the complex. Once in a while there is a very complicated pattern, probably copied from a picture or a fashion garment, followed by a series of simpler ones based on the same principles. I think the knitter was really trying to understand the structure of lace, and in so doing, has taught me much about it. The beauty of this sampler lies not so much in how it looks, but in what it can teach to those who study it.

The sampler averages 3½ in. (9cm) in width, with about 45 to 50 stitches, including selvedges, in each of its 91 patterns. That's a gauge of approximately 13 or 14 stitches per inch (51 to 58 stitches per 10cm). At 15 ft. (457cm) in length, it is one of the longest samplers I have ever seen, yet it is unfinished. The needles holding the stitches after Pattern 91 are steel wire, 1.25mm in diameter (American size 0000, English size 16). The thread used is a 3-ply, natural-color cotton, approximately size 50 or 60. All the lace patterns are knitted in stockinette stitch, with the knit side as the right side. The patterns are separated from each other by six rows of reverse stockinette stitch. The selvedges have the first stitch slipped every row throughout the entire length. At the beginning of the sampler is a decorative little hem. Instructions for it are given on p. 105.

When I worked as a volunteer in the Department of Costumes and Textiles at The Brooklyn Museum in Brooklyn, New York, one of the projects I undertook was the documentation of this sampler. My job was to figure out how all the patterns were made. I started the project with great confidence, as I was a skilled hand knitter and had been knitting lace for many years, following complicated patterns in books both old and new. But I soon discovered how little I really knew about the principles of lace knitting and about the structure of lace. I had been knitting lace, but I didn't know much *about* lace! My scribbled pad of graph paper, heap of tangled knitting and feelings of abject frustration told the story. So I started again, this time with the simplest pattern of all, Pattern 1.

I charted that one successfully, then started up the ladder of complexity. I worked most of the time from front-view and back-view photographs and with a magnifying glass. I learned as I went, drawing eyelets and decreases on my grid where I thought they should go, then knitting a few rows to see if it looked right. When it didn't, I had to figure out why, and gradually I learned about the peculiar unbalanced nature of knitted loops, how layering them upon each other with an eyelet to one side produces tension and creates bias, why some eyelets are separated by one thread and some with two, and on and on. The fruits of my investigations are what this book is about.

The book

The elements and techniques of lace knitting are simple, but their combinations and resulting effects are complex. For a growing number of knitters, the fascination of creating a complex effect from such simple elements is compelling. The desire to learn about lace knitting goes beyond fashion and into the realm of art and architecture, for designing or building a knitted lace pattern requires an understanding of the system of factors that develop and balance the pattern. You have to know the possibilities as well as the limitations inherent in this system, how to work with them and around them, and how to work the new design into the whole of the finished product. It's a wonderful challenge to fit together the elements of the design — to decide which stitches should bias and which should be straight, where the lines of eyelets and decreases will be, how prominent or how hidden they should be, and so on. How wonderful to be able to take charge of the building of this interlocking looped structure so that it becomes a new whole of grace and beauty! This book and the 19th-century sampler it explores are intended to help you understand the craft, as well as the art, of knitted lace.

To help you use the sampler to its fullest as a resource, this book is divided into two parts. Part I presents the sampler's 91 patterns, pictured and accompanied by knitting instructions. The instructions are given in both charted and written form. You can work from the chart or the written instructions or both.

Part II is a lace-knitting workshop that explores how to go beyond the sampler and incorporate its patterns and teachings in your own knitting. Chapter 1 of Part II considers what distinguishes lace knitting from other forms of knitting and gives general advice on knitting lace. Chapter 2 explores the sampler patterns in depth to clarify how knitted lace is designed and structured. This chapter identifies the patterning elements used throughout the sampler and explains their structures so that you can recombine the elements in your own way. Sprinkled throughout this chapter are swatches knitted in a variety of yarns that use a few of the patterns or combinations of patterns. These will help you visualize the possibilities for some of the patterns, and they also show the effects of using different types of yarn with lace patterns.

Chapter 3 contains exercises that take you through the creation of a pattern from scratch, the translation of a pattern from written to charted form and the documentation of a pattern from an actual piece of knitting or a photograph. Chapter 4 contains four garment projects that you can knit, which are examples of how to incorporate lace patterns in your own designs.

A reference section at the back of the book explains the abbreviations used in the written instructions and gives complete instructions, for hand knitters and for machine knitters using hand-transfer methods, for all the stitches used in the patterns. This section also explains how to use the charts to knit the patterns by hand and by machine. Finally, you'll find a Bibliography, a classification of the patterns by type and motif, and an index of techniques.

You can see the sampler in its entirety on p. ii, p. 2 (the front, or knit, side) and p. 3 (the back, or purl, side). The numbers alongside the sampler correspond to the pattern's position in the sampler; the patterns are referred to by number throughout the book.

The charts

Part of the goal of this book is to encourage and help knitters learn how to use gridded charts for patterned knitting. Until recently in the United States, instructions for knitted lace patterns have usually been written out rather than charted. This stems in no small measure from the publications and traditions we import from Great Britain, where patterns are nearly always written out. In other European countries where lace knitting is popular, principally Germany and other German-speaking countries, lace patterns are normally charted, as they have been for generations.

It is my belief that only the most determined knitters are willing to wade through lines of text (with their inevitable errors) to learn about and knit lace, and that many knitters in this country are unaware of the advantages of charting patterns in general and lace patterns in particular. One of the principal advantages of charts for lace knitting is their visual impact—you can get a very good idea what a pattern will look like and how it's constructed before knitting it, as you can see if you look through the photos of the sampler patterns and their accompanying charts in Part I. Also, while you're knitting, you can quickly read the charted pattern and remember groups of stitches, even groups of rows, making the knitting proceed much more smoothly than it might if you used only the written instructions. In the case of complex patterns, charts let you readily see the individual yarn overs and decreases within the larger context of the complete pattern repeat.

Furthermore, modifying a design or creating a totally new one is quite easy when you use gridded charts. You can fit together parts and pieces of diverse patterns to create new ones simply by lifting them out on tracing paper and refitting them on a new grid, like pieces in a puzzle. Chapter 3 explains how to do this.

In addition to the freedom gained by working from charts, you can also tap into foreign-language publications and gain access to a wealth of charted patterns. As long as you can figure out how to interpret the gridded symbols, which generally isn't difficult because most symbols are pictographs of the action or stitches they represent, you can take advantage of a great range of design styles. I have books and magazines from Germany, Austria and Switzerland dating from the end of the last century that contain charts I can follow and interpret without knowing a word of German. Nowadays, knitting and crochet patterns in Japanese books and magazines are presented entirely in charted form, and the garment shapes are diagrammed. I find that the patterns are not difficult to follow, despite my inability to read the accompanying notes.

Most knitters who have used charts for lace knitting know that there is no standardized method for making charts, nor is there a standardized list of symbols. The system of symbols and notation that I've used in this book is one that is rapidly gaining popularity in the United States and other English-speaking countries. Among others, two American knitting magazines — *Vogue Knitting* and *Knitter's* — have been using this system exclusively for some time. It is derived from the Japanese Symbolcraft system of notation used in the machine-knitting and hand-knitting publications of Nihon Vogue, Ondori and others that reach these shores. The pictographic symbols accurately copy the look of the knitting action or of the stitches produced by that action. Thus it is easy to visualize the appearance of the whole pattern in grid form, and to remember the action that the symbol stands for. All the patterns in this book are given in charted form using the Symbolcraft notation, and most have accompanying written instructions.

Although I advocate using charts for patterned knitting of all types, I also advocate the availability of written instructions for nonpatterned knitting of a complex structure. There are a few patterns in the sampler that fall into this category. For example, it's difficult to make Pattern 79 (a fisherman's rib) look sensible on a chart without using special symbols.

In the reference section you'll find a complete explanation of how to read the charts. Pages 193-198 explain how to interpret the symbols and work the stitches if you're knitting the patterns by hand; and pp. 202-205 explain how to work the stitches on the machine using hand-transfer methods.

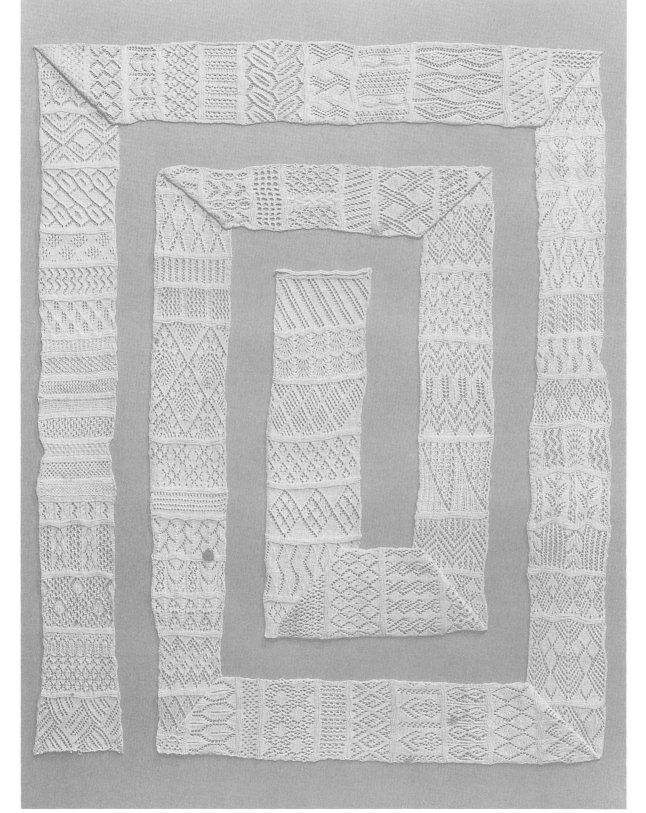

PART I

THE
SAMPLER
PATTERNS

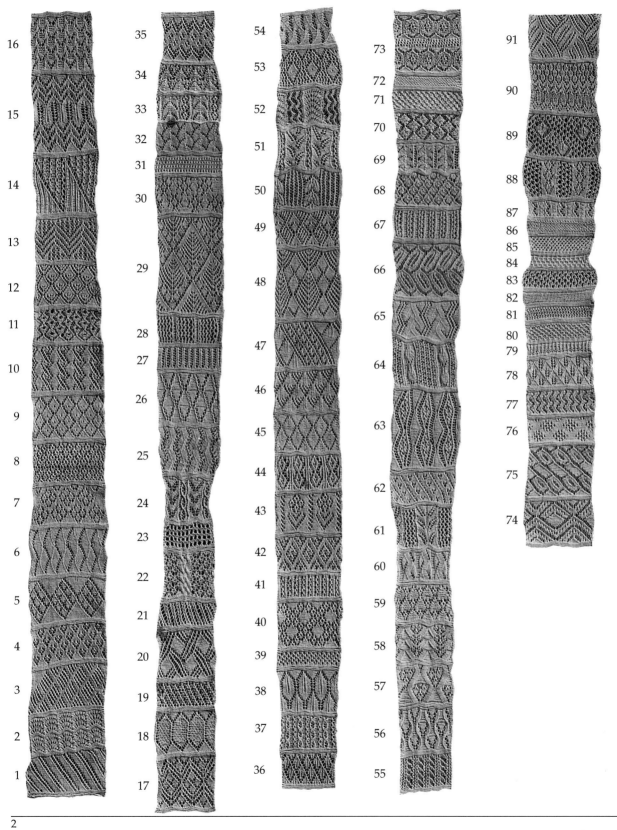

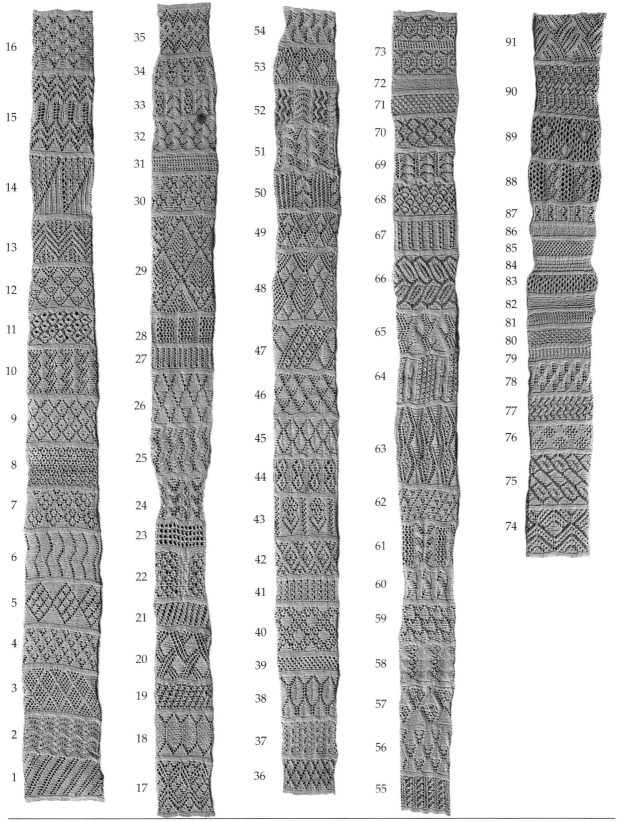

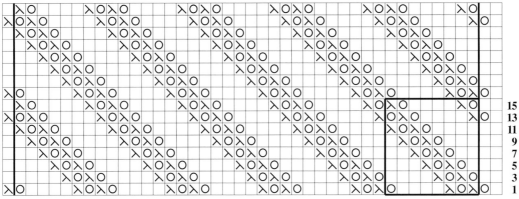

Repeat: 8 sts, 16 Rs.
Add 3 edge sts: 1 at L, 2 at Rt.
Even Rs: P all sts.

Multiple of 8 sts, plus 3.
Even Rs 2-16 (wrong side): P all sts.

Row 1: k1, yo, *ssk, yo, ssk, k4, yo*, ssk. **Row 3:** k2, *{yo, ssk} 2 times, k4*, k1. **Row 5:** k2, *k1, {yo, ssk} 2 times, k3*, k1. **Row 7:** k2, *k2, {yo, ssk} 2 times, k2*, k1. **Row 9:** k2, *k3, {yo, ssk} 2 times, k1*, k1. **Row 11:** k2, *k4, {yo, ssk} 2 times*, k1. **Row 13:** k1, yo, *ssk, k4, yo, ssk, yo*, ssk. **Row 15:** k2, *yo, ssk, k4, yo, ssk*, k1.
Rep Rs 1-16.

In the reference section at the back of the book, you'll find a complete explanation of how to read the charts. Pages 193-198 explain how to interpret the symbols and work the stitches if you're knitting the patterns by hand; pp. 199-205 explain how to work the stitches on the machine using hand-transfer methods; and p. 190 explains all the written knitting abbreviations.

Note: An alternative double decrease to that shown in the sampler is shown in rows 10 and 12 on the chart and can be used on all even-numbered rows.

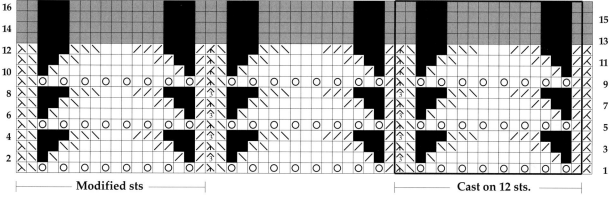

— Modified sts —   Cast on 12 sts. —

Repeat: 12 sts, 16 Rs.
Add 1 edge st at Rt.
Modified sts at L: Rs 1-12.

Multiple of 12 sts, plus 1.
Rs 1, 5, 9 have multiple of 18 sts, plus 1.
Rs 2, 6, 10 have multiple of 16 sts, plus 1.
Rs 3, 7, 11 have multiple of 14 sts, plus 1.
⋉ = P 1 st, sl 1 st kwise, return both sts to L ndl. Psso, return st to Rt ndl.

Row 1: k2tog, *{k1, yo} 8 times, k1, sl 1-k2tog-psso*, end last rep ssk.
Row 2: ⋉, *p15, p3tog*, end last rep p2tog. **Row 3:** k2tog, *k13, sl 1-k2tog-psso*, end last rep ssk. **Row 4:** ⋉, *p11, p3tog*, end last rep p2tog.

Rows 5-8: Rep Rs 1-4. **Rows 9-12:** Rep Rs 1-4. **Row 13:** Purl. **Row 14:** Knit.
Row 15: Purl. **Row 16:** Knit.
Rep Rs 1-16 for an allover pattern.

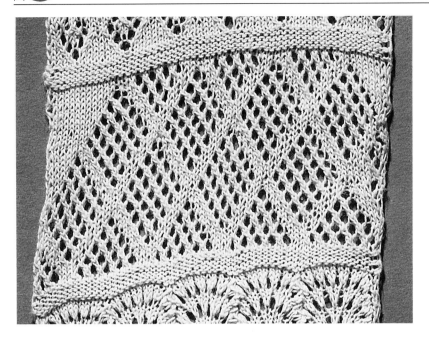

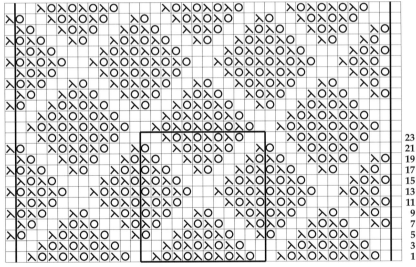

Repeat: 12 sts, 24 Rs.
Add 2 edge sts: 1 each side.
Modified sts at Rt: Rs 5, 9, 13, 17, 21.
Even Rs: P all sts.

├──── **Modified sts** ────┤

Multiple of 12 sts, plus 2.
Even Rs 2-24 (wrong side): P all sts.

Row 1: k1, *k1, {yo, ssk} 5 times, k1*,

k1. **Row 3:** k1, *k2, {yo, ssk} 4 times, k2*, k1. **Row 5:** k4, {yo, ssk} 3 times, k2, yo, *ssk, k2, {yo, ssk} 3 times, k2, yo*, ssk. **Row 7:** k1, *yo, ssk, k2, {yo, ssk} 2 times, k2, yo, ssk*, k1.
Row 9: {k2, yo, ssk} 3 times, yo, *ssk, {yo, ssk, k2} 2 times, yo, ssk, yo*, ssk.
Row 11: k1, *{yo, ssk} 2 times, k4, {yo,

ssk} 2 times*, k1. **Row 13:** k2, {yo, ssk} 2 times, k2, {yo, ssk} 2 times, yo, *{ssk, yo} 2 times, ssk, k2 {yo, ssk} 2 times, yo*, ssk. **Row 15:** Rep R 11. **Row 17:** Rep R 9. **Row 19:** Rep R 7. **Row 21:** Rep R 5.
Row 23: Rep R 3.
Rep Rs 1-24.

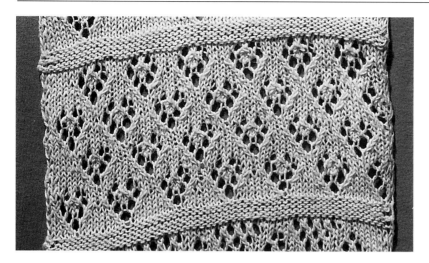

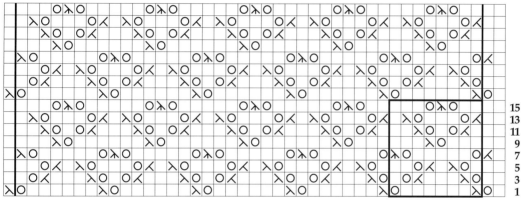

15
13
11
9
7
5
3
1

├─ **Modified st** ─┤

Repeat: 8 sts, 16 Rs.
Add 3 edge sts: 1 at L, 2 at Rt.
Modified st at L: R 7.
Even Rs: P all sts.

Multiple of 8 sts, plus 3.
Even Rs 2-16 (wrong side): P all sts.

Row 1: k1, yo, *ssk, k6, yo*, ssk.
Row 3: k2, *yo, ssk, k3, k2tog, yo, k1*, k1. **Row 5:** k2, *k1, yo, ssk, k1, k2tog, yo, k2*, k1. **Row 7:** k1, k2tog, *yo, k5, yo, sl 1-k2tog-psso*, end last rep ssk, k1. **Row 9:** k2, *k3, yo, ssk, k3*, k1. **Row 11:** k2, *k1, k2tog, yo, k1, yo, ssk, k2*, k1. **Row 13:** k2, *k2tog, yo, k3, yo, ssk, k1*, k1. **Row 15:** k2, *k2, yo, sl 1-k2tog-psso, yo, k3*, k1.
Rep Rs 1-16.

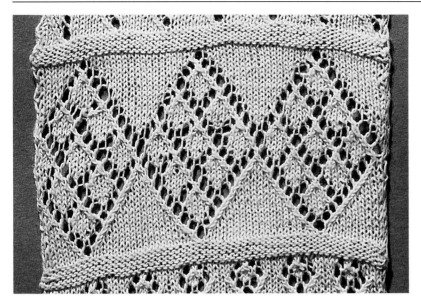

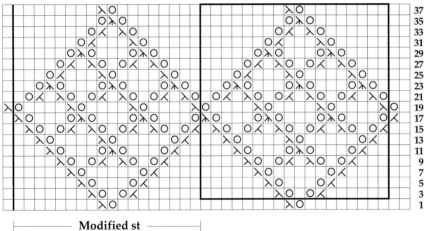

├─────────── **Modified st** ───────────┤

Repeat: 18 sts, 38 Rs.
Add 3 edge sts: 1 at L, 2 at Rt.
Modified st at L: R 17.
Even Rs: P all sts.

Multiple of 18 sts, plus 3.
Even Rs 2-38 (wrong side): P all sts.

Row 1: k2, *k8, yo, ssk, k8*, k1.
Row 3: k2, *k6, k2tog, yo, k1, yo, ssk, k7*, k1. **Row 5:** k2, *k5, k2tog, yo, k3, yo, ssk, k6*, k1. **Row 7:** k2, *k4, k2tog, yo, k5, yo, ssk, k5*, k1. **Row 9:** k2, *k3, {k2tog, yo, k1, yo, ssk, k1} 2 times, k3*, k1. **Row 11:** k2, *k2, k2tog, yo, k3, yo, sl 1-k2tog-psso, yo, k3, yo, ssk, k3*, k1. **Row 13:** k2, *k1, k2tog, yo, k5, yo, ssk, k4, yo, ssk, k2*, k1. **Row 15:** k2, *{k2tog, yo, k1, yo, ssk, k1} 3 times*, k1. **Row 17:** k1, k2tog, *yo, k3, {yo, sl 1-k2tog-psso, yo, k3} 2 times, yo, sl 1-k2tog-psso, end last rep ssk*, k1. **Row 19:** k1, yo, *ssk, k4, {yo, ssk, k4} 2 times, yo*, ssk. **Row 21:** k2, *{yo, ssk, k1, k2tog, yo, k1} 3 times*, k1.

{k2tog, yo, k1, yo, ssk, k1} 2 times, k3*, k1. **Row 23:** k2, *{k1, yo, sl 1-k2tog-psso, yo, k2} 3 times*, k1. **Row 25:** k2, *{k2, yo, ssk, k2} 2 times, k1, k2tog, yo, k3*, k1. **Row 27:** k2, *k3, {yo, ssk, k1, k2tog, yo, k1} 2 times, k3}, k1. **Row 29:** k2, *k4, {yo, sl 1-k2tog-psso, yo, k3} 2 times, k2*, k1. **Row 31:** k2, *k5, yo, ssk, k3, k2tog, yo, k6*, k1. **Row 33:** k2, *k6, yo, ssk, k1, k2tog, yo, k7*, k1. **Row 35:** k2, *k7, yo, sl 1-k2tog-psso, yo, k8*, k1. **Row 37:** Rep R 1.
Rep Rs 3-38 for an allover pattern.

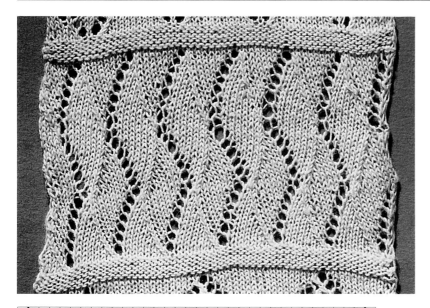

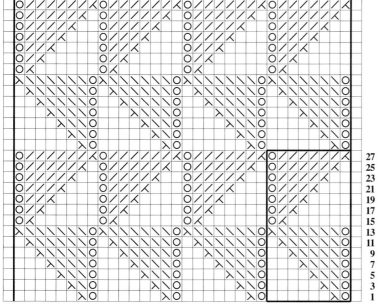

																		27
																		25
																		23
																		21
																		19
																		17
																		15
																		13
																		11
																		9
																		7
																		5
																		3
																		1

Repeat: 8 sts, 28 Rs.
Add 2 edge sts: 1 each side.
Even Rs: P all sts.

Multiple of 8 sts, plus 2.
Even Rs 2-28 (wrong side): P all sts.

Row 1: k1, *yo, ssk, k6*, k1. **Row 3:** k1, *yo, k1, ssk, k5*, k1. **Row 5:** k1, *yo, k2, ssk, k4*, k1. **Row 7:** k1, *yo, k3, ssk, k3*, k1. **Row 9:** k1, *yo, k4, ssk, k2*, k1. **Row 11:** k1, *yo, k5, ssk, k1*, k1. **Row 13:** k1, *yo, k6, ssk*, k1. **Row 15:** k1, *k6, k2tog, yo*, k1. **Row 17:** k1, *k5, k2tog, k1, yo*, k1.

Row 19: k1, *k4, k2tog, k2, yo*, k1.
Row 21: k1, *k3, k2tog, k3, yo*, k1.
Row 23: k1, *k2, k2tog, k4, yo*, k1.
Row 25: k1, *k1, k2tog, k5, yo*, k1.
Row 27: k1, *k2tog, k6, yo*, k1.
Rep Rs 1-28.

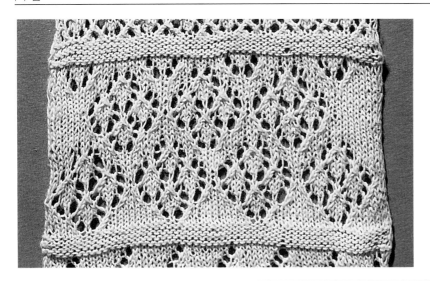

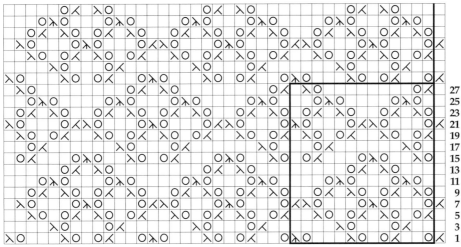

├──── **Modified sts** ────┤

Repeat: 13 sts, 28 Rs.
Add 1 edge st at Rt.
Modified sts at L: Rs 1, 7, 21.
Even Rs: P all sts.

Multiple of 13 sts, plus 1.
Even Rs 2-28 (wrong side): P all sts.

Row 1: k2tog, *yo, k2, k2tog, yo, k1, yo, ssk, k3, yo, sl 1-k2tog-psso*, end last rep ssk. **Row 3:** k1, *k2, k2tog, yo, k3, yo, ssk, k4*. **Row 5:** k1, *{k2tog, yo, k1, yo, ssk, k1} 2 times, k1*.
Row 7: k2tog, *yo, k3, yo, sl 1-k2tog-psso, yo, k3, yo, ssk, k2tog*, end last rep k1. **Row 9:** k1, *{yo, ssk, k1, k2tog, yo, k1} 2 times, k1*. **Row 11:** k1, *{k1, yo, sl 1-k2tog-psso, yo, k2} 2 times, k1*. **Row 13:** k1, *k3, yo, ssk, k1, k2tog, yo, k5*. **Row 15:** k1, *yo, ssk, k2, yo, sl 1-k2tog-psso, yo, k3, k2tog, yo, k1*. **Row 17:** k1, *k1, yo, ssk, k6, k2tog, yo, k2*. **Row 19:** k1, *k2tog, yo,

k1, yo, ssk, k2, k2tog, yo, k1, yo, ssk, k1*. **Row 21:** k2tog, *yo, k3, yo, ssk, k2tog, yo, k3, yo, sl 1-k2tog-psso*, end last rep ssk. **Row 23:** k1, *yo, ssk, k1, k2tog, yo, k2, yo, ssk, k1, k2tog, yo, k1*. **Row 25:** k1, *k1, yo, sl 1-k2tog-psso, yo, k4, yo, sl 1-k2tog-psso, yo, k2*. **Row 27:** k1, *k2tog, yo, k8, yo, ssk, k1*.
Rep Rs 1-28.

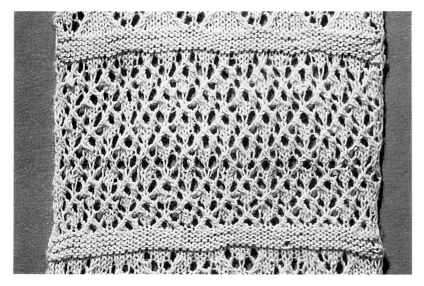

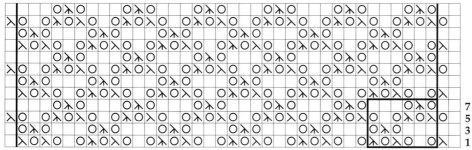

⊢Modified st ⊣

Repeat: 6 sts, 8 Rs.
Add 3 edge sts: 1 at L, 2 at Rt.
Modified st at L: R 1.
Even Rs: P all sts.

Multiple of 6 sts, plus 3.
Even Rs 2-8 (wrong side): P all sts.

Row 1: k1, ssk, *yo, k1, yo, ssk, yo,
s1-k2tog-psso*, end last rep ssk, k1.
Row 3: k2, *k3, yo, sl 1-k2tog-psso,
yo*, k1. **Row 5:** k1, yo, *ssk, yo,
sl 1-k2tog-psso, yo, k1, yo*, ssk.
Row 7: k2, *yo, sl 1-k2tog-psso, yo,
k3*, k1.
Rep Rs 1-8.

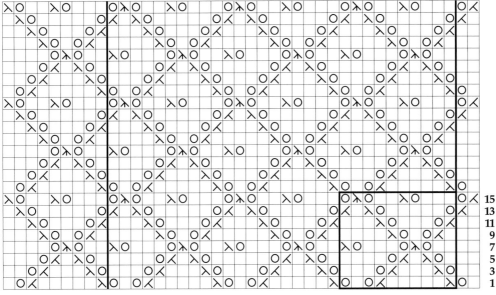

Repeat: 10 sts, 16 Rs.
Add 11 edge sts: 9 at L, 2 at Rt.
Even Rs: P all sts.

Multiple of 10 sts, plus 1.
Even Rs 2-16 (wrong side): P all sts.

Row 1: k1, yo, *ssk, k5, k2tog, yo, k1, yo*, ssk, k5, k2tog, yo, k1. **Row 3:** k2, *yo, ssk, k3, k2tog, yo, k3*, end last rep k2. **Row 5:** k2, *k1, yo, ssk, k1, k2tog, yo, k4*, end last rep k3. **Row 7:** k2, *k2, yo, sl 1-k2tog-psso, yo, k3, yo, ssk*, end last rep k4. **Row 9:** k2, *k1, k2tog, yo, k1, yo, ssk, k4*, end last rep k3. **Row 11:** k2, *k2tog, yo, k3, yo, ssk, k3*, end last rep k2. **Row 13:** k1, k2tog, *yo, k5, yo, ssk, k1, k2tog*, yo, k5, yo, ssk, k1. **Row 15:** k2tog, yo, *k3, yo, ssk, k2, yo, sl 1-k2tog-psso, yo*, end last rep ssk.
Rep Rs 1-16.

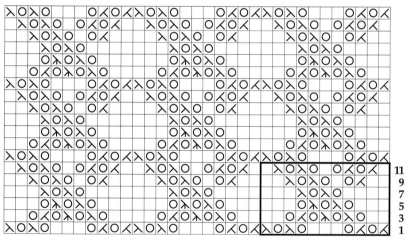

Repeat: 11 sts, 12 Rs.
Even Rs: P all sts.

Multiple of 11 sts.
Even Rs 2-12 (wrong side): P all sts.

Row 1: *{k2tog, yo} 2 times, k3, {yo, ssk} 2 times*. **Row 3:** *k2, yo, ssk, yo, sl 1-k2tog-psso, yo, k2tog, yo, k2*. **Row 5:** *k3, yo, ssk, yo, sl 1-k2tog-psso, yo, k3*. **Row 7:** *k4, {yo, ssk} 2 times, k3*. **Row 9:** *k2, k2tog, yo, k1, {yo, ssk} 2 times, k2*. **Row 11:** *k1, {k2tog, yo} 2 times, k1, {yo, ssk) 2 times, k1*.
Rep Rs 1-12.

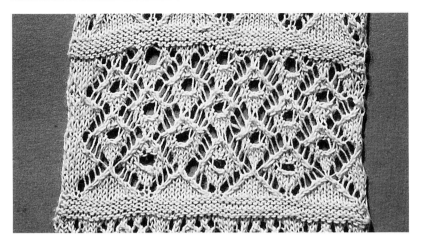

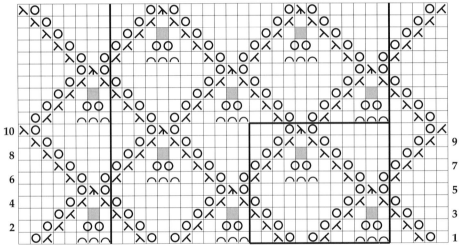

Repeat: 12 sts, 10 Rs.

Add 13 edge sts: 8 at L, 5 at Rt.

Preparation: K at least 1 R of plain sts before starting pattern.

Row 3: k1, p1, k1 into double yo of R 2.

Row 8: p1, k1, p1 into double yo of R 7.

Multiple of 12 sts, plus 13.
Preparation row: On the wrong side of work, p 1 R.
⊠ = P 1 st, sl 1 st kwise, return both sts to L ndl. Psso, return st to Rt ndl.

⋋ = P2tog, then sl 1 st kwise. Return both sts to L ndl. Psso, return to Rt ndl.

Row 1: k1, yo, ssk, k2, *bind off 3 sts, k2, k2tog, yo, k1, yo, ssk, k2*, bind off 3 sts, k2, k2tog, yo, k1. **Row 2:** p2, yo, p2tog, p1, yo twice, *p1, ⋋, yo, p3, yo, p2tog, p1, yo twice*, p1, ⋋, yo, p2. **Row 3:** k3, yo, ssk, *{k1, p1, k1} in yo twice below, k2tog, yo, k5, yo, ssk*, {k1, p1, k1} in yo twice below, k2tog, yo, k3. **Row 4:** p4, yo, p2tog, p1, ⋋, *yo, p7, yo, p2tog, p1, ⋋*, yo, p4.

Row 5: k5, *yo, sl 1-k2tog-psso, yo, k9, *yo, sl 1-k2tog-psso, yo, k5. **Row 6:** p4, ⋋, yo, p1, yo, *p2tog, p2, bind off 3 sts, p2, ⋋, yo, p1, yo*, p2tog, p4. **Row 7:** k3, k2tog, yo, *k3, yo, ssk, k1, yo twice, k1, k2tog, yo*, k3, yo, ssk, k3. **Row 8:** p2, ⋋, yo, p4, *p1, yo, p2tog, {p1, k1, p1} in yo twice below, ⋋, yo, p4*, p1, yo, p2tog, p2. **Row 9:** k1, k2tog, yo, k2, *k5, yo, ssk, k1, k2tog, yo, k2*, k5, yo, ssk, k1. **Row 10:** ⋋, yo, p6, *p3, yo, ⋋, yo, p6*, p3, yo, ⋋.
Rep Rs 1-10.

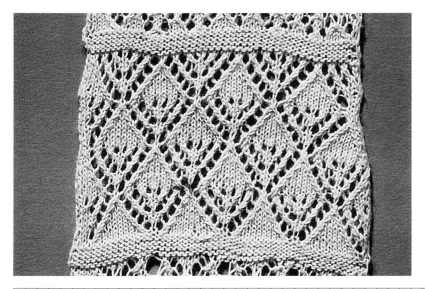

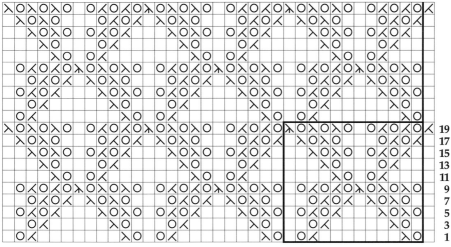

| Modified st |

Repeat: 12 sts, 20 Rs.
Add 1 edge st at Rt.
Modified st at L: R 19.
Even R: P all sts.

Multiple of 12 sts, plus 1.
Even Rs 2-20 (wrong side): P all sts.

Row 1: k1, *yo, ssk, k7, k2tog, yo, k1*.
Row 3: k1, *k1, yo, ssk, k5, k2tog, yo, k2*. **Row 5:** k1, *{yo, ssk} 2 times, k3, {k2tog, yo} 2 times, k1*. **Row 7:** k1, *k1, {yo, ssk} 2 times, k1, {k2tog, yo} 2 times, k2*. **Row 9:** k1, *{yo, ssk} 2 times, yo, sl 1-k2tog-psso, yo, {k2tog, yo} 2 times, k1*. **Row 11:** k1, *k3, k2tog, yo, k1, yo, ssk, k4*. **Row 13:** k1, *k2, k2tog, yo, k3, yo, ssk, k3*.

Row 15: k1, *k1, {k2tog, yo} 2 times, k1, {yo, ssk} 2 times, k2*. **Row 17:** k1, *{k2tog, yo} 2 times, k3, {yo, ssk} 2 times, k1*. **Row 19:** k2tog, *yo, {k2tog, yo} 2 times, k1, {yo, ssk} 2 times, yo, sl 1-k2tog-psso*, end last rep ssk.
Rep Rs 1-20.

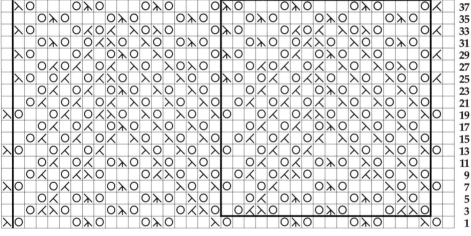

— Modified sts —

Repeat: 18 sts, 38 Rs.
Add 3 edge sts: 1 at L, 2 at Rt.
Modified sts at L: Rs 25, 29, 33, 37.
Even Rs: P all sts.

Multiple of 18 sts, plus 3.
Even Rs 2-38 (wrong side): P all sts.

Row 1: k1, yo, *ssk, {k3, yo, sl 1-k2tog-psso, yo} 2 times, k4, yo*, ssk. **Row 3:** k2, *yo, ssk, k2tog, yo, k3, yo, sl 1-k2tog-psso, yo, k3, yo, ssk, k2tog, yo, k1*, k1. **Row 5:** k2, *k1, yo, ssk, k1, yo, sl 1-k2tog-psso, yo, k3, yo, sl 1-k2tog-psso, yo, k1, k2tog, yo, k2*, k1. **Row 7:** k1, yo, *ssk, k1, yo, ssk, k3, yo, sl 1-k2tog-psso, yo, k3, k2tog, yo, k2, yo*, ssk. **Row 9:** k2, *yo, ssk, k1, yo, ssk, k2tog, yo, k3, yo, ssk, {k2tog, yo, k1} 2 times*, k1. **Row 11:** k2, *{k1, yo, ssk} 2 times, k1, yo, sl 1-k2tog-psso, yo, {k1, k2tog, yo} 2 times, k2*, k1. **Row 13:** k1, yo, *ssk, {k1, yo, ssk} 2 times, k2, {k1, k2tog, yo} 2 times, k2, yo*, ssk. **Row 15:** k2, *{yo, ssk, k1} 3 times, {k2tog, yo, k1} 3 times*, k1. **Row 17:** Rep R 11. **Row 19:** k1, yo, *ssk, {k1, yo, ssk} 3 times, {k2tog, yo, k1} 2 times, k1, yo*, ssk. **Row 21:** Rep R 15. **Row 23:** Rep R 11. **Row 25:** k1, k2tog, *yo, {k1, yo, ssk} 3 times, {k2tog, yo, k1} 2 times, yo, sl 1-k2tog-psso*, end last rep ssk, k1. **Row 27:** k2, *k1, yo, ssk, {yo, ssk, k1} 2 times, k2tog, yo, k1, {k2tog, yo} 2 times, k2*, k1. **Row 29:** k1, k2tog, *yo, k3, yo, ssk,

(Pattern 13 continued)
k1, yo, sl 1-k2tog-psso, yo, k1, k2tog, yo, k3, yo, sl 1-k2tog-psso*, end last rep ssk, k1. **Row 31:** k2, *k1, yo, sl 1-k2tog-psso, yo, {k1, yo, ssk} 2 times, k2tog, yo, k1, yo, sl 1-k2tog-psso, yo, k2*, k1. **Row 33:** k1, k2tog, *yo, k3, {yo, ssk} 2 times, k1, {k2tog, yo} 2 times, k3, yo, sl 1-k2tog-psso*, end last rep ssk, k1. **Row 35:** k2, *{k1, yo, sl 1-k2tog-psso, yo, k2} 3 times*, k1.
Row 37: k1, k2tog, *{yo, k3, yo, sl 1-k2tog-psso} 3 times*, end last rep ssk, k1. Rep Rs 3-38 for an allover pattern.

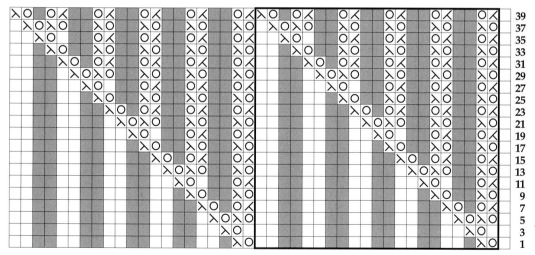

Repeat: 21 sts, 40 Rs.
Add 1 edge st at Rt.
Even Rs: P on p sts and yo (white squares), k on k sts (gray squares).

(Pattern 14 continued)
Multiple of 21 sts, plus 1.

Row 1: k1, *yo, ssk, p1, {k2, p2} 4 times, k2*. **Row 2:** *{p2, k2} 4 times, p2, k1, p2*, p1. **Row 3:** k1, *k1, yo, ssk, {k2, p2} 4 times, k2*. **Row 4:** *{p2, k2} 4 times, p5*, p1. **Row 5:** k1, *{yo, ssk} 2 times, k1, {p2, k2} 4 times*. **Row 6:** Rep R 4. **Row 7:** k1, *k2tog, yo, p1, yo, ssk, {p2, k2} 4 times*. **Row 8:** *{p2, k2} 4 times, p2, k1, p2*, p1. **Row 9:** k1, yo, ssk, p2, yo, ssk, p1, {k2, p2} 3 times, k2*. **Row 10:** *{p2, k2} 3 times, p2, k1, p2, k2, p2*, p1. **Row 11:** k1, *k2tog, yo, p2, k1, yo, ssk, {k2, p2} 3 times, k2*. **Row 12:** *{p2, k2} 3 times, p5, k2, p2*, p1. **Row 13:** k1, *yo, ssk, p2, {yo, ssk} 2 times, k1, {p2, k2} 3 times*.

Row 14: Rep R 12. **Row 15:** k1, k2tog, yo, p2, k2tog, yo, p1, yo, ssk, {p2, k2} 3 times*. **Row 16:** *{p2, k2} 3 times, p2, k1, p2, k2, p2*, p1. **Row 17:** k1, *{yo, ssk, p2} 2 times, yo, ssk, p1, {k2, p2} 2 times, k2*. **Row 18:** *{p2, k2} 2 times, p2, k1, {p2, k2} 2 times, p2*, p1. **Row 19:** k1, *{k2tog, yo, p2} 2 times, k1, yo, ssk, {p2, k2} 2 times, k2*. **Row 20:** *{p2, k2} 2 times, p5, {k2, p2} 2 times*, p1. **Row 21:** k1, *{yo, ssk, p2} 2 times, {yo, ssk} 2 times, k1, {p2, k2} 2 times*. **Row 22:** Rep R 20. **Row 23:** k1, *{k2tog, yo, p2} 2 times, k2tog, yo, p1, yo, ssk, {p2, k2} 2 times*. **Row 24:** *{p2, k2} 2 times, p2, k1, p2, {k2, p2} 2 times*, p1. **Row 25:** k1, *{yo, ssk, p2} 3 times, yo, ssk, p1, k2, p2, k2*. **Row 26:** *p2, k2, p2, k1, p2, {k2, p2} 3 times*, p1.

Row 27: k1, *{k2tog, yo, p2} 3 times, k1, yo, ssk, k2, p2, k2*. **Row 28:** *p2, k2, p5, {k2, p2} 3 times*, p1. **Row 29:** k1, *{yo, ssk, p2} 3 times, {yo, ssk} 2 times, k1, p2, k2*. **Row 30:** Rep R 28. **Row 31:** k1, *{k2tog, yo, p2} 3 times, k2tog, yo, p1, yo, ssk, p2, k2*. **Row 32:** *p2, k2, p2, k1, p2, {k2, p2} 3 times*, p1. **Row 33:** k1, *{yo, ssk, p2} 4 times, yo, ssk, p1, k2*. **Row 34:** *p2, k1, p2, {k2, p2} 4 times*, p1. **Row 35:** k1, *{k2tog, yo, p2} 4 times, k1, yo, ssk, k2*. **Row 36:** *p5, {k2, p2} 4 times*, p1. **Row 37:** k1, *{yo, ssk, p2} 4 times, {yo, ssk} 2 times, k1*. **Row 38:** Rep R 36. **Row 39:** k1, *{k2tog, yo, p2} 4 times, k2tog, yo, p1, yo, ssk*. **Row 40:** *p2, k1, p2, {k2, p2} 4 times*, p1.
Rep Rs 1-40 for an allover pattern.

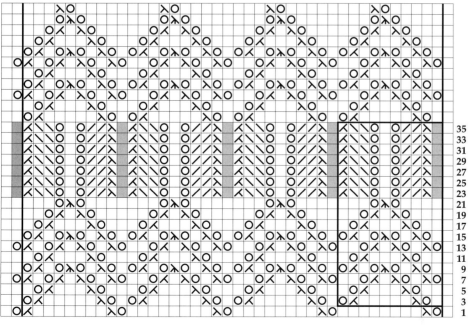

Repeat: 10 sts, 34 Rs.
Add 3 edge sts: 2 at
 L, 1 at Rt.
Modified sts at L: Rs 1,
 7, 13.
Even Rs 2-22: P all sts.
Even Rs 24-36: P, but
 k single st between
 dec (gray squares).

⊢— Modified sts —⊣

(Pattern 15 continued)

Multiple of 10 sts, plus 3.
Even Rs 2-22 (wrong side): P all sts.
Even Rs 24-36 (wrong side): P1, k1, *p9, k1*, p1.

Row 1: k1, *yo, ssk, k8*, end last rep k7, k2tog, yo, k1. **Row 3:** k1, *k1, yo, ssk, k5, k2tog, yo*, k2. **Row 5:** k1, *k2, yo, ssk, k3, k2tog, yo, k1*, k2. **Row 7:** k1, *{yo, ssk, k1} 2 times, k2tog, yo, k2*, end last rep k1, k2tog, yo, k1. **Row 9:** k1, *k1, yo, ssk, k1, yo, sl 1-k2tog-psso, yo, k1, k2tog, yo*, k2. **Row 11:** Rep R 5. **Row 13:** Rep R 7. **Row 15:** Rep R 9. **Row 17:** Rep R 5.

Row 19: k1, *k3, yo, ssk, k1, k2tog, yo, k2*, k2. **Row 21:** k1, *k4, yo, sl 1-k2tog-psso, yo, k3*, k2. **Row 23:** k1, *p1, ssk, k2, yo, k1, yo, k2, k2tog*, p1, k1. **Rows 25, 27, 29, 31, 33, 35:** Rep R 23. Rep Rs 3-36 for an allover pattern.

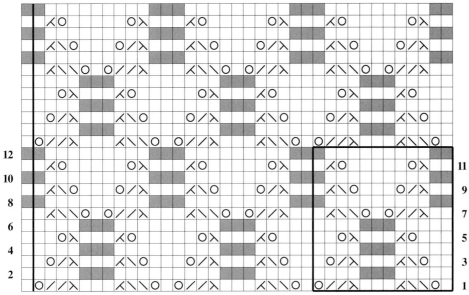

Repeat: 12 sts, 12 Rs.
Add 1 edge st at L.

Multiple of 12 sts, plus 1.

Row 1: *k1, yo, k2, k2tog, k3, ssk, k2, yo*, k1. **Row 2:** p1, *p4, k3, p5*.

Row 3: *k2, yo, k1, k2tog, k3, ssk, k1, yo, k1*, k1. **Row 4:** Rep R 2.
Row 5: *k3, yo, k2tog, k3, ssk, yo, k2*, k1. **Row 6:** Rep R 2. **Row 7:** *k2, ssk, k2, yo, k1, yo, k2, k2tog, k1*, k1.

Row 8: k1, *k1, p9, k2*. **Row 9:** *k2, ssk, k1, yo, k3, yo, k1, k2tog, k1*, k1.
Row 10: Rep R 8. **Row 11:** *k2, ssk, yo, k5, yo, k2tog, k1*, k1. **Row 12:** Rep R 8.
Rep Rs 1-12.

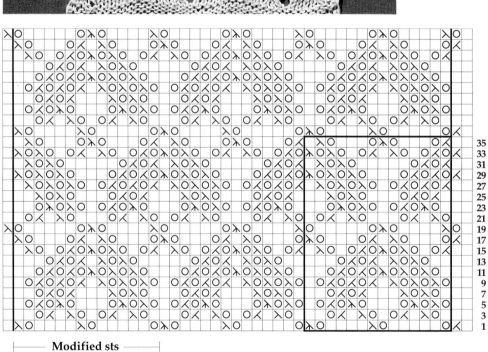

├─── **Modified sts** ───┤

Repeat: 14 sts, 36 Rs.
Add 3 edge sts: 1 at L, 2 at Rt.
Modified sts at L: Rs 1, 17, 29, 33.
Even Rs: P all sts.

Multiple of 14 sts, plus 3.
Even Rs 2-36 (wrong side): P all sts.

Row 1: k1, k2tog, *yo, k5, yo, ssk, k4, yo, sl 1-k2tog-psso*, end last rep ssk, k1. **Row 3:** k2, *k1, {yo, ssk, k1, k2tog, yo, k1} 2 times, k1*, k1. **Row 5:** k2, *yo, ssk, yo, sl 1-k2tog-psso, yo, k3, yo, sl 1-k2tog-psso, yo, k2tog, yo, k1*, k1. **Row 7:** k2, *k1, {yo, ssk} 2 times, k3, {k2tog, yo} 2 times, k2*, k1. **Row 9:** k2,

{yo, ssk} 3 times, k1, {k2tog, yo} 3 times, k1, k1. **Row 11:** k2, *k1, {yo, ssk} 2 times, yo, sl 1-k2tog-psso, yo, {k2tog, yo} 2 times, k2*, k1. **Row 13:** k2, *k2, {yo, ssk} 2 times, k1, {k2tog, yo} 2 times, k3*, k1. **Row 15:** k2, *k2tog, yo, k1, yo, ssk, yo, sl 1-k2tog-psso, yo, k2tog, yo, k1, yo, ssk, k1*, k1.

(Pattern 17 continued)

Row 17: k1, k2tog, *yo, k3, yo, ssk, k1, k2tog, yo, k3, yo, sl 1-k2tog-psso*, end last rep ssk, k1. **Row 19:** k1, yo, *ssk, k4, yo, sl 1-k2tog-psso, yo, k5, yo*, ssk. **Row 21:** k2, *yo, ssk, k1, k2tog, yo, k3, yo, ssk, k1, k2tog, yo, k1*, k1. **Row 23:** k2, *k1, yo, sl 1-k2tog-psso,

yo, k2tog, yo, k1, yo, ssk, yo, sl 1-k2tog-psso, yo, k2*, k1. **Row 25:** k2, *k1, {k2tog, yo} 2 times, k3, {yo, ssk} 2 times, k2*, k1. **Row 27:** k2, *{k2tog, yo} 3 times, k1, {yo, ssk} 3 times, k1*, k1. **Row 29:** k1, k2tog, *yo, {k2tog, yo} 2 times, k3, {yo, ssk} 2 times, yo, sl 1-k2tog-psso*, end last rep ssk, k1.

Row 31: k2, *{k2tog, yo} 2 times, k5, {yo, ssk} 2 times, k1*, k1. **Row 33:** k1, k2tog, *yo, k2tog, yo, k1, yo, ssk, k1, k2tog, yo, k1, yo, ssk, yo, sl 1-k2tog-psso*, end last rep ssk, k1. **Row 35:** k2, *k2tog, yo, k3, yo, sl 1-k2tog-psso, yo, k3, yo, ssk, k1*, k1.
Rep Rs 1-36.

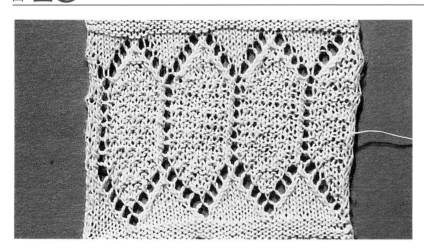

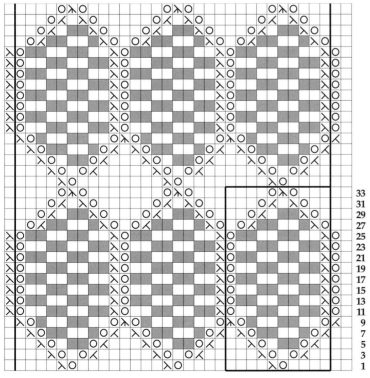

⊢ **Modified st** ⊣

Repeat: 10 sts, 34 Rs.
Add 3 edge sts: 1 at L, 2 at Rt.
Modified st at L: R 9.
Even Rs: P on p sts and yo (white squares), k on k sts (gray squares).

(*Pattern 18 continued*)
Multiple of 10 sts, plus 3.

Row 1: k2, *k4, yo, ssk, k4*, k1.
Row 2: Purl. **Row 3:** k2, *k2, k2tog, yo, k1, yo, ssk, k3*, k1. **Row 4:** Purl.
Row 5: k2, *k1, k2tog, yo, p2, k1, yo, ssk, k2*, k1. **Row 6:** p1, *p5, k2, p3*, p2. **Row 7:** k2, *k2tog, yo, p1, k2, p2, yo, ssk, k1*, k1. **Row 8:** p1, *p3, k2, p2,

k1, p2*, p2. **Row 9:** k1, k2tog, *yo, k2, p2, k2, p1, yo, sl 1-k2tog-psso*, end last rep ssk, k1. **Row 10:** p1, *p2, k1, p2, k2, p3*, p2. **Row 11:** k1, yo, *ssk, {p2, k2} 2 times, yo*, ssk. **Row 12:** p1, *p3, k2, p2, k2, p1*, p2. **Row 13:** k1, yo, *ssk, {k2, p2} 2 times, yo*, ssk.
Row 14: p1, *p1, k2, p2, k2, p3*, p2.
Rows 15, 19, 23: Rep R 11. **Rows 16, 20, 24:** Rep R 12. **Rows 17, 21, 25:** Rep

R 13. **Rows 18, 22, 26:** Rep R 14.
Row 27: k2, *yo, ssk, p1, k2, p2, k2tog, yo, k1*, k1. **Row 28:** Rep R 8.
Row 29: k2, *k1, yo, ssk, p2, k1, k2tog, yo, k2*, k1. **Row 30:** Rep R 6.
Row 31: k2, *k2, yo, ssk, k1, k2tog, yo, k3*, k1. **Row 32:** Purl. **Row 33:** k2, *k3, yo, sl 1-k2tog-psso, yo, k4*, k1.
Row 34: Purl.
Rep Rs 1-34.

Pattern 19

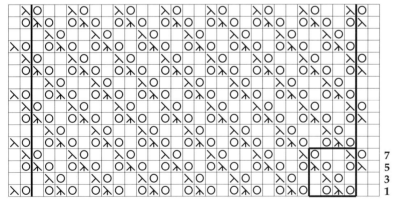

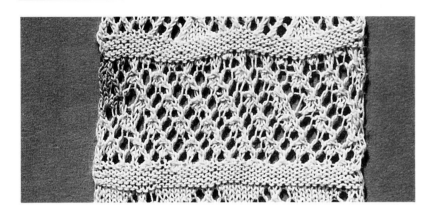

Repeat: 4 sts, 8 Rs.
Add 4 edge sts: 2 each side.
Even Rs: P all sts.

Multiple of 4 sts, plus 4.
Even Rs 2-8 (wrong side): P all sts.

Row 1: k2, *yo, sl 1-k2tog-psso, yo, k1*, yo, ssk. **Row 3:** k2, *k1, yo, ssk,

k1*, k2. **Row 5:** k1, ssk, *yo, k1, yo, sl 1-k2tog-psso*, yo, k1. **Row 7:** k1, yo, *ssk, k2, yo*, ssk, k1.
Rep Rs 1-8.

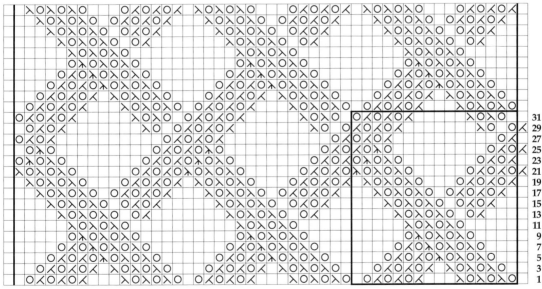

├──── **Modified sts** ────┤

Repeat: 16 sts, 32 Rs.
Add 2 edge sts: 1 each side.
Modified sts at L: Rs 21, 25, 29.
Even Rs: P all sts.

Multiple of 16 sts, plus 2.
Even Rs 2-32 (wrong side): P all sts.

Row 1: k1, *{yo, ssk} 3 times, k3,

{k2tog, yo} 3 times, k1*, k1. **Row 3:** k1, *k1, {yo, ssk} 3 times, k1, {k2tog, yo} 3 times, k2*, k1. **Row 5:** k1, *k2, {yo, ssk} 2 times, yo, sl 1-k2tog-psso, yo, {k2tog, yo} 2 times, k3*, k1. **Row 7:** k1, *k3, {yo, ssk} 2 times, yo, sl 1-k2tog-psso, yo, k2tog, yo, k4*, k1. **Row 9:** k1, *k4, {yo, ssk} 2 times, yo, sl 1-k2tog-psso,

yo, k5*, k1. **Row 11:** k1, *k5, {yo, ssk} 3 times, k5*, k1. **Row 13:** k1, *k3, k2tog, yo, k1, {yo, ssk} 3 times, k4*, k1. **Row 15:** k1, *k2, {k2tog, yo} 2 times, k1, {yo, ssk} 3 times, k3*, k1. **Row 17:** k1, *k1, {k2tog, yo} 3 times, k1, {yo, ssk} 3 times, k2*, k1. **Row 19:** k1, *{k2tog, yo} 3 times, k3, {yo, ssk} 3 times, k1*,

(*Pattern 20 continued*)
k1. **Row 21:** k2tog, *yo, {k2tog, yo} 2 times, k5, {yo, ssk} 2 times, yo, sl 1-k2tog-psso*, end last rep ssk, k1.
Row 23: k1, {k2tog, yo} 2 times, k7, yo, ssk, yo, sl 1-k2tog-psso, yo*, k1.
Row 25: k2tog, *yo, k2tog, yo, k9, yo, sl 1-k2tog-psso, yo, k2tog*, end last rep k2. **Row 27:** k1, *k2tog, yo, k10, {k2tog, yo} 2 times*, k1. **Row 29:** k2tog, *yo, k1, yo, ssk, k7, {k2tog, yo} 2 times, k2tog*, end last rep k2. **Row 31:** k1, *k1, {yo, ssk} 2 times, k5, {k2tog, yo} 3 times*, k1.
Rep Rs 1-32.

Pattern 21

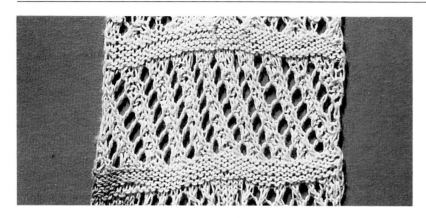

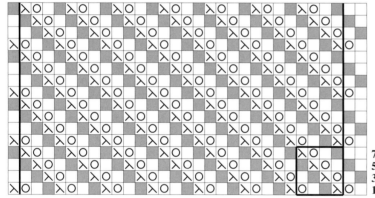

Repeat: 4 sts, 8 Rs.
Add 3 edge sts: 1 at L, 2 at Rt.
Even Rs: P on p sts and yo (white squares), k on k sts (gray squares).

Multiple of 4 sts, plus 3.

Row 1: k1, yo, *ssk, p1, k1, yo*, ssk.
Row 2: p1, *p2, k1, p1*, p2. **Row 3:** p1, k1, *yo, ssk, p1, k1*, k1. **Row 4:** p1, *p1, k1, p2*, p1, k1. **Row 5:** k1, p1, *k1, yo, ssk, p1*, k1. **Row 6:** p1, *k1, p3*, k1, p1. **Row 7:** k2, *p1, k1, yo, ssk*, p1.
Row 8: k1, *p3, k1*, p2.
Rep Rs 1-8.

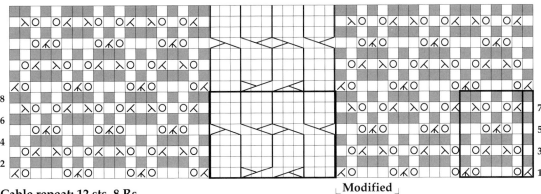

Cable repeat: 12 sts, 8 Rs.
Ground repeat: 6 sts, 8 Rs.
  Add 1 edge st at Rt.
  Modified st at L: R 1.
Combined repeat of 3 ground,
  1 cable: 31 sts, 8 Rs.

Multiple of 31 sts.
The division between patterns is marked by a slash (/).
⬚ = Ssk, return st to L ndl, pnso, return st to Rt ndl.

Row 1: *k2tog, {yo, k3, yo, ⬚} 2 times, yo, k3, yo, k2tog, / k3, sl3 sts onto extra ndl and hold in back of work, k next 3 sts, then k held sts, k3*.
Row 2: *p12, / {k1, p1, k3, p1} 3 times, k1*. **Row 3:** *k1, {yo, ssk, k1, k2tog, yo, k1} 3 times, / k12*. **Row 4:** Rep R 2.
Row 5: *k1, {k1, yo, ⬚, yo, k2} 3 times, / {sl3 sts onto extra ndl and hold in front of work, k next 3 sts, then k held sts} 2 times*. **Row 6:** *p12, / {k2, p1, k1, p1, k1} 3 times, k1*. **Row 7:** *k1, {k2tog, yo, k1, yo, ssk, k1} 3 times, / k12*. **Row 8:** Rep R 6.
Rep Rs 1-8.

Ground pattern when used alone:
Multiple of 6 sts, plus 1.

Row 1: k2tog, *yo, k3, yo, ⬚*, end last rep k2tog. **Row 2:** *k1, p1, k3, p1*, k1.
Row 3: k1, *yo, ssk, k1, k2tog, yo, k1*.
Row 4: Rep R 2. **Row 5:** k1, *k1, yo, ⬚, yo, k2*. **Row 6:** *k2, p1, k1, p1, k1*, k1.
Row 7: k1, *k2tog, yo, k1, yo, ssk, k1*.
Row 8: Rep R 6.
Rep Rs 1-8.

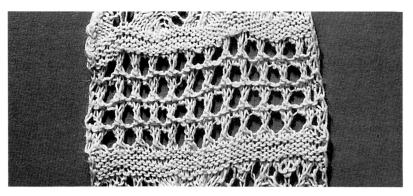

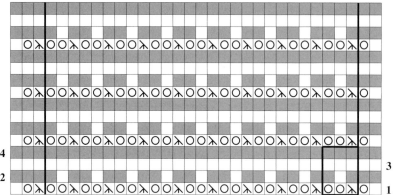

Repeat: 3 sts, 4 Rs.
Add 5 edge sts: 3 at L, 2 at Rt.

Multiple of 3 sts, plus 5.

Row 1: k1, yo, *sl 1-k2tog-psso, yo twice*, sl 1-k2tog-psso, yo, k1.
Row 2: k3, *{k1, p1} in yo twice below, k1*, k2.
Row 3: Knit.
Row 4: Knit.
Rep Rs 1-4.

Note: In the sampler, the fern decreases are not paired. On the chart, they are paired as on the right side in the lower repeat and as on the left side in the upper repeat.

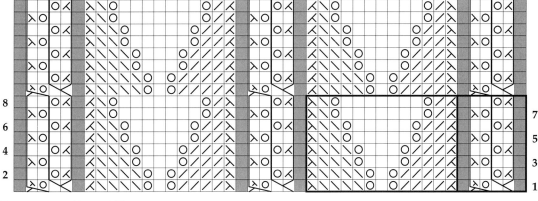

Fern repeat: 13 sts, 8 Rs.
Cable repeat: 6 sts, 8 Rs.
Combined repeat of 1 cable,
** 1 fern: 19 sts, 8 Rs.**

Combined repeat 19 sts

Multiple of 19 sts.
The division between patterns is marked by a slash (/).
⊠ = P 1 st, sl 1 st kwise, return both sts to L ndl. Psso, return st to Rt ndl.

Row 1: *p1, sl 2 sts onto extra ndl and hold in front of work, k next 2 sts, yo, ssk 2 sts off extra ndl, p1, / k2tog, k4, yo, k1, yo, k4, ssk*. **Row 2:** *⊠, p4, yo, p1, yo, p4, p2tog, / k1, p2, yo, p2tog, k1*. **Row 3:** *p1, k2, yo, ssk, p1, / k2tog, {k3, yo} 2 times, k3, ssk*. **Row 4:** *⊠, {p3, yo} 2 times, p3, p2tog, / k1, p2, yo, p2tog, k1*. **Row 5:** *p1, k2, yo, ssk, p1, / k2tog, k2, yo, k5, yo, k2, ssk*. **Row 6:** *⊠, p2, yo, p5, yo, p2, p2tog, / k1, p2, yo, p2tog, k1*. **Row 7:** *p1, k2, yo, ssk, p1, / k2tog, k1, yo, k7, yo, k1, ssk*. **Row 8:** *⊠, p1, yo, p7, yo, p1, p2tog, / k1, p2, yo, p2tog, k1*. Rep Rs 1-8.

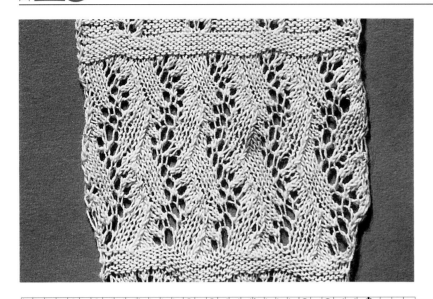

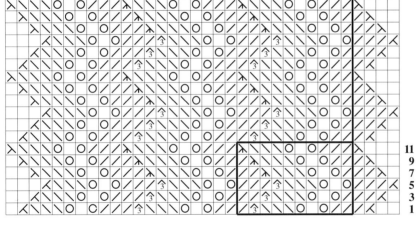

	11
	9
	7
	5
	3
	1

├── **Modified sts** ──┤

Repeat: 10 sts, 12 Rs.
Add 4 edge sts at Rt.
Modified sts at L: All odd Rs.
Even Rs: P all sts.

Multiple of 10 sts, plus 4.
Even Rs 2-12 (wrong side): P all sts.

Row 1: k2, k2tog, k1, *k2, yo, k1, yo, k3, k3tog, k1*, end last rep k2tog, k1.
Row 3: k1, k2tog, k2, *k1, yo, k1, yo, k3, k3tog, k2*, end last rep k2tog, k2.
Row 5: k2tog, k3, *yo, k1, yo, k3, k3tog, k3*, end last rep k2tog, k3. **Row 7:** k1, ssk, k2, *k1, yo, k1, yo, k3, sl 1-k2tog-psso, k2*, end last rep ssk, k2. **Row 9:** k2, ssk, k1, *k2, yo, k1, yo, k3, sl 1-k2tog-psso, k1*, end last rep ssk, k1.
Row 11: k3, ssk, *k3, yo, k1, yo, k3, sl 1-k2tog-psso*, end last rep ssk.
Rep Rs 1-12.

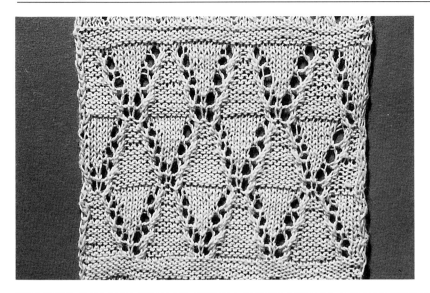

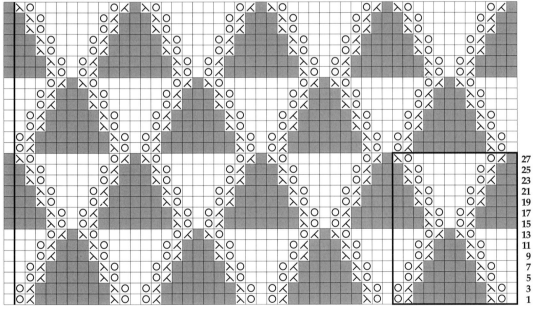

Repeat: 12 sts, 28 Rs.

Add 1 edge st at L.

Even Rs: P on p sts and yo (white squares), k on k sts (gray squares).

Multiple of 12 sts, plus 1.

Rows 1, 3: *k1, yo, ssk, p7, k2tog, yo*, k1. **Rows 2, 4:** k1, *p2, k7, p3*.

Rows 5, 7: *k2, yo, ssk, p5, k2tog, yo, k1*, k1. **Rows 6, 8:** p1, *p3, k5, p4*. **Rows 9, 11:** *k3, yo, ssk, p3, k2tog, yo, k2*, k1. **Rows 10, 12:** p1, *p4, k3, p5*. **Row 13:** *k4, yo, ssk, p1, k2tog, yo, k3*, k1. **Row 14:** p1, *p5, k1, p6*. **Rows 15, 17:** *p4, k2tog, yo, k1, yo, ssk, p3*, p1. **Rows 16, 18:** k1, *k3, p5,

k4*. **Rows 19, 21:** *p3, k2tog, yo, k3, yo, ssk, p2*, p1. **Rows 20, 22:** k1, *k2, p7, k3*. **Rows 23, 25:** *p2, k2tog, yo, k5, yo, ssk, p1*, p1. **Rows 24, 26:** k1, *k1, p9, k2*. **Row 27:** *p1, k2tog, yo, k7, yo, ssk*, p1. **Row 28:** k1, *p11, k1*. Rep Rs 1-28.

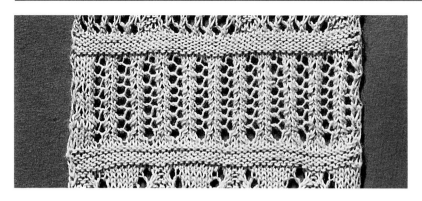

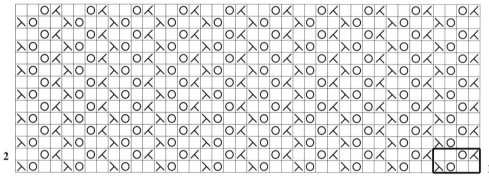

2

1

Repeat: 4 sts, 2 Rs.

Multiple of 4 sts.

Row 1: *k2, yo, ssk*.
Row 2: *p2, yo, p2tog*.
Rep Rs 1-2.

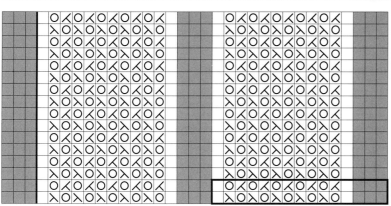

Repeat: 15 sts, 4 Rs.
Add 3 edge sts at L.
Even Rs: P on p sts and yo
  (white squares), k on k sts
  (gray squares).

Multiple of 15 sts, plus 3.

Row 1: *p3, k1, {yo, ssk} 5 times, k1*, p3.
Row 2: k3, *p12, k3*.
Row 3: *p3, k1, {k2tog, yo} 5 times, k1*, p3.
Row 4: Rep R 2.
Rep Rs 1-4.

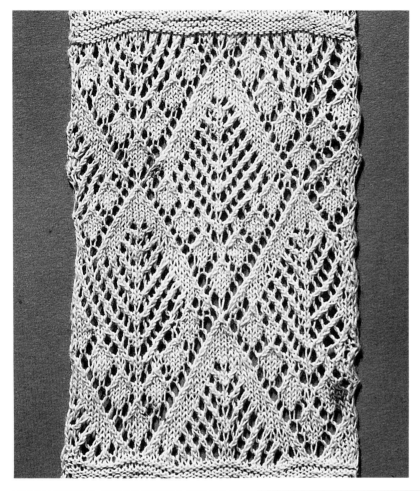

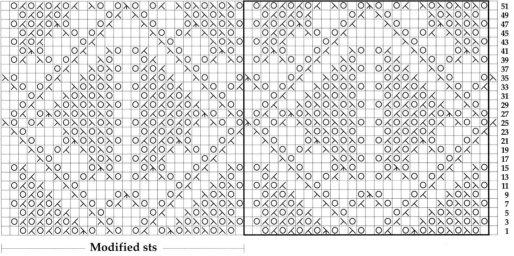

Modified sts

Repeat: 28 sts, 52 Rs.
Add 1 edge st at Rt.
Modified sts at L: Rs 25, 35.
Even Rs: P all sts.

(Pattern 29 continued)

Multiple of 28 sts, plus 1.

Even Rs 2-52 (wrong side): P all sts.

Row 1: k1, *k1, {yo, ssk} 3 times, yo, sl 1-k2tog-psso, yo, k1, k2tog, yo, k1, yo, ssk, k1, yo, sl 1-k2tog-psso, yo, {k2tog, yo} 3 times, k2*. **Row 3:** k1, *{yo, ssk} 4 times, k2, k2tog, yo, k3, yo, ssk, k2, {k2tog, yo} 4 times, k1*. **Row 5:** k1, *k1, {yo, ssk} 3 times, k2, k2tog, yo, k5, yo, ssk, k2, {k2tog, yo} 3 times, k2*. **Row 7:** k1, *{yo, ssk} 3 times, k2, {k2tog, yo, k1, yo, ssk, k1} 2 times, k1, {k2tog, yo} 3 times, k1*. **Row 9:** k1, *k1, {yo, ssk} 2 times, k2, k2tog, yo, k3, yo, sl 1-k2tog-psso, yo, k3, yo, ssk, k2, {k2tog, yo} 2 times, k2*. **Row 11:** k1, *{yo, ssk} 2 times, k2, k2tog, yo, k11, yo, ssk, k2, {k2tog, yo} 2 times, k1*. **Row 13:** k1, *k1, yo, ssk, k2, {k2tog, yo, k1, yo, ssk, k1} 3 times, k1, k2tog, yo, k2*. **Row 15:** k1, *yo, ssk, k2, k2tog, yo, k3, {yo, sl 1-k2tog-psso, yo, k3} 2 times, yo, ssk, k2, k2tog, yo, k1*. **Row 17:** k1, *k3, k2tog, yo, k4, {k2tog, yo} 2 times, k1, {yo, ssk} 2 times, k4,

yo, ssk, k4*. **Row 19:** k1, *k2, k2tog, yo, k1, yo, ssk, k1, {k2tog, yo} 2 times, k3, {yo, ssk} 2 times, k1, k2tog, yo, k1, yo, ssk, k3*. **Row 21:** k1, *k1, k2tog, yo, k3, yo, sl 1-k2tog-psso, yo, {k2tog, yo} 2 times, k1, {yo, ssk} 2 times, yo, sl 1-k2tog-psso, yo, k3, yo, ssk, k2*. **Row 23:** k1, *k2tog, yo, k4, {k2tog, yo} 3 times, k3, {yo, ssk} 3 times, k4, yo, ssk, k1*. **Row 25:** k2tog, *yo, k1, yo, ssk, k1, {k2tog, yo} 4 times, k1, {yo, ssk} 4 times, k1, k2tog, yo, k1, yo, sl 1-k2tog-psso*, end last rep ssk. **Row 27:** k1, *yo, ssk, k1, yo, sl 1-k2tog-psso, yo, {k2tog, yo} 3 times, k3, {yo, ssk} 3 times, yo, sl 1-k2tog-psso, yo, k1, k2tog, yo, k1*. **Row 29:** k1, *k1, yo, ssk, k2, {k2tog, yo} 4 times, k1, {yo, ssk} 4 times, k2, k2tog, yo, k2*. **Row 31:** k1, *k2, yo, ssk, k2, {k2tog, yo} 3 times, k3, {yo, ssk} 3 times, k2, k2tog, yo, k3*. **Row 33:** k1, *k2tog, yo, k1, yo, ssk, k2, {k2tog, yo} 3 times, k1, {yo, ssk} 3 times, k2, k2tog, yo, k1, yo, ssk, k1*. **Row 35:** ssk, *yo, k3, yo, ssk, k2, {k2tog, yo} 2 times, k3, {yo, ssk} 2 times, k2, k2tog, yo, k3, yo, sl 1-k2tog-

psso*, end last rep ssk. **Row 37:** k1, *k5, yo, ssk, k2, {k2tog, yo} 2 times, k1, {yo, ssk} 2 times, k2, k2tog, yo, k6*. **Row 39:** k1, *yo, ssk, k1, k2tog, yo, k1, yo, ssk, k2, k2tog, yo, k3, yo, ssk, k2, k2tog, yo, k1, yo, ssk, k1, k2tog, yo, k1*. **Row 41:** k1, *k1, yo, sl 1-k2tog-psso, yo, k3, yo, ssk, k2, k2tog, yo, k1, yo, ssk, k2, k2tog, yo, k3, yo, sl 1-k2tog-psso, yo, k2*. **Row 43:** k1, *{yo, ssk} 2 times, k4, yo, ssk, k7, k2tog, yo, k4, {k2tog, yo} 2 times, k1*. **Row 45:** k1, *k1, {yo, ssk} 2 times, k1, k2tog, yo, k1, yo, ssk, k5, k2tog, yo, k1, yo, ssk, k1, {k2tog, yo} 2 times, k2*. **Row 47:** k1, *{yo, ssk} 2 times, yo, sl 1-k2tog-psso, yo, k3, yo, ssk, k3, k2tog, yo, k3, yo, sl 1-k2tog-psso, yo, {k2tog, yo} 2 times, k1*. **Row 49:** k1, *k1, {yo, ssk} 3 times, k4, yo, ssk, k1, k2tog, yo, k4, {k2tog, yo} 3 times, k2*. **Row 51:** k1, *{yo, ssk} 4 times, k1, k2tog, yo, k1, yo, sl 1-k2tog-psso, yo, k1, yo, ssk, k1, {k2tog, yo} 4 times, k1*.

Rep Rs 1-52 for an allover pattern.

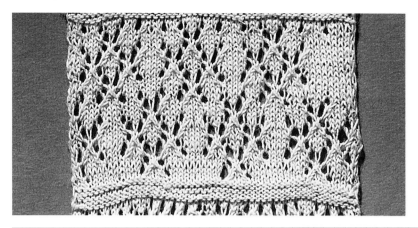

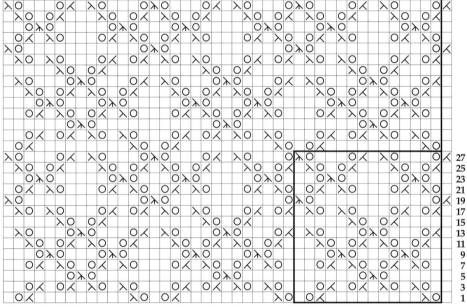

—— **Modified sts** ——|

Repeat: 14 sts, 28 Rs.
Add 1 edge st at Rt.
Modified sts at L: Rs 19, 27.
Even Rs: P all sts.

Multiple of 14 sts, plus 1.
Even Rs 2-28 (wrong side): P all sts.

Row 1: k1, *yo, ssk, k9, k2tog, yo, k1*.
Row 3: k1, *{k1, yo, ssk} 2 times, {k1, k2tog, yo} 2 times, k2*. **Row 5:** k1, *k5,

yo, sl 1-k2tog-psso, yo, k6*. **Row 7:** k1, *k1, {yo, ssk, k1, k2tog, yo, k1} 2 times, k1*. **Row 9:** k1, *k2, {yo, sl 1-k2tog-psso, yo, k3} 2 times*. **Row 11:** k1, *k1, {k2tog, yo, k1, yo, ssk, k1} 2 times, k1*.
Row 13: k1, *k2tog, yo, k3, yo, sl 1-k2tog-psso, yo, k3, yo, ssk, k1*.
Row 15: k1, *k4, k2tog, yo, k1, yo, ssk, k5*. **Row 17:** k1, *{k2tog, yo, k1} 2 times, k2, {yo, ssk, k1} 2 times*.
Row 19: k2tog, *yo, k11, yo, sl 1-k2tog-

psso*, end last rep ssk. **Row 21:** k1, *yo, ssk, k1, k2tog, yo, k3, yo, ssk, k1, k2tog, yo, k1*. **Row 23:** k1, *k1, yo, sl 1-k2tog-psso, yo, k5, yo, sl 1-k2tog-psso, yo, k2*. **Row 25:** k1, *k2tog, yo, k1, yo, ssk, k3, k2tog, yo, k1, yo, ssk, k1*. **Row 27:** k2tog, *yo, k3, yo, ssk, k1, k2tog, yo, k3, yo, sl 1-k2tog-psso*, end last rep ssk.
Rep Rs 1-28.

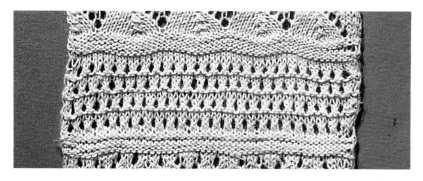

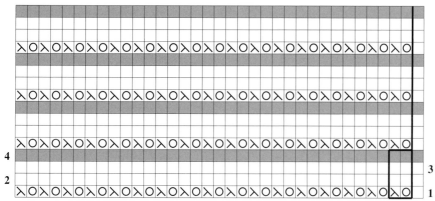

Repeat: 2 sts, 4 Rs.
Add 1 edge st at Rt.

Multiple of 2 sts, plus 1.

Row 1: k1, *yo, ssk*.
Row 2: Purl.
Row 3: Knit.
Row 4: Knit.
Rep Rs 1-4.

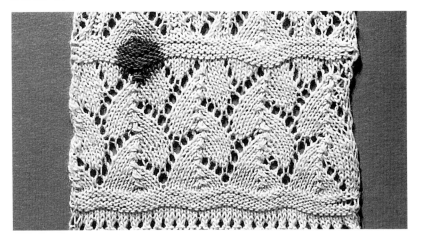

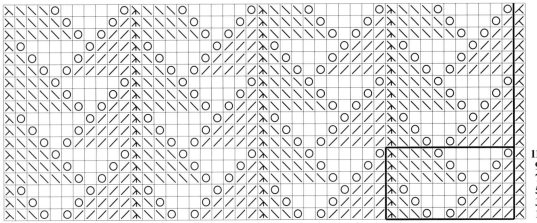

├── **Modified sts** ──┤

Repeat: 11 sts, 12 Rs.
Add 1 edge st at Rt.
Modified sts at L: All odd Rs.
Even Rs: P all sts.

Multiple of 11 sts, plus 1.
Even Rs 2-12 (wrong side): P all sts.

Row 1: k2tog, *k5, yo, k1, yo, k2,
sl 1-k2tog-psso*, end last rep ssk.
Row 3: k2tog, *k4, yo, k3, yo, k1,
sl 1-k2tog-psso*, end last rep ssk.
Row 5: k2tog, *k3, yo, k5, yo, sl 1-k2tog-

psso*, end last rep ssk. **Row 7:** k2tog,
k2, yo, k1, yo, k5, sl 1-k2tog-psso,
end last rep ssk. **Row 9:** k2tog, *k1, yo,
k3, yo, k4, sl 1-k2tog-psso*, end last
rep ssk. **Row 11:** k2tog, *yo, k5, yo, k3,
sl 1-k2tog-psso*, end last rep ssk.
Rep Rs 1-12.

Note: To make the pattern a repeating unit, the diamond has been enlarged by two stitches and two rows on the chart.

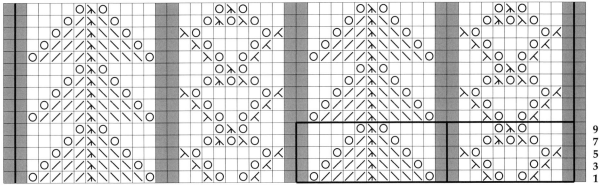

9
7
5
3
1

Combined repeat 24 sts

Horseshoe repeat: 13 sts, 10 Rs.
Diamond repeat: 11 sts, 10 Rs.
Combined repeat of 1 diamond,
  1 horseshoe: 24 sts, 10 Rs.
  Add 2 edge sts: 1 each side.
Even Rs: P on p sts and yo
  (white squares), k on k sts
  (gray squares).

Multiple of 24 sts, plus 2.
The division between patterns is
marked by a slash (/).
Even Rs 2-10 (wrong side): k1, / *k1,
p11, k1, / k1, p9, k1*, k1.

Row 1: p1, *p1, k2, k2tog, yo, k1, yo,
ssk, k2, p1, / p1, yo, k4, sl 1-k2tog-
psso, k4, yo, p1*, p1. **Row 3:** p1, *p1,
k1, k2tog, yo, k3, yo, ssk, k1, p1, / p1,
k1, yo, k3, sl 1-k2tog-psso, k3, yo, k1,

p1*, p1. **Row 5:** p1, *p1, k2tog, yo, k5,
yo, ssk, p1, / p1, k2, yo, k2, sl 1-k2tog-
psso, k2, yo, k2, p1*, p1. **Row 7:** p1,
*p1, k2, yo, ssk, yo, sl 1-k2tog-psso,
yo, k2, p1, / p1, k3, yo, k1, sl 1-k2tog-
psso, k1, yo, k3, p1*, p1. **Row 9:** p1,
*p1, k3, yo, sl 1-k2tog-psso, yo, k3, p1,
/ p1, k4, yo, sl 1-k2tog-psso, yo, k4,
p1*, p1.
Rep Rs 1-10.

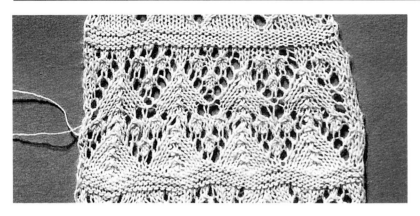

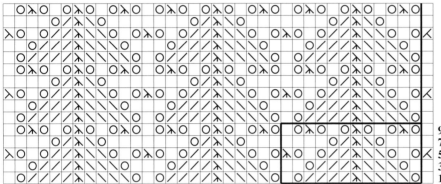

						9
						7
						5
						3
						1

├─── **Modified st** ───┤

Repeat: 12 sts, 10 Rs.
Add 1 edge st at Rt.
Modified st at L: R 5.
Even Rs: P all sts.

Multiple of 12 sts, plus 1.
Even Rs 2-10 (wrong side): P all sts.

Row 1: k1, *yo, k4, sl 1-k2tog-psso, k4, yo, k1*. **Row 3:** k1, *k1, yo, k3, sl 1-k2tog-psso, k3, yo, k2*. **Row 5:** k2tog, *yo, k1, yo, k2, sl 1-k2tog-psso, k2, yo, k1, yo, sl 1-k2tog-psso*, end last rep ssk. **Row 7:** k1, *k3, yo, k1, sl 1-k2tog-psso, k1, yo, k4*. **Row 9:** k1, *{yo, sl 1-k2tog-psso, yo, k1} 3 times*.
Rep Rs 1-10.

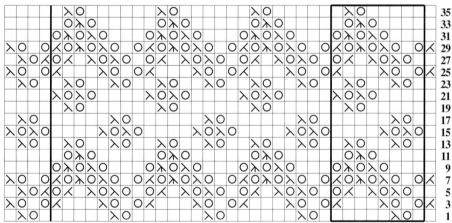

Repeat: 8 sts, 36 Rs.
Add 5 edge sts: 4 at L, 1 at Rt.
Even Rs: P all sts.

Multiple of 8 sts, plus 5.
Even Rs 2-36 (wrong side): P all sts.

Row 1: k1, *k1, yo, ssk, k5*, k1, yo, ssk, k1. **Row 3:** k2tog, *yo, k1, yo, ssk, k3, k2tog*, yo, k1, yo, ssk. **Row 5:** k1, *k1, {yo, ssk} 2 times, k1, k2tog, yo*, k2tog, yo, ssk, k1. **Row 7:** k2tog, *yo, k1, yo, ssk, yo, sl 1-k2tog-psso, yo, k2tog*, yo, k1, yo, ssk. **Row 9:** k1, *k3, yo, ssk, yo, sl 1-k2tog-psso, yo*, k4. **Row 11:** k1, *k4, yo, sl 1-k2tog-psso, yo, k1*, k4. **Row 13:** k1, *k1, yo, ssk, k2, yo, ssk, k1*, k1, yo, ssk, k1. **Row 15:** k1, *{yo, ssk} 2 times, k4*, {yo, ssk} 2 times. **Row 17:** k1, *k1, yo, ssk, k5*, k1, yo, ssk, k1. **Row 19:** k1, *k5, yo, ssk, k1*, k4. **Row 21:** k1, *k4, {yo, ssk} 2 times*, k4. **Row 23:** k1, *{k1, yo, ssk, k1} 2 times*, k1, yo, ssk, k1. **Row 25:** Rep R 3. **Row 27:** Rep R 5. **Row 29:** Rep R 7. **Row 31:** Rep R 9. **Row 33:** Rep R 11. **Row 35:** Rep R 19.
Rep Rs 1-36 for an allover pattern.

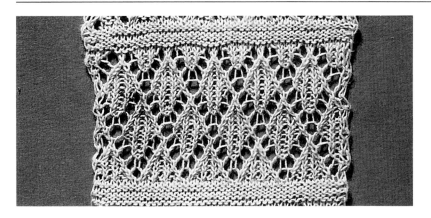

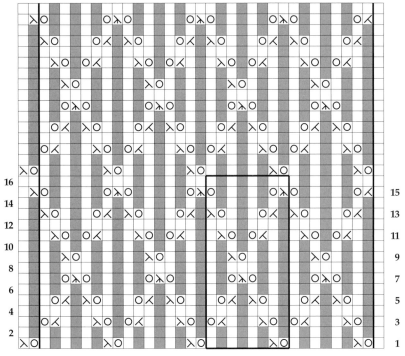

Repeat: 8 sts, 16 Rs.
Add 3 edge sts: 2 at L, 1 at Rt.
Modified st at Rt: R 15.

⊢ **Modified st** ⊣

Multiple of 8 sts, plus 3.

Row 1: k1, *yo, ssk, {p1, k1} 3 times*, yo, ssk. **Row 2:** p1, k1, *{p1, k1} 4 times*, p1. **Row 3:** k1, *p1, yo, ssk, k1, p1, k1, k2tog, yo*, p1, k1. **Row 4:** p1, k1, *{p3, k1} 2 times*, p1. **Row 5:** k1, *p1, k1, yo, ssk, p1, k2tog, yo, k1*, p1, k1. **Row 6:** Rep R 2. **Row 7:** k1, *p1, k1, p1, yo, sl 1-k2tog-psso, yo, p1, k1*, p1, k1. **Row 8:** p1, k1, *p1, k1, p3, k1, p1, k1*, p1. **Row 9:** k1, *{p1, k1} 2 times, yo, ssk, p1, k1*, p1, k1. **Row 10:** Rep R 2. **Row 11:** k1, *p1, k1, k2tog, yo, p1, yo, ssk, k1*, p1, k1. **Row 12:** Rep R 4. **Row 13:** k1, *p1, k2tog, yo, k1, p1, k1, yo, ssk*, p1, k1. **Row 14:** Rep R 2. **Row 15:** k1, k2tog, *yo, {p1, k1} 2 times, p1, yo, sl 1-k2tog-psso*, end last rep ssk, k1. **Row 16:** p2, *{p1, k1} 3 times, p2*, p1.
Rep Rs 1-16.

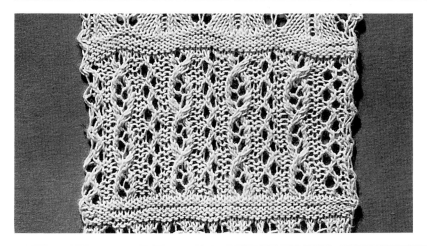

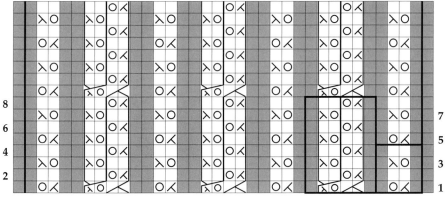

Cable repeat: 6 sts, 8 Rs.
Ground repeat: 4 sts, 4 Rs.
Combined repeat of 1 ground,
  1 cable: 10 sts, 8 Rs.
   Add 2 edge sts: 1 each side.

├─ **Combined repeat** ─┤
  10 sts

Multiple of 10 sts, plus 2.
The division between patterns is
marked by a slash (/).
Rs 2-8 (wrong side): k1, *k1, p2, yo,
p2tog, k1, / k1, p2, k1*, k1.

Row 1: p1, *p1, k2tog, yo, p1, / p1,
sl 2 sts onto extra ndl and hold in back
of work, k next 2 sts, yo, ssk the 2 sts
off extra ndl, p1*, p1. **Row 3:** p1, *p1,
yo, ssk, p1, / p1, k2, yo, ssk, p1*, p1.
Row 5: p1, *p1, k2tog, yo, p1, / p1, k2,
yo, ssk, p1*, p1. **Row 7:** Rep R 3.
Rep Rs 1-8.

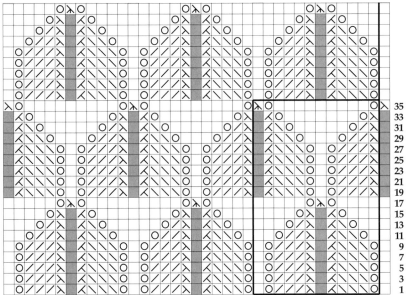

|————— Modified st —————|

Repeat: 12 sts, 36 Rs.
Add 1 edge st at Rt.
Modified st at L: R 35.
Even Rs: P, but k single st
between dec (gray squares).

Multiple of 12 sts, plus 1.
Even Rs 2-16 (wrong side): *p6, k1,
p5*, p1.

Even Rs 20-34 (wrong side): *k1, p11*, k1.
Even Rs 18, 36 (wrong side): P all sts.

Rows 1, 3, 5, 7, 9: k1, *yo, k3, k2tog,
p1, ssk, k3, yo, k1*. **Row 11:** k1, *k1,
yo, k2, k2tog, p1, ssk, k2, yo, k2*.
Row 13: k1, *k2, yo, k1, k2tog, p1, ssk,
k1, yo, k3*. **Row 15:** k1, *k3, yo, k2tog,
p1, ssk, yo, k4*. **Row 17:** k1, *k4, yo,

sl 1-k2tog-psso, yo, k5*. **Rows 19, 21,
23, 25, 27:** p1, *ssk, k3, yo, k1, yo, k3,
k2tog, p1*. **Row 29:** p1, *ssk, k2, yo,
k3, yo, k2, k2tog, p1*. **Row 31:** p1,
ssk, k1, yo, k5, yo, k1, k2tog, p1.
Row 33: p1, *ssk, yo, k7, yo, k2tog,
p1*. **Row 35:** ssk, *yo, k9, yo, sl 1-
k2tog-psso*, end last rep ssk.
Rep Rs 1-36.

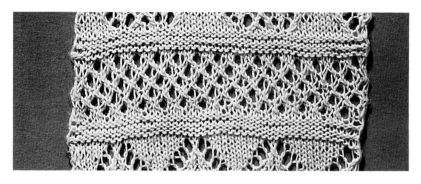

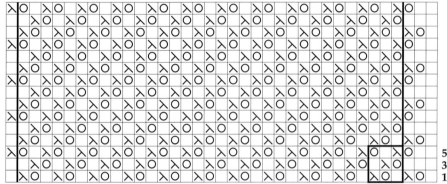

Repeat: 3 sts, 6 Rs.
Add 4 edge sts: 1 at L, 3 at Rt.
Even Rs: P all sts.

Multiple of 3 sts, plus 4.
Even Rs 2-6 (wrong side): P all sts.

Row 1: *k1, yo, ssk*, k1.
Row 3: k3, *yo, ssk, k1*, k1.
Row 5: k2, yo, *ssk, k1, yo*, ssk.
Rep Rs 1-6.

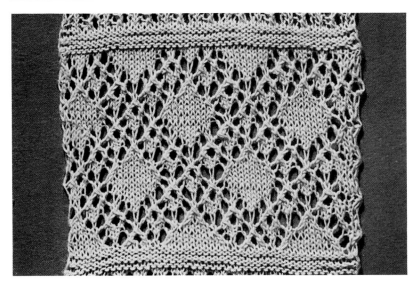

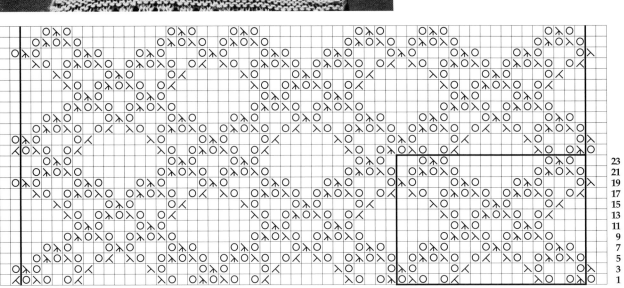

Repeat: 18 sts, 24 Rs.
Add 4 edge sts: 2 each side.
Even Rs: P all sts.

Multiple of 18 sts, plus 4.
Even Rs 2-24 (wrong side): P all sts.

Row 1: k1, yo, *sl 1-k2tog-psso, yo, k1, yo, ssk, k7, k2tog, yo, k1, yo, ssk, yo*, k2tog, k1. **Row 3:** k1, ssk, *yo, k3, yo, ssk, k5, k2tog, yo, k3, yo, sl 1-k2tog-psso*, yo, k1. **Row 5:** k2, *yo, ssk, yo, sl 1-k2tog-psso, yo, k1, yo, ssk, k1, k2tog, yo, k1, yo, ssk, yo, sl 1-k2tog-psso, yo, k1*, k2. **Row 7:** k2, *{k1, yo, sl 1-k2tog-psso, yo, k2} 3 times*, k2. **Row 9:** k2, *k3, {yo, ssk, yo, sl 1-k2tog-psso, yo, k1} 2 times, k3*, k2. **Row 11:** k2, *k4, {yo, sl 1-k2tog-psso, yo, k3} 2 times, k2*, k2. **Row 13:** k2, *k3, k2tog, yo, k1, yo, ssk, yo, sl 1-k2tog-psso, yo, k1, yo, ssk, k4*, k2. **Row 15:** k2, *k2, k2tog, yo, k3, yo, sl 1-k2tog-psso, yo, k3, yo, ssk, k3*, k2. **Row 17:** k2, *k2tog, yo, k1, {yo, ssk, yo, sl 1-k2tog-psso, yo, k1} 2 times, yo, ssk, k1*, k2. **Row 19:** k1, ssk, *yo, k3, {yo, sl 1-k2tog-psso, yo, k3} 2 times, yo, sl 1-k2tog-psso*, yo, k1. **Row 21:** k2, *yo, ssk, yo, sl 1-k2tog-psso, yo, k7, yo, ssk, yo, sl 1-k2tog-psso, yo, k1*, k2. **Row 23:** k2, *k1, yo, sl 1-k2tog-psso, yo, k9, yo, sl 1-k2tog-psso, yo, k2*, k2.
Rep Rs 1-24.

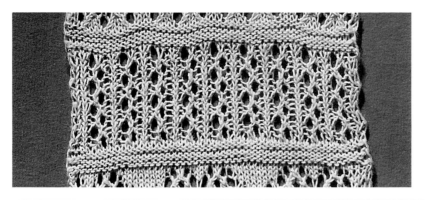

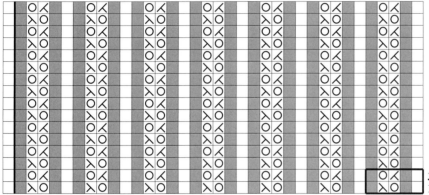

3
1

Repeat: 5 sts, 4 Rs.
Add 1 edge st at L.
Even Rs: P on p sts and yo
  (white squares), k on k sts
  (gray squares).

Multiple of 5 sts, plus 1.

Row 1: *k1, p1, yo, ssk, p1*, k1.
Row 2: p1, *k1, p2, k1, p1*.
Row 3: *k1, p1, k2tog, yo, p1*, k1.
Row 4: Rep R 2.
Rep Rs 1-4.

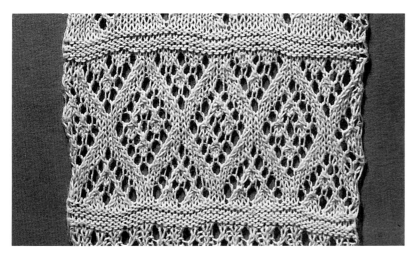

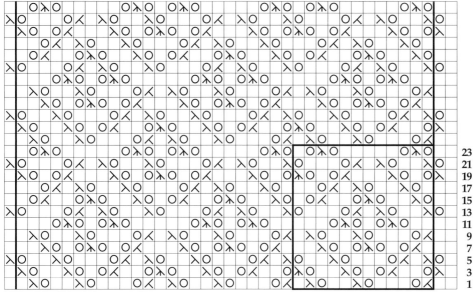

|—— Modified sts ——|

Repeat: 12 sts, 24 Rs.
Add 3 edge sts: 1 at L, 2 at Rt.
Modified sts at L: Rs 3, 19.
Even Rs: P all sts.

Multiple of 12 sts, plus 3.
Even Rs 2-24 (wrong side): P all sts.

Row 1: k2, *k2tog, yo, k3, yo, ssk, k2, yo, ssk, k1*, k1. **Row 3:** k1, ssk, *yo,

k2, k2tog, yo, k1, yo, ssk, k2, yo, sl 1-k2tog-psso*, end last rep ssk, k1.
Row 5: k1, yo, *ssk, k1, k2tog, yo, k3, yo, ssk, k2, yo*, ssk. **Row 7:** k2, *k1, k2tog, yo, k1, yo, sl 1-k2tog-psso, yo, k1, yo, ssk, k2*, k1. **Row 9:** k2, *k2tog, yo, k3, yo, ssk, k2, yo, ssk, k1*, k1. **Row 11:** k2, *k2, {yo, sl 1-k2tog-psso, yo, k1} 2 times, k2*, k1. **Row 13:** k1, yo, *ssk, k2, yo, ssk, k1, k2tog, yo, k3, yo*, ssk. **Row 15:** k2, *yo, ssk, k2, yo,

sl 1-k2tog-psso, yo, k2, k2tog, yo, k1*, k1. **Row 17:** k2, *k1, yo, ssk, k2, yo, ssk, k1, k2tog, yo, k2*, k1. **Row 19:** k1, ssk, *yo, k1, yo, ssk, k3, k2tog, yo, k1, yo, sl 1-k2tog-psso*, end last rep ssk, k1. **Row 21:** k1, yo, *ssk, k2, yo, ssk, k1, k2tog, yo, k3, yo*, ssk. **Row 23:** k2, *yo, sl 1-k2tog-psso, yo, k5, yo, sl 1-k2tog-psso, yo, k1*, k1.
Rep Rs 1-24.

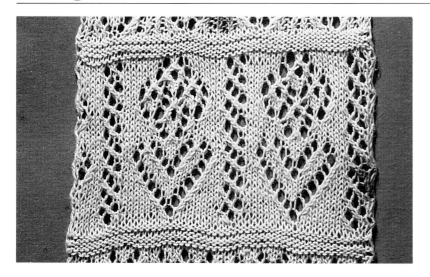

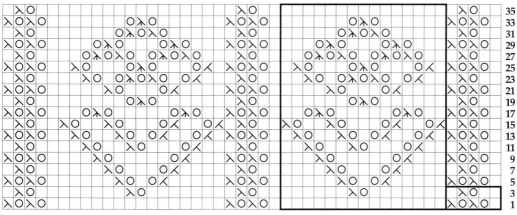

Flower repeat: 15 sts, 36 Rs.
Ground repeat: 5 sts, 4 Rs.
Combined repeat of 1 ground,
 1 flower: 20 sts, 36 Rs.
Even Rs: P all sts.

Combined repeat 20 sts

Multiple of 20 sts.
The division between patterns is
marked by a slash (/).
Even Rs 2-36 (wrong side): P all sts.

Row 1: *k1, {yo, ssk} 2 times, / k15*.
Row 3: *k2, yo, ssk, k1, / k7, yo, ssk,
k6*. **Row 5:** *k1, {yo, ssk} 2 times, / k5,
k2tog, yo, k1, yo, ssk, k5*. **Row 7:** *k2,
yo, ssk, k1, / k4, k2tog, yo, k3, yo,

ssk, k4*. **Row 9:** *k1, {yo, ssk} 2 times,
/ k3, k2tog, yo, k5, yo, ssk, k3*.
Row 11: *k2, yo, ssk, k1, / k2, k2tog, yo,
k3, {yo, ssk, k2} 2 times*. **Row 13:** *k1,
{yo, ssk} 2 times, / {k1, k2tog, yo, k1}
2 times, yo, ssk, k2, yo, ssk, k1*.
Row 15: *k2, yo, ssk, k1, / {k2tog, yo,
k2} 2 times, k1, yo, ssk, k2, yo, ssk*.
Row 17: *k1, {yo, ssk} 2 times, / k2,
yo, sl 1-k2tog-psso, yo, k5, yo, sl 1-
k2tog-psso, yo, k2*. **Row 19:** *k2, yo,
ssk, k1, / k6, yo, sl 1-k2tog-psso, yo,
k6*. **Row 21:** *k1, {yo, ssk} 2 times,
/ k4, k2tog, yo, k3, yo, ssk, k4*.
Row 23: *k2, yo, ssk, k1, / k2, k2tog,

yo, k1, yo, ssk, yo, sl 1-k2tog-psso,
yo, k1, yo, ssk, k2*. **Row 25:** *k1, {yo,
ssk} 2 times, / k1, k2tog, yo, k3, yo,
sl 1-k2tog-psso, yo, k3, yo, ssk, k1*.
Row 27: *k2, yo, ssk, k1, / k2, {yo, ssk,
yo, sl 1-k2tog-psso, yo, k1} 2 times, k1*.
Row 29: *k1, {yo, ssk} 2 times, / {k3,
yo, sl 1-k2tog-psso, yo} 2 times, k3*.
Row 31: *k2, yo, ssk, k1, / k5, yo, ssk,
yo, sl 1-k2tog-psso, yo, k5*. **Row 33:** *k1,
{yo, ssk} 2 times, / k6, yo, sl 1-k2tog-
psso, yo, k6*. **Row 35:** *k2, yo, ssk,
k1, / k15*.
Rep Rs 1-36 for an allover pattern.

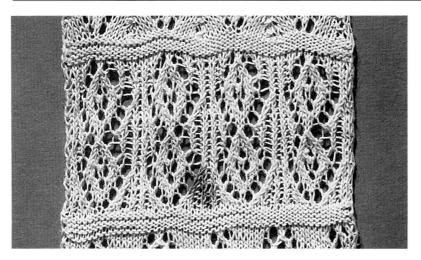

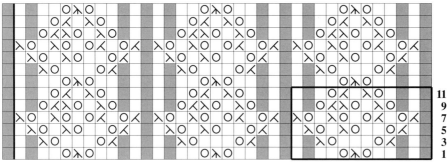

Repeat: 12 sts, 12 Rs.
Add 1 edge st at L.
Even Rs: P on p sts and yo
  (white squares), k on k sts
  (gray squares).

Multiple of 12 sts, plus 1.

Row 1: *p1, k1, p1, k2, yo, sl 1-k2tog-psso, yo, k2, p1, k1*, p1. **Row 2:** k1, *p1, k1, p7, k1, p1, k1*. **Row 3:** *p1, k1, p1, k2tog, yo, k3, yo, ssk, p1, k1*, p1. **Row 4:** Rep R 2. **Row 5:** *p1, k1, k2tog, yo, k2, {yo, ssk, k1} 2 times*, p1. **Row 6:** k1, *p11, k1*. **Row 7:** *p1, {k2tog, yo, k1} 2 times, yo, ssk, k1, yo, ssk*, p1. **Row 8:** Rep R 6. **Row 9:** *p1, k1, p1, yo, ssk, k1, yo, ssk, k2tog, yo, p1, k1*, p1. **Row 10:** Rep R 2. **Row 11:** *p1, k1, p1, k1, yo, ssk, k1, k2tog, yo, k1, p1, k1*, p1. **Row 12:** Rep R 2.
Rep Rs 1-12.

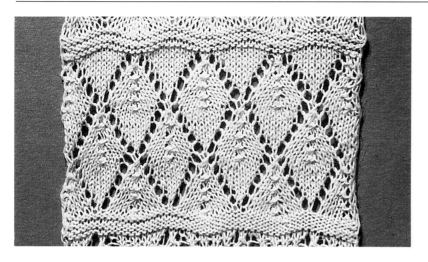

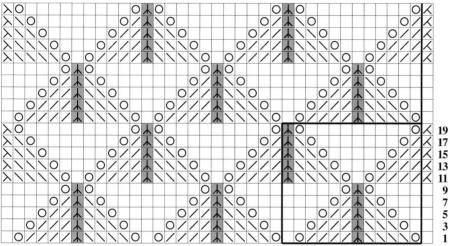

—— **Modified sts** ——

Repeat: 12 sts, 20 Rs.
Add 1 edge st at Rt.
Modified sts at L: Rs 11, 13,
   15, 17, 19.
Even Rs: P all sts.

Multiple of 12 sts, plus 1.
Even Rs 2-20 (wrong side): P all sts.
⋏ = P2tog, then sl 1 st kwise. Return both sts to L ndl, psso, return to Rt ndl.

Row 1: k1, *yo, k4, ⋏, k4, yo, k1*.
Row 3: k1, *k1, yo, k3, ⋏, k3, yo, k2*.

Row 5: k1, *k2, yo, k2, ⋏, k2, yo, k3*.
Row 7: k1, *k3, yo, k1, ⋏, k1, yo, k4*.
Row 9: k1, *k4, yo, ⋏, yo, k5*.
Row 11: k2tog, *k4, yo, k1, yo, k4, ⋏*, end last rep ssk. **Row 13:** k2tog, *k3, yo, k3, yo, k3, ⋏*, end last rep ssk.
Row 15: k2tog, *k2, yo, k5, yo, k2, ⋏*, end last rep ssk. **Row 17:** k2tog, *k1, yo, k7, yo, k1, ⋏*, end last rep ssk.
Row 19: k2tog, *yo, k9, yo, ⋏*, end last rep ssk.
Rep Rs 1-20.

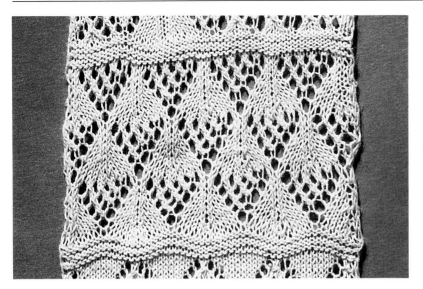

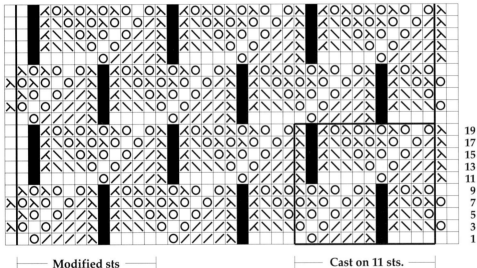

Modified sts ——— **Cast on 11 sts.**

19
17
15
13
11
9
7
5
3
1

Repeat: 11 sts, 20 Rs.
Add 3 edge sts: 1 at L, 2 at Rt.
Modified sts at L: Rs 11, 13, 15, 17, 19.
Even Rs: P all sts.

Multiple of 11 sts, plus 3.
Even Rs 2-20 (wrong side): P all sts.

Row 1: k2, *k4, ssk, k4, yo, k1*, k1.
Row 3: k1, yo, *k3, k2tog, ssk, k3, yo, k1, yo*, ssk. **Row 5:** k2, *yo, k2, k2tog, ssk, k2, yo, k1, yo, ssk*, k1. **Row 7:** k1, yo, *ssk, yo, k1, k2tog, ssk, k1, yo, k1, yo, ssk, yo*, ssk. **Row 9:** k2, *yo, ssk, yo, k2tog, ssk, yo, k1, {yo, ssk} 2 times*, k1. **Row 11:** k1, ssk, *k4, yo, k5, ssk*, end last rep k2. **Row 13:** k1, ssk, *k3, yo, k1, yo, k3, k2tog, ssk*, end last rep k2. **Row 15:** k1, ssk, *k2, yo, k1, yo, ssk, yo, k2, k2tog, ssk*, end last rep k2. **Row 17:** k1, ssk, *{k1, yo} 2 times, {ssk, yo} 2 times, k1, k2tog, ssk*, end last rep k2. **Row 19:** k1, ssk, *yo, k1, {yo, ssk} 3 times, yo, k2tog, ssk*, end last rep k2.
Rep Rs 1-20.

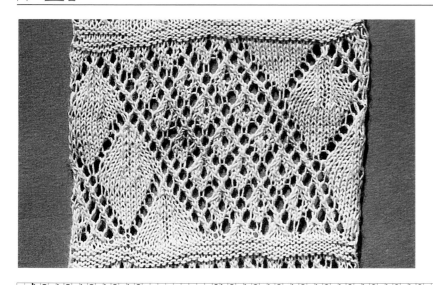

Note: To make the pattern a repeating unit, one plain stitch on each side of the ground panel has been added on the chart.

Repeat: 36 sts, 72 Rs.
Add 4 edge sts: 2 each side.
Even Rs: P all sts.

(Pattern 47 continued)

Multiple of 36 sts, plus 4.
Even Rs 2-72 (wrong side): P all sts.

Row 1: k2, *ssk, k4, yo, k2, {yo, ssk, k1, k2tog, yo, k1} 3 times, yo, ssk, k1, yo, k4, k2tog, k1*, k2. **Row 3:** k2, *ssk, k3, yo, k1, yo, ssk, k1, {yo, sl 1-k2tog-psso, yo, k3} 3 times, yo, ssk, k1, yo, k3, k2tog, k1*, k2. **Row 5:** k2, *ssk, k2, yo, k3, {yo, ssk, k1} 8 times, yo, k2, k2tog, k1*, k2. **Row 7:** k2, *ssk, k1, yo, k5, yo, ssk, k1, {yo, ssk, k1, k2tog, yo, k1} 3 times, yo, ssk, k1, yo, k1, k2tog, k1*, k2. **Row 9:** k2, *ssk, yo, k7, yo, ssk, k1, {yo, sl 1-k2tog-psso, yo, k3} 3 times, yo, ssk, k1, yo, k2tog, k1*, k2. **Row 11:** k1, ssk, *yo, k9, {yo, ssk, k1} 8 times, yo, sl 1-k2tog-psso*, yo, k1. **Row 13:** k1, yo, *k4, k2tog, k1, ssk, k4, yo, k2, {yo, ssk, k1, k2tog, yo, k1} 3 times, yo, ssk, k1, yo*, ssk, k1. **Row 15:** k2, *yo, k3, k2tog, k1, ssk, k3, yo, k1, yo, ssk, k1, {yo, sl 1-k2tog-psso, yo, k3} 3 times, yo, ssk, k1*, yo, ssk. **Row 17:** k2, *k1, yo, k2, k2tog, k1, ssk, k2, yo, k3, {yo, ssk, k1} 7 times, yo, ssk*, k2. **Row 19:** k1, yo, *ssk, k1, yo, k1, k2tog, k1, ssk, k1, yo, k5, yo, ssk, k1, {yo, ssk, k1, k2tog, yo, k1} 3 times, yo*, ssk, k1. **Row 21:** k2, *yo, ssk, k1, yo, k2tog, k1, ssk, yo, k7, yo, ssk, k1, {yo, sl 1-k2tog-psso, yo, k3} 3 times*, yo, ssk. **Row 23:** k2, *k1, yo, ssk, k1, yo, sl 1-k2tog-psso, yo, k9, {yo, ssk, k1} 6 times, yo, ssk*, k2. **Row 25:** k1, k2tog, yo, *k1, yo, ssk, k1, yo, k4, k2tog, k1, ssk, k4, yo, k2, {yo, ssk, k1,

k2tog, yo, k1} 2 times, yo, ssk, k1, k2tog*, yo, k1. **Row 27:** k2tog, yo, *k3, yo, ssk, k1, yo, k3, k2tog, k1, ssk, k3, yo, k1, yo, ssk, k1, {yo, sl 1-k2tog-psso, yo, k3} 2 times, yo, sl 1-k2tog-psso, yo*, k2. **Row 29:** k2, *{k1, yo, ssk} 2 times, k1, yo, k2, k2tog, k1, ssk, k2, yo, k3, {yo, ssk, k1} 5 times, yo, ssk*, k2. **Row 31:** k1, yo, *ssk, k1, k2tog, yo, k1, yo, ssk, k1, yo, k1, k2tog, k1, ssk, k1, yo, k5, yo, ssk, k1, {yo, ssk, k1, k2tog, yo, k1} 2 times, yo*, ssk, k1. **Row 33:** k2, *yo, sl 1-k2tog-psso, yo, k3, yo, ssk, k1, yo, k2tog, k1, ssk, yo, k7, yo, ssk, k1, {yo, sl 1-k2tog-psso, yo, k3} 2 times*, yo, ssk. **Row 35:** k2, *{k1, yo, ssk} 3 times, k1, yo, sl 1-k2tog-psso, yo, k9, {yo, ssk, k1} 4 times, yo, ssk*, k2. **Row 37:** k1, k2tog, *yo, k1, yo, ssk, k1, k2tog, yo, k1, yo, ssk, k1, yo, k4, k2tog, k1, ssk, k4, yo, k2, yo, ssk, k1, k2tog, yo, k1, yo, ssk, k1, k2tog*, yo, k1. **Row 39:** k2tog, yo, *k3, yo, sl 1-k2tog-psso, yo, k3, yo, ssk, k1, yo, k3, k2tog, k1, ssk, k3, yo, k1, yo, ssk, k1, yo, sl 1-k2tog-psso, yo, k3, yo, sl 1-k2tog-psso, yo*, k2. **Row 41:** k2, *{k1, yo, ssk} 4 times, k1, yo, k2, k2tog, k1, ssk, k2, yo, k3, {yo, ssk, k1} 3 times, yo, ssk*, k2. **Row 43:** k1, yo, *{ssk, k1, k2tog, yo, k1, yo} 2 times, ssk, k1, yo, k1, k2tog, k1, ssk, k1, yo, k5, yo, ssk, k1, k2tog, yo, k1, yo*, ssk, k1. **Row 45:** k2, *{yo, sl 1-k2tog-psso, yo, k3} 2 times, yo, ssk, k1, yo, k2tog, k1, ssk, yo, k7, yo, ssk, k1, yo, sl 1-k2tog-psso, yo, k3*, yo, ssk. **Row 47:** k2, *{k1, yo, ssk} 5 times, k1, yo, sl 1-

k2tog-psso, yo, k9, {yo, ssk, k1} 2 times, yo, ssk*, k2. **Row 49:** k1, k2tog, *{yo, k1, yo, ssk, k1, k2tog} 2 times, yo, k1, yo, ssk, k1, yo, k4, k2tog, k1, ssk, k4, yo, k2, yo, ssk, k1, k2tog*, yo, k1. **Row 51:** k2tog, yo, *{k3, yo, sl 1-k2tog-psso, yo} 2 times, k3, yo, ssk, k1, yo, k3, k2tog, k1, ssk, k3, yo, k1, yo, ssk, k1, yo, sl 1-k2tog-psso, yo*, k2. **Row 53:** k2, *{k1, yo, ssk} 6 times, k1, yo, k2, k2tog, k1, ssk, k2, yo, k3, yo, ssk, k1, yo, ssk*, k2. **Row 55:** k1, yo, *{ssk, k1, k2tog, yo, k1, yo} 3 times, ssk, k1, yo, k1, k2tog, k1, ssk, k1, yo, k5, yo, ssk, k1, yo*, ssk, k1. **Row 57:** k2, *{yo, sl 1-k2tog-psso, yo, k3} 3 times, yo, ssk, k1, yo, k2tog, k1, ssk, yo, k7, yo, ssk, k1*, yo, ssk. **Row 59:** k2, *{k1, yo, ssk} 7 times, k1, yo, sl 1-k2tog-psso, yo, k9, yo, ssk*, k2. **Row 61:** k2tog, yo, *k2, {yo, ssk, k1, k2tog, yo, k1} 3 times, yo, ssk, k1, yo, k4, k2tog, k1, ssk, k4, yo*, k2. **Row 63:** k2, *yo, ssk, k1, {yo, sl 1-k2tog-psso, yo, k3} 3 times, yo, ssk, k1, yo, k3, k2tog, k1, ssk, k3, yo, k1*, yo, ssk. **Row 65:** k2, *{k1, yo, ssk} 8 times, k1, yo, k2, k2tog, k1, ssk, k2, yo, k2*, k2. **Row 67:** k2, *k2, {yo, ssk, k1} 2 times, {k2tog, yo, k1, yo, ssk, k1} 3 times, yo, k1, k2tog, k1, ssk, k1, yo, k3*, k2. **Row 69:** k2, *k3, yo, ssk, k1, {yo, sl 1-k2tog-psso, yo, k3} 3 times, yo, ssk, k1, yo, k2tog, k1, ssk, yo, k4*, k2. **Row 71:** k2, *k4, {yo, ssk, k1} 8 times, yo, sl 1-k2tog-psso, yo, k5*, k2.
Rep Rs 1-72.

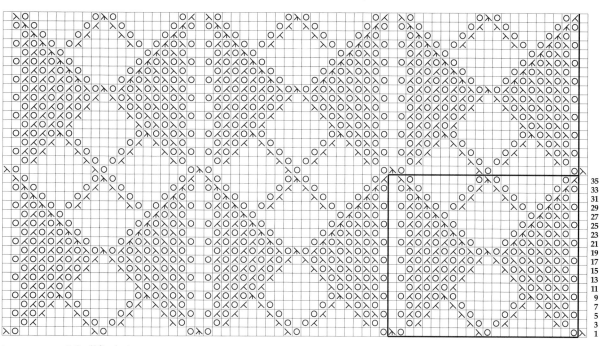

|——————— Modified st ———————|

Repeat: 22 sts, 36 Rs.
Add 1 edge st at Rt.
Modified st at L: R 1.
Even Rs: P all sts.

(*Pattern 48 continued*)

Multiple of 22 sts, plus 1.
Even Rs 2-36 (wrong side): P all sts.
⟋ = Ssk, return st to L ndl, pnso, return st to Rt ndl.

Row 1: ssk, *yo, k9, yo, ssk, k8, yo, sl 1-k2tog-psso*, end last rep ssk.
Row 3: k1, *k1, yo, ssk, k5, k2tog, yo, k1, yo, ssk, k5, k2tog, yo, k2*.
Row 5: k1, *{yo, ssk} 2 times, k3, k2tog, yo, k3, yo, ssk, k3, {k2tog, yo} 2 times, k1*. **Row 7:** k1, *k1, {yo, ssk} 2 times, k1, k2tog, yo, k5, yo, ssk, k1, {k2tog, yo} 2 times, k2*. **Row 9:** k1, *{yo, ssk} 2 times, yo, sl 1-k2tog-psso, yo, k7, yo, sl 1-k2tog-psso, yo, {k2tog, yo} 2 times, k1*. **Row 11:** k1, *k1, {yo, ssk} 3 times, k7, {k2tog, yo} 3 times, k2*. **Row 13:** k1, *{yo, ssk} 4 times, k5, {k2tog, yo} 4 times, k1*. **Row 15:** k1, *k1, {yo, ssk} 4 times, k3, {k2tog, yo} 4 times, k2*. **Row 17:** k1, *{yo, ssk} 5 times, k1, {k2tog, yo} 5 times, k1*. **Row 19:** k1, *k1, {yo, ssk} 3 times, yo, k2tog, yo, sl 1-k2tog-psso, yo, ssk, yo, {k2tog, yo} 3 times, k2*. **Row 21:** k1, *{yo, ssk} 3 times, yo, ⟋, yo, k3, yo, sl 1-k2tog-psso, yo, {k2tog, yo} 3 times, k1*. **Row 23:** k1, *k1, {yo, ssk} 2 times, yo, ⟋, yo, k5, yo, sl 1-k2tog-psso, yo, {k2tog, yo} 2 times, k2*.

Row 25: k1, *{yo, ssk} 2 times, yo, ⟋, yo, k7, yo, sl 1-k2tog-psso, yo, {k2tog, yo} 2 times, k1*. **Row 27:** k1, *k1, yo, ssk, yo, ⟋, yo, k9, yo, sl 1-k2tog-psso, yo, k2tog, yo, k2*. **Row 29:** k1, *yo, ssk, yo, ⟋, yo, k1, yo, ssk, k5, k2tog, yo, k1, yo, sl 1-k2tog-psso, yo, k2tog, yo, k1*. **Row 31:** k1, *k1, yo, ⟋, yo, k3, yo, ssk, k3, k2tog, yo, k3, yo, sl 1-k2tog-psso, yo, k2*. **Row 33:** k1, *yo, ⟋, yo, k5, yo, ssk, k1, k2tog, yo, k5, yo, sl 1-k2tog-psso, yo, k1*.
Row 35: k1, *k2tog, yo, k7, yo, sl 1-k2tog-psso, yo, k7, yo, ssk, k1*.
Rep Rs 1-36.

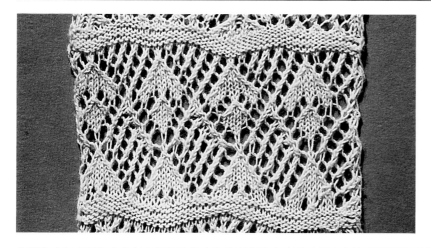

Note: The double decrease in row 11 leans left in the sampler and right on the chart.

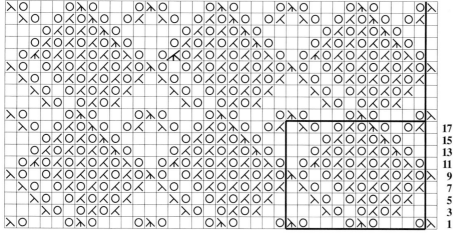

├────── **Modified sts** ──────┤

Repeat: 12 sts, 18 Rs.
Add 1 edge st at Rt.
Modified sts at L: Rs 1, 9.
Even Rs: P all sts.

Multiple of 12 sts, plus 1.
Even Rs 2-18 (wrong side): P all sts.
⊿ = Ssk, return st to L ndl, pnso, return st to Rt ndl.

Row 1: ssk, *yo, k3, yo, sl 1-k2tog-psso, yo, k3, yo, sl 1-k2tog-psso*, end last rep ssk. **Row 3:** k1, *k2, {k2tog, yo} 2 times, k1, yo, ssk, k3*. **Row 5:** k1, *k1, {k2tog, yo} 3 times, k1, yo, ssk, k2*. **Row 7:** k1, *{k2tog, yo} 4 times, k1, yo, ssk, k1*. **Row 9:** ssk, *yo, {k2tog, yo} 4 times, k1, yo, sl 1-k2tog-psso*, end last rep ssk. **Row 11:** k1, *yo, ssk, yo, {k2tog, yo} 3 times, ⊿, yo, k1*. **Row 13:** k1, *k1, yo, sl 1-k2tog-psso, yo, {k2tog, yo} 3 times, k2*. **Row 15:** k1, *k2, yo, sl 1-k2tog-psso, yo, {k2tog, yo} 2 times, k3*. **Row 17:** k1, *k2tog, yo, k1, yo, sl 1-k2tog-psso, yo, k2tog, yo, k1, yo, ssk, k1*. Rep Rs 1-18.

Note: In this pattern, the edge stitches for the leaf are provided by the ground.

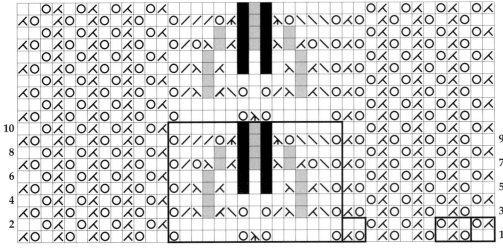

Leaf repeat: 13 sts, 10 Rs.
  Add 2 edge sts: 1 each side.
Ground repeat: 3 sts, 2 Rs.
  Add 4 edge sts: 2 each side.
Combined repeat of 3 ground,
  1 leaf: 26 sts, 10 Rs.
  Add 1 edge st at L (not shown).

Multiple of 26 sts, plus 1.
The division between patterns is marked by a slash (/).
Rows 1-4 have multiple of 28 sts plus 1.
$\boxtimes$ = Ssk, return st to L ndl, pnso, return st to Rt ndl.

Cast on 13 sts.

Combined repeat 26 sts

Row 1: *k2, {yo, k2tog} 4 times, / yo, k5, yo, sl 1-k2tog-psso, yo, k5, yo*, k1.
Row 2: p1, *p15, / p2, {yo, p2tog} 4 times*. **Row 3:** *k2, {yo, k2tog} 4 times, / yo, k1, k2tog, p1, ssk, {k1, yo} 2 times, k1, k2tog, p1, ssk, k1, yo*, k1.
Row 4: p1, *p3, k1, p7, k1, p3, / p2, {yo, p2tog} 4 times*. **Row 5:** *k2, {yo, k2tog} 4 times, / yo, k1, k2tog, p1, ssk, k3, k2tog, p1, ssk, k1, yo*, k1.
Row 6: p1, *p3, k1, p5, k1, p3, / p2, {yo, p2tog} 4 times*. **Row 7:** *k2, {yo, k2tog} 4 times, / yo, k1, yo, k2tog, p1, ssk, p1, k2tog, p1, ssk, yo, k1, yo*, k1. **Row 8:** p1, *p4, {k1, p1} 2 times, k1, p4, / p2, {yo, p2tog} 4 times*. **Row 9:** *k2, {yo, k2tog} 4 times, / yo, k3, yo, sl 1-k2tog-psso, p1, $\boxtimes$, yo, k3, yo*, k1. **Row 10:** p1, *p6, k1, p6, / p2, {yo, p2tog} 4 times*.
Rep Rs 1-10.

(Pattern 50 continued)
Leaf pattern when used alone:
Multiple of 14 sts, plus 1.

Row 1: *p1, yo, k5, yo, sl 1-k2tog-psso, yo, k5, yo*, p1. **Row 2:** k1, *p15*, k1. **Row 3:** *p1, yo, k1, k2tog, p1, ssk, {k1, yo} 2 times, k1, k2tog, p1, ssk, k1, yo*, p1. **Row 4:** k1, *p3, k1, p7, k1, p3*, k1.

Row 5: *p1, yo, k1, k2tog, p1, ssk, k3, k2tog, p1, ssk, k1, yo*, p1. **Row 6:** k1, *p3, k1, p5, k1, p3*, k1. **Row 7:** *p1, yo, k1, yo, k2tog, p1, ssk, p1, k2tog, p1, ssk, yo, k1, yo*, p1. **Row 8:** k1, *p4, {k1, p1} 2 times, k1, p4*, k1. **Row 9:** *p1, yo, k3, yo, sl 1-k2tog-psso, p1, , yo, k3, yo*, p1. **Row 10:** k1, *p6, k1, p6*, k1.
Rep Rs 1-10.

Ground pattern when used alone:
Multiple of 3 sts, plus 4.

Row 1: k2, *yo, k2tog, k1*, yo, k2tog.
Row 2: p2, *yo, p2tog, p1*, yo, p2tog.
Rep Rs 1-2.

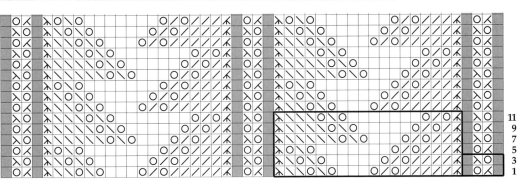

Note: In the sampler, the fern decreases are not paired. On the chart, they are paired as on the right side of the sampler.

Fern repeat: 18 sts, 12 Rs.
Ground repeat: 4 sts, 4 Rs.
Combined repeat of 1 ground, 1 fern: 22 sts, 12 Rs.
Even Rs: P, but k single st each side of fern (gray squares).

Multiple of 22 sts.
The division between patterns is marked by a slash (/).

— Combined repeat 22 sts —

Even Rs 2-12 (wrong side): *p18, / k1, p2, k1*.
$\mathcal{K}$ = Ssk, return st to L ndl, pnso, return st to Rt ndl.

Row 1: *p1, k2tog, yo, p1, / $\mathcal{K}$, k5, yo, k1, yo, k3, yo, k1, yo, k2, sl 1-k2tog-psso*. **Row 3:** *p1, yo, ssk, p1, / $\mathcal{K}$, k4, yo, k1, yo, k5, {yo, k1} 2 times, sl 1-k2tog-psso*. **Row 5:** *p1, k2tog, yo, p1, / $\mathcal{K}$, k3, yo, k1, yo, k7, yo, k1, yo, sl 1-k2tog-psso*. **Row 7:** *p1, yo, ssk, p1, / $\mathcal{K}$, k2, yo, k1, yo, k3, yo, k1, yo, k5, sl 1-k2tog-psso*. **Row 9:** *p1, k2tog, yo, p1, / $\mathcal{K}$, {k1, yo} 2 times, k5, yo, k1, yo, k4, sl 1-k2tog-psso*. **Row 11:** *p1, yo, ssk, p1, / $\mathcal{K}$, yo, k1, yo, k7, yo, k1, yo, k3, sl 1-k2tog-psso*.
Rep Rs 1-12.

Note: In the sampler, the fan decreases are not paired. On the chart, they are paired as on the right side in the lower repeat and as on the left side in the upper repeat.

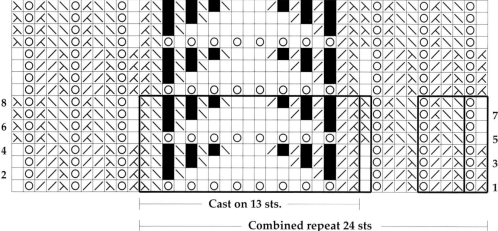

Cast on 13 sts.

Combined repeat 24 sts

Fan repeat: 13 sts, 4 Rs.
Zigzag repeat: 4 sts, 8 Rs.
  Add 3 edge sts: 1 at L, 2 at Rt.
Combined repeat of 2 zigzag,
  1 fan: 24 sts, 8 Rs.

Multiple of 24 sts.
The division between patterns is marked by a slash (/).
Rs 1 and 5: 30-st rep.
Rs 2 and 6: 28-st rep.
Rs 3 and 7: 26-st rep.
⊠ = P 1 st, sl 1 st kwise, return both sts to L ndl. Psso, return st to Rt ndl.

Row 1: *k2tog, yo, {ssk, k2, yo} 2 times, k1, / k2tog, {k1, yo} 8 times, k1, ssk*.
Row 2: *⊠, p15, p2tog, / p1, {yo, p2, ⊠}, 2 times, yo, p2tog*. **Row 3:** *k2tog, yo, {ssk, k2, yo} 2 times, k1, / k2tog, k13, ssk*. **Row 4:** *⊠, p11, p2tog, / p1, {yo, p2, ⊠} 2 times, yo, p2tog*.
Row 5: *k1, yo, {k2, k2tog, yo} 2 times, ssk, / k2tog, {k1, yo} 8 times, k1, ssk*.
Row 6: *⊠, p15, p2tog, / ⊠, {yo, p2tog, p2} 2 times, yo, p1*. **Row 7:** *k1, yo, {k2, k2tog, yo} 2 times, ssk, / k2tog, k13, ssk*. **Row 8:** *⊠, p11, p2tog, / ⊠, {yo, p2tog, p2} 2 times, yo, p1*.
Rep Rs 1-8.

Zigzag pattern when used alone:
Multiple of 4 sts, plus 3.

Row 1: k2tog, yo, *ssk, k2, yo*, k1.
Row 2: p1, *yo, p2, ⊠*, yo, p2tog.
Rows 3 and 4: Rep Rs 1 and 2.
Row 5: k1, yo, *k2, k2tog, yo*, ssk.
Row 6: ⊠, *yo, p2tog, p2*, yo, p1.
Rows 7 and 8: Rep Rs 5 and 6.
Rep Rs 1-8.

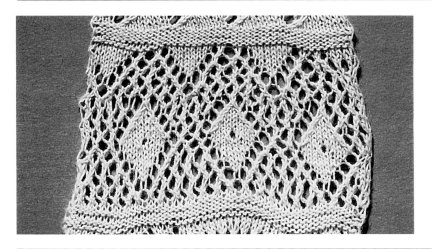

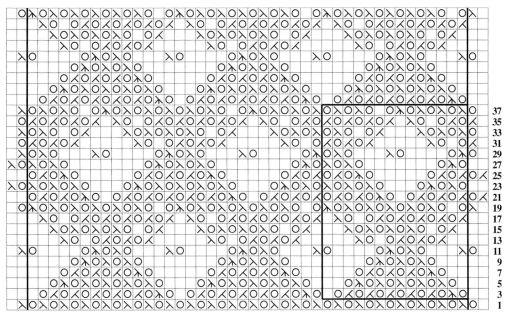

Repeat: 14 sts, 36 Rs.
Add 4 edge sts: 2 each side.
Even Rs: P all sts.

Multiple of 14 sts, plus 4.
Even Rs 2-38 (wrong side): P all sts.

Row 1: k1, yo, *{ssk, yo} 7 times*, ssk, k1. **Row 3:** k2, *yo, sl 1-k2tog-psso, yo, {k2tog, yo} 5 times, k1*, k2. **Row 5:** k2, *k1, {yo, ssk} 4 times, yo, sl 1-k2tog-

psso, yo, k2*, k2. **Row 7:** k2, *k2, yo, sl 1-k2tog-psso, yo, {k2tog, yo} 3 times, k3*, k2. **Row 9:** k2, *k3, {yo, ssk} 2 times, yo, sl 1-k2tog-psso, yo, k4*, k2. **Row 11:** k1, yo, *ssk, k3, yo, ssk, yo, sl 1-k2tog-psso, yo, k4, yo*, ssk, k1. **Row 13:** k2, *k2, {k2tog, yo} 3 times, k1, yo, ssk, k3*, k2. **Row 15:** k2, *k1, k2tog, yo, k1, {yo, ssk} 4 times, k2*, k2. **Row 17:** k2, *{k2tog, yo} 5 times, k1, yo, ssk, k1*, k2. **Row 19:** k1, ssk, *yo,

k1, {yo, ssk} 5 times, yo, sl 1-k2tog-psso*, yo, k1. **Row 21:** k2tog, yo, *{k2tog, yo} 3 times, k1, yo, sl 1-k2tog-psso, yo, {k2tog, yo} 2 times*, k2. **Row 23:** k2, *yo, ssk, yo, sl 1-k2tog-psso, yo, k3, {yo, ssk} 3 times*, yo, ssk. **Row 25:** k2tog, yo, *{k2tog, yo} 2 times, k5, yo, sl 1-k2tog-psso, yo, k2tog, yo*, k2. **Row 27:** k2, *yo, sl 1-k2tog-psso, yo, k7, {yo, ssk} 2 times*, yo, ssk. **Row 29:** k1, yo, *sl 1-k2tog-psso, yo,

(Pattern 53 continued)
k4, yo, ssk, k3, yo, ssk, yo*, ssk, k1.
Row 31: k1, k2tog, *yo, k1, yo, ssk, k5, {k2tog, yo} 2 times, k2tog*, yo, k1.

Row 33: k1, yo, *{ssk, yo} 2 times, ssk, k3, k2tog, yo, k1, yo, ssk, yo*, ssk, k1.
Row 35: k1, k2tog, *yo, k2tog, yo, k1, yo, ssk, k1, {k2tog} 3 times, k2tog*,

yo, k1. **Row 37:** k1, yo, *{ssk, yo} 3 times, sl 1-k2tog-psso, yo, k1, {yo, ssk} 2 times, yo*, ssk, k1.
Rep Rs 3-38 for an allover pattern.

Pattern 54

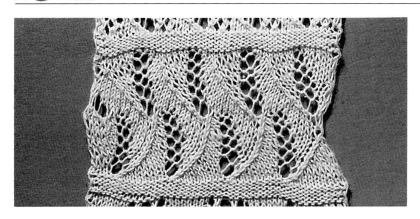

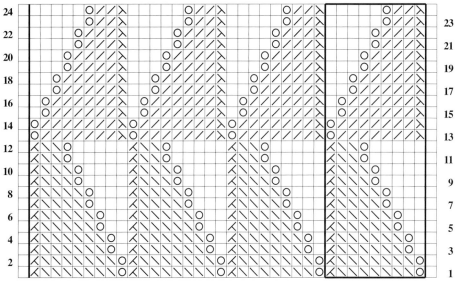

Repeat: 9 sts, 24 Rs.
Add 2 edge sts: 1 each side.

Multiple of 9 sts, plus 2.
◩ = P 1 st, sl 1 st kwise, return both sts to L ndl. Psso, return st to Rt ndl.

Row 1: k1, *yo, k7, k2tog*, k1. **Row 2:** p1, *p2tog, p7, yo*, p1. **Row 3:** k1, *k1, yo, k6, k2tog*, k1. **Row 4:** p1, *p2tog, p6, yo, p1*, p1. **Row 5:** k1, *k2, yo, k5, k2tog*, k1. **Row 6:** p1, *p2tog, p5, yo, p2*, p1. **Row 7:** k1, *k3, yo, k4, k2tog*, k1. **Row 8:** p1, *p2tog, p4, yo, p3*, p1. **Row 9:** k1, *k4, yo, k3, k2tog*, k1. **Row 10:** p1, *p2tog, p3, yo, p4*, p1. **Row 11:** k1, *k5, yo, k2, k2tog*, k1. **Row 12:** p1, *p2tog, p2, yo, p5*, p1. **Row 13:** k1, *ssk, k7, yo*, k1. **Row 14:** p1, *yo, p7, ◩*, p1. **Row 15:** k1, *ssk, k6, yo, k1*, k1. **Row 16:** p1, *p1, yo, p6, ◩*, p1. **Row 17:** k1, *ssk, k5, yo, k2*, k1. **Row 18:** p1, *p2, yo, p5, ◩*, p1. **Row 19:** k1, *ssk, k4, yo, k3*, k1. **Row 20:** p1, *p3, yo, p4, ◩*, p1. **Row 21:** k1, *ssk, k3, yo, k4*, k1. **Row 22:** p1, *p4, yo, p3, ◩*, p1. **Row 23:** k1, *ssk, k2, yo, k5*, k1. **Row 24:** p1, *p5, yo, p2, ◩*, p1.
Rep Rs 1-24 for an allover pattern.

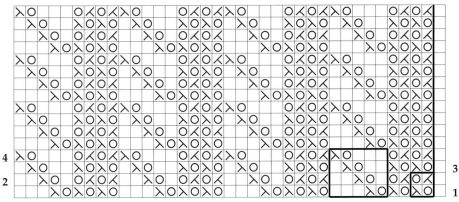

Diagonal repeat: 5 sts, 4 Rs.
  Add 1 edge st at Rt.
Ground repeat: 2 sts, 2 Rs.
  Add 2 edge sts: 1 each side.
Combined repeat of 2 ground,
  1 diagonal: 9 sts, 4 Rs.
  Add 1 edge st at Rt.

⌐— **Combined** —⌐
 repeat 9 sts

Multiple of 9 sts, plus 1.
The division between patterns is
marked by a slash (/).
⊠ = P 1 st, sl 1 st kwise, return both sts
to L ndl. Psso, return st to Rt ndl.

Row 1: k1, *{yo, ssk} 2 times, / yo, ssk,
k3*. **Row 2:** *p2, ⊠, yo, p1, / {yo, p2tog}
2 times*, p1. **Row 3:** k1, *{yo, ssk} 2 times,
/ k2, yo, ssk, k1*. **Row 4:** *⊠, yo, p3, /
{yo, p2tog} 2 times*, p1.
Rep Rs 1-4.

Diagonal pattern when used alone:
Multiple of 5 sts, plus 1.

Row 1: k1, *yo, ssk, k3*. **Row 2:** *p2,
⊠, yo, p1*, p1. **Row 3:** k1, *k2, yo, ssk,
k1*. **Row 4:** *⊠, yo, p3*, p1.
Rep Rs 1-4.

Ground pattern when used alone:
Multiple of 2 sts, plus 2.

Row 1: k1, *yo, ssk*, k1.
Row 2: p1, *yo, p2tog*, p1.
Rep Rs 1-2.

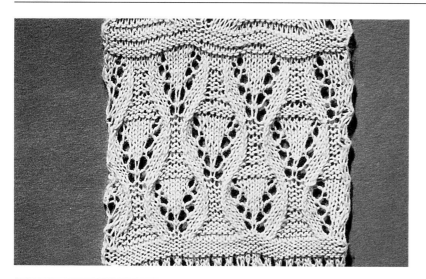

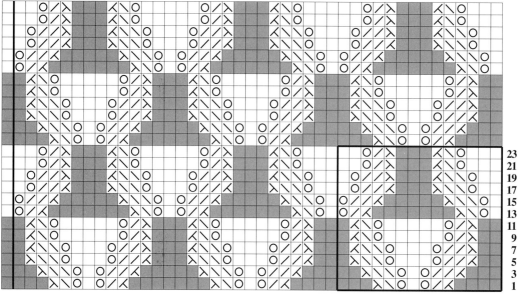

23 21 19 17 15 13 11 9 7 5 3 1

Repeat: 14 sts, 24 Rs.
Add 1 edge st at L.
Even Rs: P on p sts and yo (white squares), k on k sts (gray squares).

Multiple of 14 sts, plus 1.

Row 1: *p4, k2tog, {k1, yo} 2 times, k1, ssk, p3*, p1. **Row 2:** k1, *k3, p7, k4*.

Row 3: *p3, k2tog, k2, yo, k1, yo, k2, ssk, p2*, p1. **Row 4:** k1, *k2, p9, k3*. **Row 5:** *p2, k2tog, k2, yo, k3, yo, k2, ssk, p1*, p1. **Row 6:** k1, *k1, p11, k2*. **Row 7:** *p2, ssk, k2, yo, k3, yo, k2, k2tog, p1*, p1. **Row 8:** Rep R 6. **Row 9:** *p2, ssk, k1, yo, k5, yo, k1, k2tog, p1*, p1. **Row 10:** Rep R 6. **Row 11:** Rep R 9. **Row 12:** Rep R 6. **Row 13:** *k1, yo, k1, ssk, p7, k2tog, k1, yo*, k1. **Row 14:** p1,

p3, k7, p4. **Row 15:** *k1, yo, k2, ssk, p5, k2tog, k2, yo*, k1. **Row 16:** p1, *p4, k5, p5*. **Row 17:** *k2, yo, k2, ssk, p3, k2tog, k2, yo, k1*, k1. **Row 18:** p1, *p5, k3, p6*. **Row 19:** *k2, yo, k2, k2tog, p3, ssk, k2, yo, k1*, k1. **Row 20:** Rep R 18. **Row 21:** *k3, yo, k1, k2tog, p3, ssk, k1, yo, k2*, k1. **Row 22:** Rep R 8. **Row 23:** Rep R 21. **Row 24:** Rep R 18. Rep R 1-24.

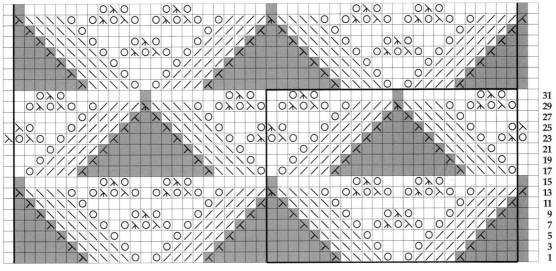

Modified sts

Repeat: 24 sts, 32 Rs.
Add 3 edge sts: 1 at L, 2 at Rt.
Modified sts at L: Rs 13, 25.
Even Rs: P on p sts and yo
(white squares), k on k sts
(gray squares).

Multiple of 24 sts, plus 3.
◪ = P 1 st, sl 1 st kwise, return both sts to L ndl. Psso, return st to Rt ndl.

◪ = P1, then sl 2 tog kwise. Return all 3 sts to L ndl, p2sso, return to Rt ndl.

Row 1: k1, p1, *p5, p2tog, k4, yo, k1, yo, k4, ◪, p6*, k1. **Row 2:** p1, *k7, p11, k6*, k1, p1. **Row 3:** k1, p1, *p4, p2tog, k4, yo, k3, yo, k4, ◪, p5*, k1. **Row 4:** p1, *k6, p13, k5*, k1, p1. **Row 5:** k1, p1, *p3, p2tog, k4, yo, k5, yo, k4, ◪, p4*, k1. **Row 6:** p1, *k5, p15, k4*, k1, p1.

Row 7: k1, p1, *p2, p2tog, k4, yo, k1, yo, ssk, yo, sl 1-k2tog-psso, yo, k1, yo, k4, ◪, p3*, k1. **Row 8:** p1, *k4, p17, k3*, k1, p1. **Row 9:** k1, p1, *p1, p2tog, k4, yo, k3, yo, sl 1-k2tog-psso, yo, k3, yo, k4, ◪, p2*, k1. **Row 10:** p1, *k3, p19, k2*, k1, p1. **Row 11:** k1, p1, *p2tog, k4, yo, k11, yo, k4, ◪, p1*, k1. **Row 12:** p1, *k2, p21, k1*, k1, p1. **Row 13:** k1, p2tog, *k4, yo, k1, {yo, ssk, yo, sl 1-k2tog-psso,

(Pattern 57 continued)
yo, k1} 2 times, yo, k4, ◣*, end last rep ◣, k1. **Row 14:** p1, *k1, p23*, k1, p1. **Row 15:** k1, p1, *k7, {yo, sl 1-k2tog-psso, yo, k3} 2 times, k4, p1*, k1. **Row 16:** Rep R 14. **Row 17:** k2, *yo, k4, ◣, p11, p2tog, k4, yo, k1*, k1. **Row 18:** p1, *p6, k13, p5*, p2. **Row 19:** k2, *k1, yo, k4, ◣, p9, p2tog, k4, yo, k2*, k1. **Row 20:** p1, *p7, k11, p6*, p2. **Row 21:** k2, *k2, yo, k4, ◣, p7, p2tog, k4, yo, k3*, k1. **Row 22:** p1, *p8, k9, p7*, p2. **Row 23:** k1, yo, *sl 1-k2tog-psso, yo, k1, yo, k4, ◣, p5, p2tog, k4, yo, k1, yo, ssk, yo*, ssk. **Row 24:** p1, *p9, k7, p8*, p2. **Row 25:** k1, ssk, *yo, k3, yo, k4, ◣, p3, p2tog, k4, yo, k3, yo, sl 1-k2tog-psso*, end last rep ssk, k1. **Row 26:** p1, *p10, k5, p9*, p2. **Row 27:** k2, *k5, yo, k4, ◣, p1, p2tog, k4, yo, k6*, k1. **Row 28:** p1, *p11, k3, p10*, p2. **Row 29:** k2, *yo, ssk, yo, sl 1-k2tog-psso, yo, k1, yo, k4, ◣, k4, yo, k1, yo, ssk, yo, sl 1-k2tog-psso, yo, k1*, k1. **Row 30:** p1, *p12, k1, p11*, p2. **Row 31:** k2, *k1, yo, sl 1-k2tog-psso, yo, k7, p1, k7, yo, sl 1-k2tog-psso, yo, k2*, k1. **Row 32:** Rep R 30.

Rep Rs 1-32.

Pattern 58

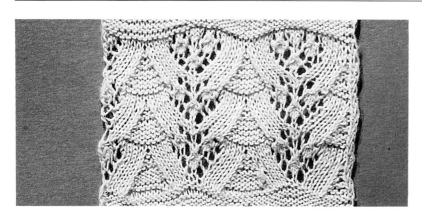

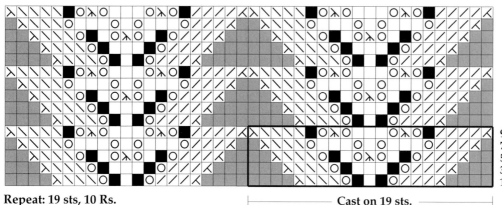

Repeat: 19 sts, 10 Rs.
Even Rs: P on p sts and yo (white squares), k on k sts (gray squares).

Cast on 19 sts.

9
7
5
3
1

Multiple of 19 sts.
Rows 7 and 8 have multiple of 21 sts.

Row 1: *p4, k2tog, k3, yo, k1, yo, k3, ssk, p4*. **Row 2:** *k4, p11, k4*. **Row 3:** *p3, k2tog, k3, yo, k3, yo, k3, ssk, p3*. **Row 4:** *k3, p13, k3*. **Row 5:** *p2, k2tog, k3, yo, k1, yo, sl 1-k2tog-psso, yo, k1, yo, k3, ssk, p2*. **Row 6:** *k2, p15, k2*. **Row 7:** *p1, k2tog, k3, yo, k3, yo, k1, yo, k3, yo, k3, ssk, p1*. **Row 8:** *k1, p19, k1*.
Row 9: *k2tog, k4, yo, sl 1-k2tog-psso, yo, k3, yo, sl 1-k2tog-psso, yo, k4, ssk*. **Row 10:** Purl.
Rep Rs 1-10.

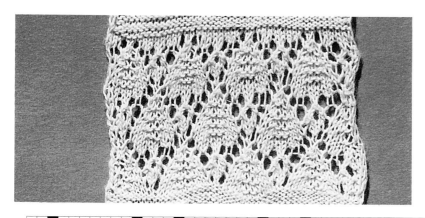

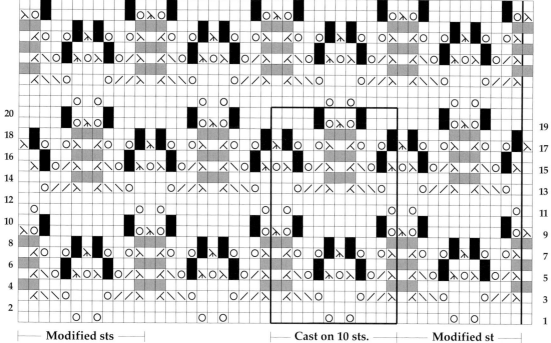

Modified sts — Cast on 10 sts. — Modified st

Repeat: 10 sts, 20 Rs.
Add 1 edge st at Rt.
Modified sts at L: Rs 9, 17.
Modified st at Rt: R 15.

Multiple of 10 sts, plus 1.
Rows 1-4 and 11-14 have multiple of
12 sts, plus 1.

Row 1: k1, *k4, yo, k1, yo, k5*.
Row 2: Purl. **Row 3:** k1, *ssk, k2, yo, k3, yo, k2, k2tog, k1*. **Row 4:** *k2, p9, k1*, k1. **Row 5:** k1, *ssk, k1, yo, ssk, yo, sl 1-k2tog-psso, yo, k1, k2tog, k1*. **Row 6:** *k2, p7, k1*, k1. **Row 7:** k1, *ssk, yo, k1, yo, sl 1-k2tog-psso, yo, k1, yo, k2tog, k1*. **Row 8:** Rep R 6. **Row 9:** ssk, *yo, k7, yo, sl 1-k2tog-psso*, end last rep ssk. **Row 10:** Purl. **Row 11:** k1, *yo, k9, yo, k1*. **Row 12:** Purl. **Row 13:** k1, *k1, yo, k2, k2tog, k1, ssk, k2, yo, k2*.

Row 14: *p5, k3, p4*, p1. **Row 15:** k1, ssk, *yo, k1, k2tog, k1, ssk, k1, yo, ssk, yo, sl 1-k2tog-psso*, end last rep ssk, k1. **Row 16:** *p4, k3, p3*, p1. **Row 17:** ssk, *yo, k1, yo, k2tog, k1, ssk, yo, k1, yo, sl 1-k2tog-psso*, end last rep ssk. **Row 18:** Rep R 16. **Row 19:** k1, *k3, yo, sl 1-k2tog-psso, yo, k4*. **Row 20:** Purl.
Rep Rs 1-20.

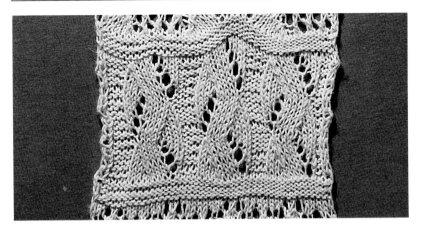

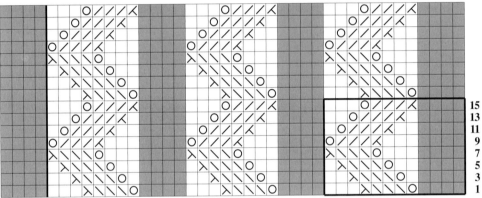

Repeat: 12 sts, 16 Rs.
Add 4 edge sts at L.
**Even Rs: P on p sts and yo
(white squares), k on k sts
(gray squares).**

Multiple of 12 sts, plus 4.
Even Rs 2-16 (wrong side): k4, *p8, k4*.

Row 1: *p4, yo, k3, ssk, k3*, p4.
Row 3: *p4, k1, yo, k3, ssk, k2*, p4.
Row 5: *p4, k2, yo, k3, ssk, k1*, p4.
Row 7: *p4, k3, yo, k3, ssk*, p4.
Row 9: *p4, k3, k2tog, k3, yo*, p4.
Row 11: *p4, k2, k2tog, k3, yo, k1*, p4.
Row 13: *p4, k1, k2tog, k3, yo, k2*, p4.
Row 15: *p4, k2tog, k3, yo, k3*, p4.
Rep Rs 1-16.

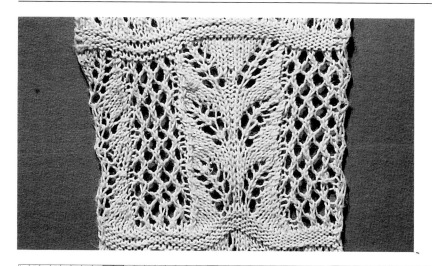

Note: In the sampler, the fern decreases are not paired. On the chart, they are paired as on the left side of the sampler.

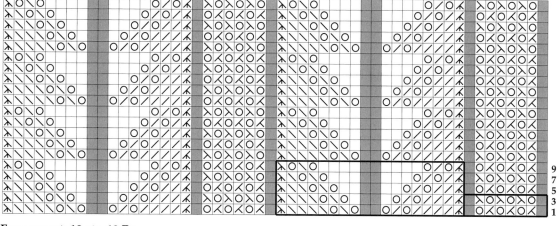

							9
---	---	---	---	---	---	---	7
							5
							3
							1

Combined repeat 26 sts

Fern repeat: 18 sts, 10 Rs.
Ground repeat: 8 sts, 4 Rs.
Combined repeat of 1 ground,
 1 fern: 26 sts, 20 Rs.
Even Rs: P on p sts and yo
 (white squares), k on k sts
 (gray squares).

Multiple of 26 sts.
The division between patterns is marked by a slash (/).
Even Rs 2-20 (wrong side): *p8, k2, p8, / k1, p6, k1*.
◩ = Ssk, return st to L ndl, pnso, return st to R ndl.

Row 1: *p1, {k2tog, yo} 3 times, p1, / ◩, k4, yo, k1, yo, p2, yo, k1, yo, k4, sl 1-k2tog-psso*. **Row 3:** *p1, {yo, ssk} 3 times, p1, / ◩, k3, {yo, k1} 2 times, p2, {k1, yo} 2 times, k3, sl 1-k2tog-psso*. **Row 5:** *p1, {k2tog, yo} 3 times, p1, / ◩, k2, yo, k1, yo, k2, p2, k2, yo, k1, yo, k2, sl 1-k2tog-psso*. **Row 7:** *p1, {yo, ssk} 3 times, p1, / ◩, {k1, yo} 2 times, k3, p2, k3, {yo, k1} 2 times, sl 1-k2tog-psso*. **Row 9:** *p1, {k2tog, yo} 3 times, p1, / ◩, yo, k1, yo, k4, p2, k4, yo, k1, yo, k1, yo, sl 1-k2tog-psso*. **Row 11:** *p1, {yo, ssk} 3 times, p1, / ◩, k4, yo, k1,

yo, p2, yo, k1, yo, k4, sl 1-k2tog-psso*.
Row 13: *p1, {k2tog, yo} 3 times, p1, / ◩, k3, {yo, k1} 2 times, p2, {k1, yo} 2 times, k3, sl 1-k2tog-psso*. **Row 15:** *p1, {yo, ssk} 3 times, p1, / ◩, k2, yo, k1, yo, k2, p2, k2, yo, k1, yo, k2, sl 1-k2tog-psso*. **Row 17:** *p1, {k2tog, yo} 3 times, p1, / ◩, {k1, yo} 2 times, k3, p2, k3, {yo, k1} 2 times, sl 1-k2tog-psso*. **Row 19:** *p1, {yo, ssk} 3 times, p1, / ◩, yo, k1, yo, k4, p2, k4, yo, k1, yo, sl 1-k2tog-psso*.
Rep Rs 1-20.

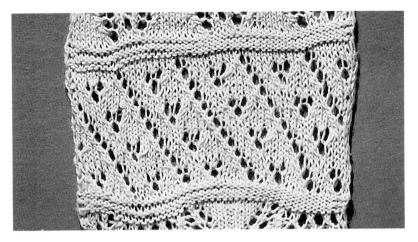

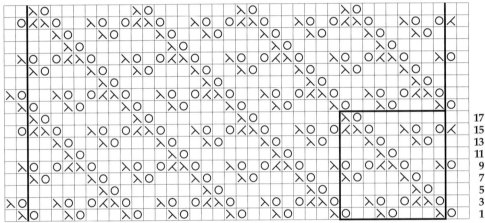

Repeat: 9 sts, 18 Rs.
Add 4 edge sts: 2 each side.
Even Rs: P all sts.

Multiple of 9 sts, plus 4.
Even Rs 2-18 (wrong side): P all sts.

Row 1: k1, yo, *ssk, k3, yo, ssk, k2, yo*, ssk, k1. **Row 3:** k2, *yo, ssk, k2tog, yo, k1, yo, ssk, k2*, yo, ssk. **Row 5:** k2, *k1, yo, ssk, k6*, k2. **Row 7:** k2, *k2, yo, ssk, k3, yo, ssk*, k2. **Row 9:** k1, yo, *ssk, k2, yo, ssk, k2tog, yo, k1, yo*, ssk, k1. **Row 11:** k2, *k4, yo, ssk, k3*, k2. **Row 13:** k2, *k1, {yo, ssk, k2} 2 times*, k2. **Row 15:** k1, k2tog, *yo, k1, yo, ssk, k2, yo, ssk, k2tog*, yo, k1. **Row 17:** k2, *k7, yo, ssk*, k2. Rep Rs 1-18.

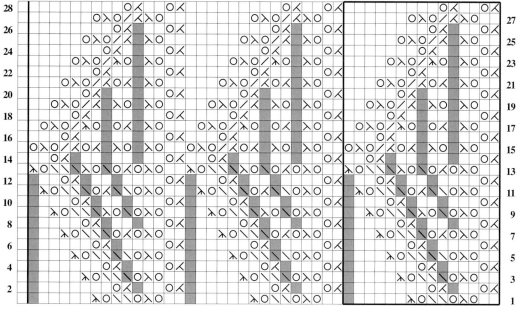

Repeat: 15 sts, 28 Rs.
Add 1 edge st at L.

(*Pattern 63 continued*)
Multiple of 15 sts, plus 1.

Row 1: *k2, yo, ssk, yo, k2, yo, sl 1-k2tog-psso, k5, p1*, k1. **Row 2:** p1, *k1, p7, yo, p2tog, k1, p2, yo, p2tog*. **Row 3:** *k2, yo, ssk, yo, p1, k2, yo, sl 1-k2tog-psso, k4, p1*, k1. **Row 4:** p1, *k1, p6, yo, p2tog, k1, p3, yo, p2tog*. **Row 5:** *k2, yo, ssk, yo, k1, p1, k2, yo, sl 1-k2tog-psso, k3, p1*, k1. **Row 6:** p1, *k1, p5, yo, p2tog, k1, p4, yo, p2tog*. **Row 7:** *k2, yo, ssk, yo, k2tog, yo, p1, k2, yo, sl 1-k2tog-psso, k2, p1*, k1. **Row 8:** p1, *k1, p4, yo, p2tog, k1, p2, k1, p2, yo, p2tog*. **Row 9:** *k2, yo, ssk, yo, p1, yo, ssk, p1, k2, yo, sl 1-k2tog-psso, k1, p1*, k1. **Row 10:** p1, *k1, p3, yo, p2tog, k1, p2, k1, p3, yo, p2tog*. **Row 11:** *k2, yo, ssk, yo, k1, p1, k2tog, yo, p1, k2, yo, sl 1-k2tog-psso, p1*, k1. **Row 12:** p1, *k1, p2, yo, p2tog, k1, p2, k1, p4, yo, p2tog*. **Row 13:** *k2, yo, ssk, yo, k2tog, yo, p1, yo, ssk, p1, k2, yo, sl 1-k2tog-psso*, k1. **Row 14:** p1, *p2, yo, p2tog, k1, p2, k1, p2, k1, p2, yo, p2tog*. **Row 15:** *k2, {yo, ssk, p1} 2 times, k2tog, yo, k2tog, k1, yo, ssk, yo*, k1. **Row 16:** p1, *p3, yo, p2tog, {p2, k1} 2 times, p2, yo, p2tog*. **Row 17:** *k2, yo, ssk, p1, k2tog, yo, p1, yo, sl 1-k2tog-psso, k1, yo, ssk, yo, k1*, k1. **Row 18:** p1, *p4, yo, p2tog, p1, {k1, p2} 2 times, yo, p2tog*. **Row 19:** *k2, yo, ssk, p1, yo, ssk, p1, k2tog, k1, yo, ssk, yo, k2*, k1. **Row 20:** p1, *p5, yo, p2tog, {k1, p2} 2 times, yo, p2tog*. **Row 21:** *k2, yo, ssk, p1, k2tog, yo, k2tog, k1, yo, ssk, yo, k3*, k1. **Row 22:** p1, *p6, yo, p2tog, p2, k1, p2, yo, p2tog*. **Row 23:** *k2, yo, ssk, p1, yo, sl 1-k2tog-psso, k1, yo, ssk, yo, k4*, k1. **Row 24:** p1, *p7, yo, p2tog, p1, k1, p2, yo, p2tog*. **Row 25:** *k2, yo, ssk, p1, k2tog, k1, yo, ssk, yo, k5*, k1. **Row 26:** p1, *p8, yo, p2tog, k1, p2, yo, p2tog*. **Row 27:** *k2, yo, ssk, k2tog, k1, yo, ssk, yo, k6*, k1. **Row 28:** p1, *p9, yo, p2tog, p2, yo, p2tog*.
Rep Rs 1-28 for an allover pattern.

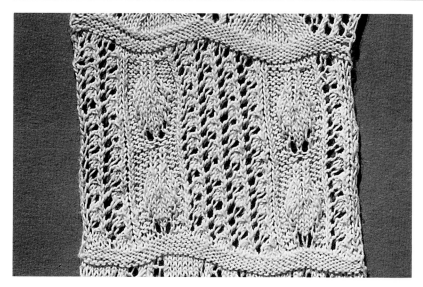

Note: To improve the pattern's symmetry, the single column of knit stitches at the left of the leaf panel has been omitted on the chart.

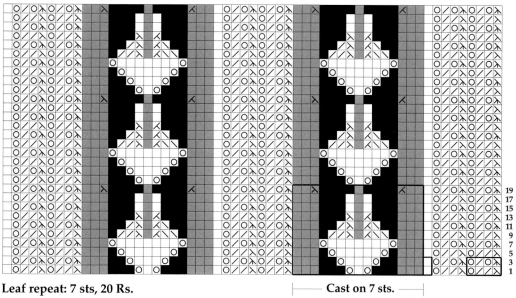

Leaf repeat: 7 sts, 20 Rs.
Ground repeat: 4 sts, 4 Rs.
  Add 1 edge st at L.
Combined repeat of 2 ground,
  1 leaf: 16 sts, 20 Rs.
Even Rs: P on p sts and yo
  (white squares), k on k sts
  (gray squares).

— Cast on 7 sts. —

— Combined repeat 16 sts —

Multiple of 16 sts.
The division between patterns is marked by a slash (/).
⊠ = P 1 st, sl 1 st kwise, return both sts to L ndl. Psso, return st to Rt ndl.

Row 1: *{ssk, k2, yo} 2 times, k1, / p3, yo, k1, yo, p3* (18 st rep). **Row 2:** *k3, p3, k3, / p9*. **Row 3:** *{sl 1-k2tog-psso, yo, k1, yo} 2 times, k1, / p3, yo, k3, yo, p3* (20 st rep). **Row 4:** *k3, p5, k3, / p9*. **Row 5:** *{ssk, k2, yo} 2 times, k1, / p3, yo, k5, yo, p3* (22 st rep). **Row 6:** *k3, p7, k3, / p9*. **Row 7:** *{sl 1-k2tog-psso, yo, k1, yo} 2 times, k1, / p3, yo, k7, yo, p3* (24 st rep). **Row 8:** *k3, p9, k3, /

(Pattern 64 continued)
p9*. **Row 9:** *{ssk, k2, yo} 2 times, k1, / p3, k2, k2tog, p1, ssk, k2, p3* (22 st rep). **Row 10:** *k3, p3, k1, p3, k3, / p9*. **Row 11:** *{sl 1-k2tog-psso, yo, k1, yo} 2 times, k1, / p3, k1, k2tog, p1, ssk, k1, p3* (20 st rep). **Row 12:** *k3, p2, k1, p2, k3, / p9*. **Row 13:** *{ssk, k2, yo} 2 times, k1, / p3, k2tog, p1, ssk, p3* (18 st rep). **Row 14:** *k3, p1, k1, p1, k3, / p9*.

Row 15: *{sl 1-k2tog-psso, yo, k1, yo} 2 times, k1, / p3, k1, p1, k1, p3* (18 st rep). **Row 16:** Rep R 14. **Row 17:** *{ssk, k2, yo} 2 times, k1, / p3, k1, p1, k1, p3* (18 st rep). **Row 18:** Rep R 14. **Row 19:** *{sl 1-k2tog-psso, yo, k1, yo} 2 times, k1, / p2, p2tog, p1, ◩, p2* (16-st rep). **Row 20:** *k7, / p9*. Rep Rs 1-20.

Ground pattern when used alone: Multiple of 4 sts, plus 1.

Row 1: *ssk, k2, yo*, k1. **Row 2:** Purl. **Row 3:** *sl 1-k2tog-psso, yo, k1, yo*, k1. **Row 4:** Purl. Rep Rs 1-4.

Pattern 65

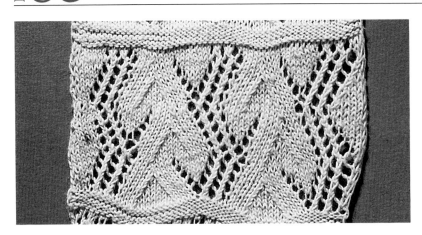

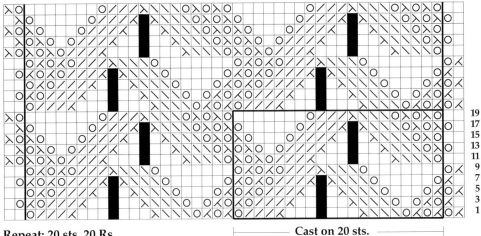

Repeat: 20 sts, 20 Rs.
Add 4 edge sts: 2 each side.
Even Rs: P all sts.

Multiple of 20 sts, plus 4.
Even Rs 2-20 (wrong side): P all sts.
Rs 1-8 and 11-18 have multiple of 19 sts, plus 4.

Row 1: k2tog, yo, *{k2tog, yo} 2 times, k3, ssk, k6, k2tog, k3, yo*, k2.
Row 3: k1, k2tog, *yo, k2tog, yo, k1, yo, k3, ssk, k4, k2tog, k3, yo, k2tog*, yo, k1. **Row 5:** k2tog, yo, *k2tog, yo, k3, yo, k3, ssk, k2, k2tog, k3, yo, k2tog, yo*, k2. **Row 7:** k1, k2tog, *yo, k5, yo, k3, ssk, k2tog, k3, {yo, k2tog} 2 times*, yo, k1. **Row 9:** k2tog, yo, *k7, yo, k3, ssk, k3, {yo, k2tog} 2 times, yo*, k2. **Row 11:** k2, *yo, k3, ssk, k6, k2tog, k3, {yo, ssk} 2 times*, yo, ssk. **Row 13:** k1,

(*Pattern 65 continued*)
yo, *ssk, yo, k3, ssk, k4, k2tog, k3, yo, k1, yo, ssk, yo*, ssk, k1.
Row 15: k2, *yo, ssk, yo, k3, ssk, k2,

k2tog, k3, yo, k3, yo, ssk*, yo, ssk.
Row 17: k1, yo, *{ssk, yo} 2 times, k3, ssk, k2tog, k3, yo, k5, yo*, ssk, k1.
Row 19: k2, *{yo, ssk} 2 times, yo, k3,

ssk, k3, yo, k7*, yo, ssk.
Rep Rs 1-20.

Pattern 66

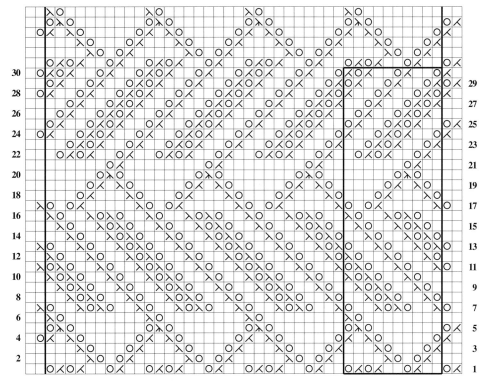

Repeat: 10 sts, 30 Rs.
Add 4 edge sts: 2 each side.

(*Pattern 66 continued*)

Multiple of 10 sts, plus 4.

◹ = P 1 st, sl 1 st kwise, return both sts to L ndl. Psso, return st to Rt ndl.

◺ = P2tog, then sl 1 st kwise. return both sts to L ndl, psso, return to Rt ndl.

Row 1: k2tog, yo, *k2, k2tog, yo, k2, {k2tog, yo} 2 times*, k2. **Row 2:** p2, *p4, ◹, yo, p1, yo, p2tog, p1*, p2. **Row 3:** k2, *k2tog, yo, k3, yo, ssk, k3*, k2. **Row 4:** p1, yo, *p2tog, p1, ◹, yo, p5, yo*, p2tog, p1. **Row 5:** k2tog, yo, *k7, yo, sl 1-k2tog-psso, yo*, k2. **Row 6:** p2, *◹, yo, p8*, p2. **Row 7:** k1, yo, *ssk, k2, {yo, ssk} 2 times, k2, yo*, ssk, k1. **Row 8:** p2, *p2, {◹, yo} 2 times, p2, ◹, yo*, p2. **Row 9:** k2, *k1, yo, ssk, k2, {yo, ssk} 2 times, k1*, k2. **Row 10:** p2, *{◺, yo} 2 times, p2, ◺, yo, p2*, p2. **Row 11:** k1, yo, *ssk, {k2, yo, ssk} 2 times, yo*, ssk, k1. **Row 12:** p2, *{◺, yo, p2} 2 times, ◺, yo*, p2. **Row 13:** k1, yo, *ssk, yo, ssk, k2, yo, ssk, k2, yo*, ssk, k1. **Row 14:** p2, *p2, ◺, yo, p2, {◺, yo} 2 times*, p2. **Row 15:** k2, *k1, {yo, ssk} 2 times, k2, yo, ssk, k1*, k2. **Row 16:** p2, *◺, yo, p2, {◺, yo} 2 times, p2*, p2. **Row 17:** k1, yo, *ssk, k5, k2tog, yo, k1, yo*, ssk, k1. **Row 18:** p2, *p3, yo, p2tog, p3, ◹, yo*, p2. **Row 19:** k2, *k1, yo, ssk, k1, k2tog, yo, k4*, k2. **Row 20:** p2, *p5, yo, ◹, yo, p2*, p2. **Row 21:** k2, *k2, k2tog, yo, k6*, k2.

Row 22: p2, *p1, {yo, p2tog} 2 times, p2, yo, p2tog, p1*, p2. **Row 23:** k2, *k2tog, yo, k2, {k2tog, yo} 2 times, k2*, k2. **Row 24:** p1, yo, *p2tog, p2, {yo, p2tog} 2 times, p2, yo*, p2tog, p1. **Row 25:** k2tog, yo, *k2, {k2tog, yo} 2 times, k2, k2tog, yo*, k2. **Row 26:** p2, *p1, yo, p2tog, p2, {yo, p2tog} 2 times, p1*, p2. **Row 27:** k2, *{k2tog, yo} 2 times, k2, k2tog, yo, k2*, k2. **Row 28:** p1, yo, *p2tog, p2, yo, p2tog, p2, yo, p2tog, yo*, p2tog, p1. **Row 29:** k2tog, yo, *{k2tog, yo, k2} 2 times, k2tog, yo*, k2. **Row 30:** p1, yo, *p2tog, {yo, p2tog, p2} 2 times, yo*, p2tog, p1.

Rep Rs 1-30 for an allover pattern.

Pattern 67

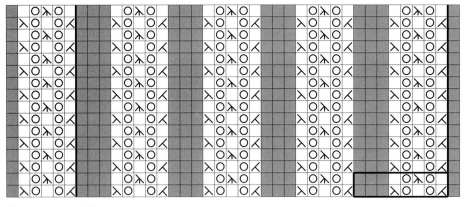

Repeat: 8 sts, 4 Rs.
Add 7 edge sts: 6 at L, 1 at Rt.
Even Rs: P on p sts and yo (white squares), k on k sts (gray squares).

Multiple of 8 sts, plus 7.

Row 1: p1, *k2tog, yo, k1, yo, ssk, p3*, k2tog, yo, k1, yo, ssk, p1. **Row 2:** k1, p5, *k3, p5*, k1. **Row 3:** p1, *k1, yo,

sl 1-k2tog-psso, yo, k1, p3*, k1, yo, sl 1-k2tog-psso, yo, k1, p1.
Row 4: Rep R 2.
Rep Rs 1-4.

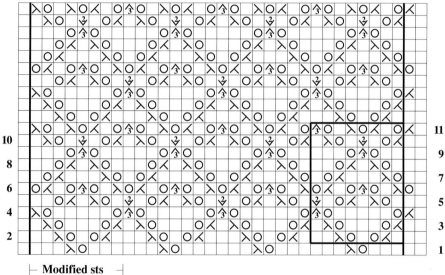

⊢ **Modified sts** ⊣

Repeat: 8 sts, 10 Rs.
Add 3 edge sts: 1 at L, 2 at Rt.
Modified sts at L: Rs 4, 5, 11.

Multiple of 8 sts, plus 3.
⊠ = P 1 st, sl 1 st kwise, return both sts to L ndl. Psso, return st to Rt ndl.

Row 1: k2, *k3, yo, ssk, k3*, k1.
Row 2: p1, *p2, ⊠, yo, p1, yo, p2tog, p1*, p2. **Row 3:** k2, *k2tog, yo, k3, yo, ssk, k1*, k1. **Row 4:** p1, p2tog, *yo, p5, yo, p3tog*, end last rep p2tog, p1.
Row 5: k2, *k1, yo, ssk, k1, k2tog, yo, k1, k into front and back of st*, end last rep k1, k1 (9 st rep). **Row 6:** p1, *yo, p2tog, p1, yo, p3tog, yo, p1, ⊠*, yo, p1. **Row 7:** k2, *yo, ssk, k3, k2tog, yo, k1*, k1. **Row 8:** p1, *p2, yo, p2tog, p1, ⊠, yo, p1*, p2. **Row 9:** k2, *k2, yo, k3tog, yo, k3*, k1. **Row 10:** p1, *p1, ⊠, yo, p1, p into front and back of st, p1, yo, p2tog*, p2 (9 st rep). **Row 11:** k1, k2tog, *yo, k1, k2tog, yo, ssk, k1, yo, k3tog*, end last rep k2tog, k1.
Rep Rs 2-11 for an allover pattern.

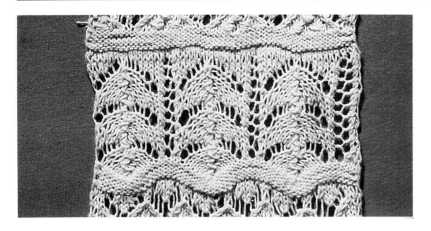

Note: In this pattern, the edge stitches for the horseshoe are provided by the ground.

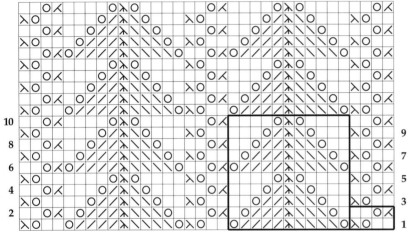

⊢ **Combined repeat 15 sts** ⊣

Horseshoe repeat: 11 sts, 10 Rs.
 Add 2 edge sts: 1 each side.
Ground repeat: 4 sts, 2 Rs.
Combined repeat of 1 ground,
 1 horseshoe: 15 sts, 10 Rs.
 Add 1 edge st at L (not shown).

Multiple of 15 sts, plus 1.
The division between patterns is
marked by a slash (/).
⊠ = P2tog, then sl 1 st kwise. Return
both sts to L ndl, psso, return to Rt ndl.

Row 1: *k2, yo, ssk, / yo, k4, sl 1-
k2tog-psso, k4, yo*, k1. **Row 2:** p1,
*p1, yo, p3, ⊠, p3, yo, p1, / p2, yo,
p2tog*. **Row 3:** *k2, yo, ssk, / k2, yo,
k2, sl 1-k2tog-psso, k2, yo, k2*, k1.
Row 4: p1, *p3, yo, p1, ⊠, p1, yo, p3,
/ p2, yo, p2tog*. **Row 5:** *k2, yo, ssk,
/ k4, yo, sl 1-k2tog-psso, yo, k4*, k1.
Row 6: p1, *yo, p4, ⊠, p4, yo, / p2, yo,
p2tog*. **Row 7:** *k2, yo, ssk, / k1, yo,
k3, sl 1-k2tog-psso, k3, yo, k1*, k1.
Row 8: p1, *p2, yo, p2, ⊠, p2, yo, p2,
/ p2, yo, p2tog*. **Row 9:** *k2, yo, ssk,
/ k3, yo, k1, sl 1-k2tog-psso, k1, yo,
k3*, k1. **Row 10:** p1, *p4, yo, ⊠, yo, p4,
/ p2, yo, p2tog*.
Rep Rs 1-10.

Horseshoe pattern when used alone:
Multiple of 12 sts, plus 1.

Row 1: *p1, yo, k4, sl 1-k2tog-psso, k4,
yo*, p1. **Row 2:** k1, *p1, yo, p3, ⊠, p3,
yo, p1, k1*. **Row 3:** *p1, k2, yo, k2,
sl 1-k2tog-psso, k2, yo, k2*, p1. **Row 4:**
k1, *p3, yo, p1, ⊠, p1, yo, p3, k1*.
Row 5: *p1, k4, yo, sl 1-k2tog-psso, yo,
k4*, p1. **Row 6:** k1, *yo, p4, ⊠, p4, yo,
k1*. **Row 7:** *p1, k1, yo, k3, sl 1-k2tog-
psso, k3, yo, k1*, p1. **Row 8:** k1, *p2,
yo, p2, ⊠, p2, yo, p2, k1*. **Row 9:** *p1,
k3, yo, k1, sl 1-k2tog-psso, k1, yo, k3*,
p1. **Row 10:** k1, *p4, yo, ⊠, yo, p4, k1*.
Rep Rs 1-10.

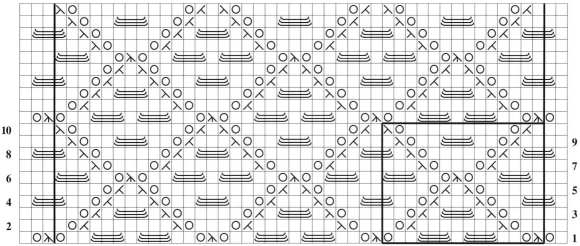

Repeat: 14 sts, 10 Rs.
Add 5 edge sts: 3 at L, 2 at Rt.

Multiple of 14 sts, plus 5.

⟋⟍ = P 1 st, sl 1 st kwise, return both sts to L ndl. Psso, return st to Rt ndl.

⟋⟍ = P2tog, then sl 1 st kwise. Return both sts to L ndl, psso, return to Rt ndl.

▤ = Wrapped sts: K if odd row/p if even row 3 sts onto extra ndl, wrap yarn counterclockwise around the 3 sts 3 times ending on wrong side of work. Sl sts to Rt ndl.

Row 1: k1, yo, *sl 1-k2tog-psso, yo, k2, ▤, k1, ▤, k2, yo*, sl 1-k2tog-psso, yo, k1. **Row 2:** p3, *p1, yo, p2tog, p7, ⟍, yo, p2*, p2. **Row 3:** k2, *k3, yo, ssk, k1, ▤, k1, k2tog, yo, k2*, k3. **Row 4:** p1, *▤, p2, yo, p2tog, p3, ⟍, yo, p2*, ▤, p1. **Row 5:** k2, *k5, yo, ssk, k1, k2tog, yo, k4*, k3. **Row 6:** p3, *▤, p2, yo, ⟍, yo, p2, ▤, p1*, p2. **Row 7:** k2, *k4, k2tog, yo, k3, yo, ssk, k3*, k3. **Row 8:** p1, *▤, p1, ⟍, yo, p5, yo, p2tog, p1*, ▤, p1. **Row 9:** k2, *k2, k2tog, yo, k2, ▤, k2, yo, ssk, k1*, k3. **Row 10:** p3, *⟍, yo, p9, yo, p2tog, p1*, p2.
Rep Rs 1-10.

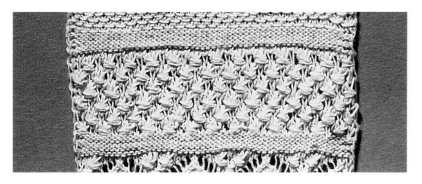

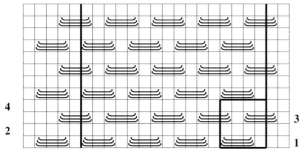

Repeat: 4 sts, 4 Rs.
Add 7 edge sts: 5 at L, 2 at Rt.

Multiple of 4 sts, plus 3.
Even Rs 2-4 (wrong side): P all sts.
▤ = Wrapped sts: K 3 sts onto
extra ndl, wrap yarn counterclockwise
around the 3 sts 3 times ending on
wrong side of work, sl sts to Rt ndl.

Row 1: k2, *k1, ▤*, k1.
Row 3: *k1, ▤*, k3.
Rep Rs 1-4.

Repeat: 2 sts, 4 Rs.
Add 3 edge sts: 2 at L, 1 at Rt.

Multiple of 2 sts, plus 3.
⊻ = With yarn in back, sl 1 st pwise.

Row 1: Knit.
Row 2: *k1, ⊻*, k1.
Row 3: Knit.
Row 4: k2, *⊻, k1*, k1.
Rep Rs 1-4.

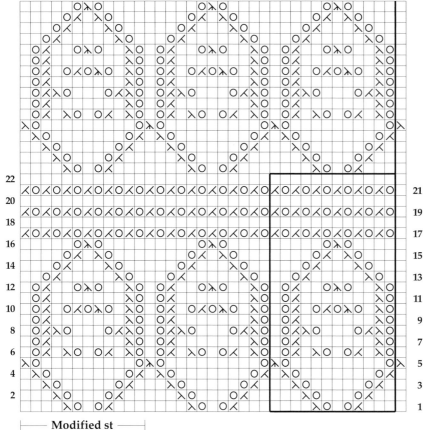

Repeat: 12 sts, 22 Rs.
Add 1 edge st at Rt.
Modified st at L: R 5.

Modified st

(Pattern 73 continued)

Multiple of 12 sts, plus 1.

⊠ = P 1 st, sl 1 st kwise, return both sts to L ndl. Psso, return st to Rt ndl.

⊠ = P2tog, then sl 1 st kwise. Return both sts to L ndl, psso, return to Rt ndl.

Row 1: k1, *k3, k2tog, yo, k1, yo, ssk, k4*. **Row 2:** *p3, ⊠, yo, p3, yo, p2tog, p2*, p1. **Row 3:** k1, *k1, k2tog, yo, k5, yo, ssk, k2*. **Row 4:** *p1, ⊠, yo, p7, yo, p2tog*, p1. **Row 5:** ssk, *yo, k9, yo, sl 1-k2tog-psso*, end last rep ssk. **Row 6:** *{p1, yo, p2tog, p1, ⊠, yo} 2 times*, p1. **Row 7:** k1, *yo, ssk, k7, k2tog, yo, k1*. **Row 8:** *p1, yo, p2tog, ⊠, yo, p3, yo, p2tog, ⊠, yo*, p1. **Row 9:** Rep R 7. **Row 10:** *{p1, yo, p2tog} 2 times, yo, ⊠, yo, p1, ⊠, yo*, p1. **Row 11:** Rep R 7. **Row 12:** *p1, yo, p2tog, p2, yo, ⊠, yo, p2, ⊠, yo*, p1. **Row 13:** k1, *k1, yo, ssk, k5, k2tog, yo, k2*. **Row 14:** *p3, yo, p2tog, p3, ⊠, yo, p2*, p1. **Row 15:** k1, *k3, yo, ssk, k1, k2tog, yo, k4*. **Row 16:** *p5, yo, ⊠, yo, p4*, p1. **Row 17:** k1, *{yo, k2tog} 6 times*. **Row 18:** Purl. **Row 19:** Rep R 17. **Row 20:** Purl. **Row 21:** Rep R 17. **Row 22:** Purl.

Rep Rs 1-22.

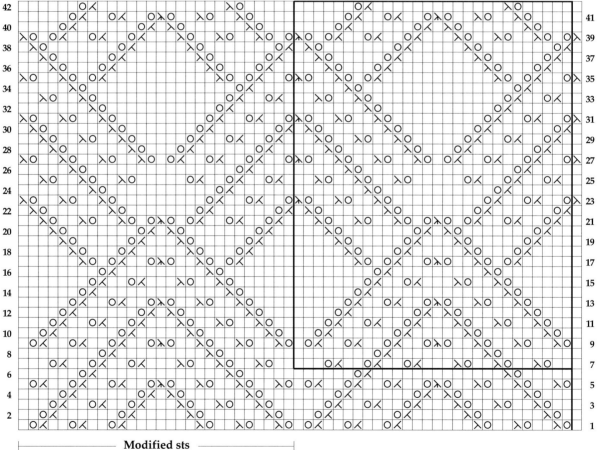

— Modified sts —

Repeat: 28 sts, 36 Rs.
Add 1 edge st at Rt.
Modified sts at L: Rs 23, 27, 31, 35, 39.

(Pattern 74 continued)

Multiple of 28 sts, plus 1.

⃠ = P 1 st, sl 1 st kwise, return both sts to L ndl. Psso, return st to Rt ndl.

Row 1: k1, *{yo, ssk, k2} 3 times, k3, {k2, k2tog, yo} 3 times, k1*. **Row 2:** *{p2, yo, p2tog, p4} 2 times, p1, ⃠, yo, p6, ⃠, yo, p1*, p1. **Row 3:** k1, *{k2, yo, ssk} 3 times, k3, {k2tog, yo, k2} 3 times, k1*. **Row 4:** *p4, yo, p2tog, p6, yo, p2tog, p1, ⃠, yo, p6, ⃠, yo, p3*, p1. **Row 5:** k1, *{yo, ssk, k2} 3 times, yo, sl 1-k2tog-psso, yo, {k2, k2tog, yo} 3 times, k1*. **Row 6:** *p6, yo, p2tog, p13, ⃠, yo, p5*, p1. **Row 7:** k1, *{k2, yo, ssk} 3 times, k3, {k2tog, yo, k2} 3 times, k1*. **Row 8:** *p8, yo, p2tog, p9, ⃠, yo, p7*, p1. **Row 9:** Rep R 5. **Row 10:** Rep R 2. **Row 11:** Rep R 3. **Row 12:** Rep R 4. **Row 13:** k1, *k4, {yo, ssk, k2} 2 times, yo, sl 1-k2tog-psso, yo, {k2, k2tog, yo} 2 times, k5*. **Row 14:** Rep R 6.

Row 15: k1, *k6, {yo, ssk, k2} 2 times, {k1, k2tog, yo, k1} 2 times, k6*. **Row 16:** Rep R 8. **Row 17:** k1, *k5, k2tog, yo, k1, yo, ssk, k2, yo, sl 1-k2tog-psso, yo, k2, k2tog, yo, k1, yo, ssk, k6*. **Row 18:** *p3, {p2, ⃠, yo, p3, yo, p2tog, p3} 2 times, p1*, p1. **Row 19:** k1, *{k3, k2tog, yo, k5, yo, ssk} 2 times, k4*. **Row 20:** *p2, {p1, ⃠, yo, p7, yo, p2tog} 2 times, p2*, p1. **Row 21:** k1, *{k1, k2tog, yo, k1} 3 times, yo, sl 1-k2tog-psso, yo, {k1, yo, ssk, k1} 3 times, k1*. **Row 22:** *{p1, ⃠, yo, p5} 2 times, p2, yo, p2tog, p6, yo, p2tog*, p1. **Row 23:** ssk, *{yo, k2, k2tog} 2 times, yo, k9, {yo, ssk, k2} 2 times, yo, sl 1-k2tog-psso*, end last rep ssk. **Row 24:** *p7, ⃠, yo, p11, yo, p2tog, p6*, p1. **Row 25:** k1, *{k1, k2tog, yo, k1} 3 times, k4, {yo, ssk, k2} 3 times*. **Row 26:** *p5, ⃠, yo, p15, yo, p2tog, p4*, p1. **Row 27:** ssk, *{yo, k2, k2tog} 3 times, yo, k1, {yo, ssk, k2} 3 times, yo, sl 1-k2tog-psso*,

end last rep ssk. **Row 28:** *{p3, ⃠, yo, p3} 2 times, yo, p2tog, p6, yo, p2tog, p2*, p1. **Row 29:** Rep R 25. **Row 30:** Rep R 22. **Row 31:** Rep R 23. **Row 32:** Rep R 24. **Row 33:** k1, *{k1, k2tog, yo, k1} 2 times, k12, {yo, ssk, k2} 2 times*. **Row 34:** Rep R 26. **Row 35:** ssk, *yo, k2, k2tog, yo, k1, yo, ssk, k11, k2tog, yo, k1, yo, ssk, k2, yo, sl 1-k2tog-psso*, end last rep ssk. **Row 36:** *p3, ⃠, yo, p3, yo, p2tog, p9, ⃠, yo, p3, yo, p2tog, p2*, p1. **Row 37:** k1, *k1, k2tog, yo, k5, yo, ssk, k7, k2tog, yo, k5, yo, ssk, k2*. **Row 38:** *p1, ⃠, yo, p7, yo, p2tog, p5, ⃠, yo, p7, yo, p2tog*, p1. **Row 39:** ssk, *yo, {k1, yo, ssk, k1} 3 times, {k2, k2tog, yo} 3 times, k1, yo, sl 1-k2tog-psso*, end last rep ssk. **Row 40:** Rep R 4. **Row 41:** Rep R 13. **Row 42:** Rep R 6.

Rep Rs 7-42 for an allover pattern.

Note: To make the pattern a repeating unit, each rectangle has been reduced by one stitch and two rows on the chart.

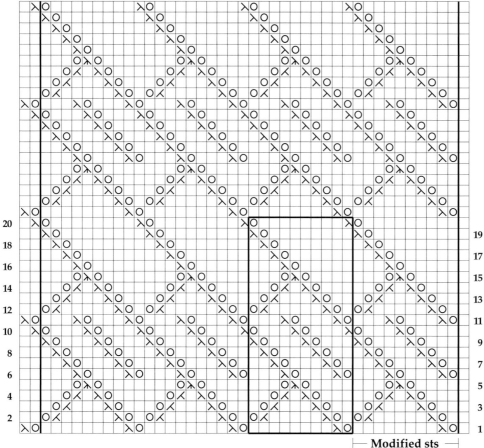

Repeat: 10 sts, 20 Rs.
Add 3 edge sts: 2 at L, 1 at Rt.
Modified sts at Rt: Rs 10, 20.

⊢ **Modified sts** ⊣

(Pattern 75 continued)
Multiple of 10 sts, plus 3.

⊠ = P 1 st, sl 1 st kwise, return both sts to L ndl. Psso, return st to Rt ndl.

Row 1: k1, *yo, ssk, k8*, yo, ssk.
Row 2: p2, *yo, p2tog, p5, ⊠, yo, p1*, p1. **Row 3:** k1, *k2, yo, ssk, k3, k2tog, yo, k1*, k2. **Row 4:** p2, *p2, yo, p2tog, p1,

⊠, yo, p3*, p1. **Row 5:** k1, *k4, yo, sl 1-k2tog-psso, yo, k3*, k2. **Row 6:** p2, *{p3, ⊠, yo} 2 times*, p1. **Row 7:** k1, *{k1, yo, ssk, k2} 2 times*, k2. **Row 8:** p2, *{p1, ⊠, yo, p2} 2 times*, p1. **Row 9:** k1, *{k3, yo, ssk} 2 times*, k2. **Row 10:** p1, ⊠, *{yo, p3, ⊠} 2 times*, end last rep p5. **Row 11:** k1, *{yo, ssk, k3} 2 times*, yo, ssk. **Row 12:** Rep R 2. **Row 13:** Rep R 3. **Row 14:**

Rep R 4. **Row 15:** Rep R 5. **Row 16:** p2, *p3, ⊠, yo, p5*, p1. **Row 17:** k1, *k6, yo, ssk, k2*, k2. **Row 18:** p2, *p1, ⊠, yo, p7*, p1. **Row 19:** k1, *k8, yo, ssk*, k2. **Row 20:** p1, ⊠, *yo, p8, ⊠*, end last rep p10.
Rep Rs 1-20.

Pattern 76

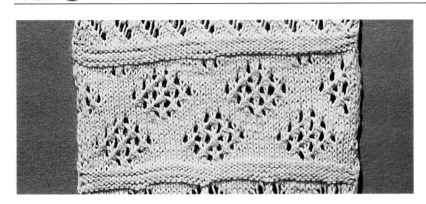

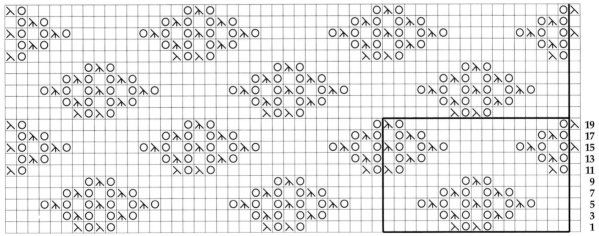

																			19
																			17
																			15
																			13
																			11
																			9
																			7
																			5
																			3
																			1

─── **Modified sts** ───

Repeat: 17 sts, 20 Rs.
Add 1 edge st at Rt.
Modified sts at L: Rs 15, 19.
Even Rs: P all sts.

Row 1: k1, *k7, {yo, ssk} 2 times, k6*. **Row 3:** k1, *k5, {yo, sl 1-k2tog-psso, yo, k1} 2 times, k4*. **Row 5:** k1, *k3, {yo, sl 1-k2tog-psso, yo, k1} 3 times, k2*. **Row 7:** Rep R 3. **Row 9:** k1, *k7, yo, sl 1-k2tog-psso, yo, k7*. **Row 11:** k1, *yo, ssk, k13, yo, ssk*. **Row 13:** k1, *yo, sl 1-k2tog-psso, yo, k10, yo, sl 1-k2tog-

psso, yo, k1*. **Row 15:** ssk, *yo, k1, yo, sl 1-k2tog-psso, yo, k6, yo, sl 1-k2tog-psso, yo, k1, yo, sl 1-k2tog-psso*, end last rep ssk. **Row 17:** k1, *yo, sl 1-k2tog-psso, yo, k10, yo, sl 1-k2tog-psso, yo, k1*. **Row 19:** ssk, *yo, k14, yo, sl 1-k2tog-psso*, end last rep ssk.
Rep Rs 1-20.

Multiple of 17 sts, plus 1.
Even Rs 2-20 (wrong side): P all sts.

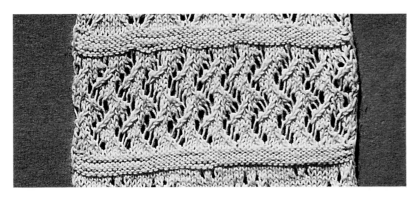

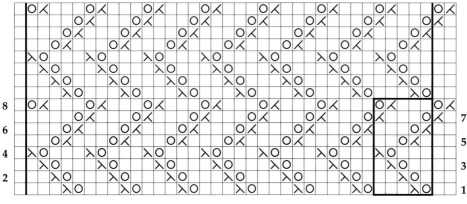

| Modified |
| st |

Repeat: 5 sts, 8 Rs.
Add 3 edge sts: 1 at L, 2 at Rt.
Modified st at L: R 7.

Multiple of 5 sts, plus 3.
⊠ = P 1 st, sl 1 st kwise, return both sts
to L ndl. Psso, return st to Rt ndl.

Row 1: k2, *yo, ssk, k3*, k1. **Row 2:** p1,
p2, ⊠, yo, p1, p2. **Row 3:** k2, *k2, yo,
ssk, k1*, k1. **Row 4:** p1, *⊠, yo, p3*,
p2. **Row 5:** k2, *k1, k2tog, yo, k2*, k1.
Row 6: p1, *p3, yo, p2tog*, p2.
Row 7: k1, k2tog, *yo, k3, k2tog*, end
last rep k2. **Row 8:** p1, *yo, p2tog, p3*,
yo, p2tog.
Rep Rs 1-8.

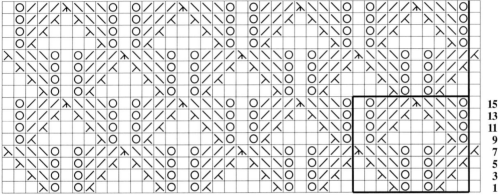

├──── **Modified st** ────┤

Repeat: 10 sts, 16 Rs.
Add 1 edge st at Rt.
Modified st at L: R 7.
Even Rs: P all sts.

Multiple of 10 sts, plus 1.
Even Rs 2-16 (wrong side): P all sts.

Row 1: k1, *k2, k2tog, yo, k1, yo, ssk,
k3*. **Row 3:** k1, *k1, k2tog, {k1, yo}
2 times, k1, ssk, k2*. **Row 5:** k1, *k2tog,
k2, yo, k1, yo, k2, ssk, k1*. **Row 7:** k2tog,
k3, yo, k1, yo, k3, sl 1-k2tog-psso,
end last rep ssk. **Row 9:** k1, *yo, ssk,
k5, k2tog, yo, k1*. **Row 11:** k1, *yo, k1,
ssk, k3, k2tog, k1, yo, k1*. **Row 13:** k1,
yo, k2, ssk, k1, k2tog, k2, yo, k1.
Row 15: k1, *yo, k3, sl 1-k2tog-psso,
k3, yo, k1*.
Rep Rs 1-16.

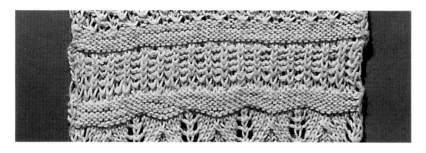

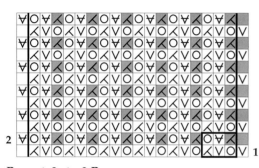

Repeat: 3 sts, 2 Rs.
Add 2 edge sts: 1 each side.

Multiple of 3 sts, plus 2.
Ⅴ = With yarn in back, sl 1 st pwise.

Row 1: sl 1, *yo, Ⅴ, k2tog*, k1.
Row 2: sl 1, *yo, Ⅴ, k2tog*, k1.
Rep Rs 1-2.

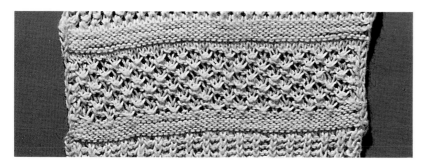

Repeat: 4 sts, 4 Rs.
Add 2 edge sts: 1 each side.

Cast
on
4 sts.

3
1

Multiple of 4 sts, plus 2.

Row 1: Knit.
Row 2: k1, *sl 1-k2tog-psso, {k1, p1, k1} in next st*, k1.
Row 3: Knit.
Row 4: k1, *{k1, p1, k1} in next st, sl 1-k2tog-psso*, k1.
Rep Rs 1-4.

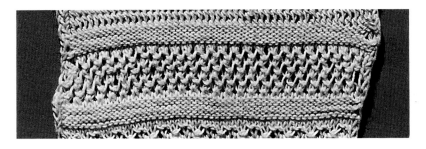

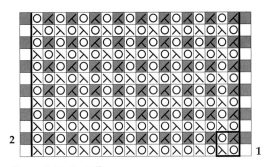

2

1

Repeat: 2 sts, 2 Rs.
Add 2 edge sts: 1 each side.

Multiple of 2 sts, plus 2.

Row 1: k1, *yo, ssk*, k1.
Row 2: k1, *yo, k2tog*, k1.
Rep Rs 1-2.

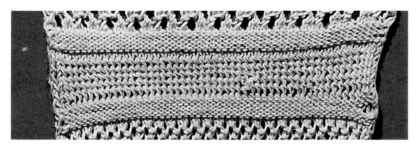

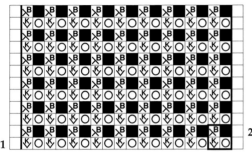

1   2

Cast on 1 st.

Repeat: 2 sts, 2 Rs.
Add 2 edge sts: 1 each side.
Odd Rs are knitted from the
    wrong side and are read L to Rt
    on the chart. Even Rs are
    knitted from the right side and
    are read Rt to L on the chart.

Multiple of 2 sts, plus 2.
Note: Cast on only one-half the
number of required sts, plus 2 edge
sts. R 1 is on wrong side of fabric,
R 2 on right side of fabric.

Row 1: p1, *with yarn in front, sl 1 st
kwise, yo*, p1.
Row 2: k1, *k2tog in backs of sts*, k1.
Rep Rs 1-2.

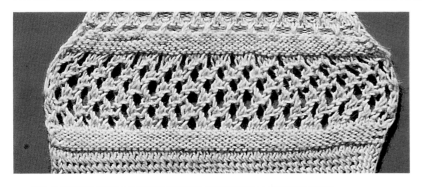

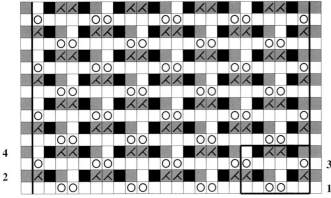

Repeat: 4 sts, 4 Rs.
Add 2 edge sts: 1 each side.

Cast on
4 sts.

Multiple of 4 sts, plus 2.

Row 1: k1, *k2, yo twice, k2*, k1.
Row 2: k1, *k2tog, {k1, p1} in yo twice below, k2tog*, k1.
Row 3: k1, *yo, k4, yo*, k1.
Row 4: k1, *p1, {k2tog} 2 times, k1*, k1.
Rep Rs 1-4.

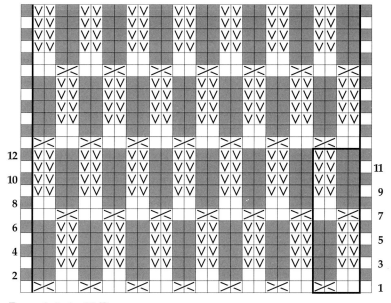

Repeat: 4 sts, 12 Rs.
Add 2 edge sts: 1 each side.

Multiple of 4 sts, plus 2.
☑ = On odd-numbered, right-side Rs, with yarn in back, sl 2 sts pwise.
☒ = On even-numbered, wrong-side Rs, with yarn in front, sl 2 sts pwise.
✕ = K the 2nd st on L ndl, then k the 1st st and drop both from L ndl tog.

Row 1: k1, *k2, ✕*, k1. **Row 2:** k1, *k2, p2*, k1. **Row 3:** k1, *☑, p2*, k1. **Row 4:** k1, *k2, ☒*, k1. **Row 5:** Rep R 3. **Row 6:** Rep R 4. **Row 7:** k1, *✕, k2*, k1. **Row 8:** k1, *p2, k2*, k1. **Row 9:** k1, *p2, ☑*, k1. **Row 10:** k1, *☒, k2*, k1. **Row 11:** Rep R 9. **Row 12:** Rep R 10.
Rep Rs 1-12.

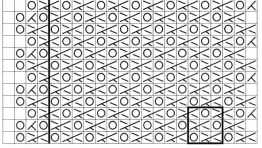

5
3
1

Repeat: 3 sts, 6 Rs.
Add 4 edge sts at L.
Modified sts at Rt: Rs 3, 5.
Even Rs: P all sts.

Modified sts

Multiple of 3 sts, plus 4.
Even Rs 2-6 (wrong side): P all sts.
⊠ = On L ndl k 3rd and 2nd sts tog, then k 1st st, and drop all from L ndl tog.

Row 1: *⊠, yo*, k1.
Row 3: k1, *⊠, yo*, k2tog, yo, k1.
Row 5: k2tog, *yo, ⊠*, yo, k2.
Rep Rs 1-6.

Pattern with the twists in the opposite direction:
Multiple of 3 sts, plus 4.
Even Rs 2-6 (wrong side): P all sts.
⊠ = On L ndl k 2nd and 3rd sts tog through back loops, then k 1st st through front loop and drop all from L ndl tog.

Row 1: k1, *yo, ⊠*.
Row 3: k1, yo, ssk, *yo, ⊠*, k1.
Row 5: k2, *yo, ⊠*, yo, ssk.
Rep Rs 1-6.

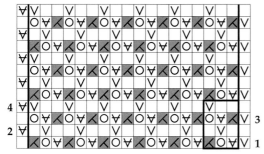

Repeat: 3 sts, 4 Rs.
Add 2 edge sts: 1 each side.

Multiple of 3 sts, plus 2.
ⱴ = With yarn in front, sl 1 st pwise.

Row 1: sl 1, *ⱴ, yo, p2tog*, k1.
Row 2: sl 1, *p1, ⱴ, p1*, p1.
Row 3: sl 1, *p2tog, ⱴ, yo*, k1.
Row 4: sl 1, *ⱴ, p2*, p1.
Rep Rs 1-4.

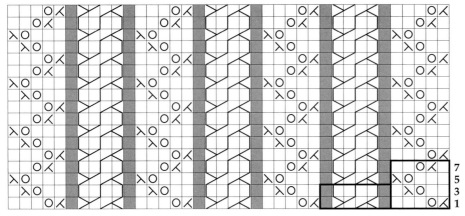

Cable repeat: 6 sts, 4 Rs.

Ground repeat: 5 sts, 8 Rs.

Combined repeat of 1 ground, 1 cable: 11 sts, 8 Rs.

Even Rs: P, but k single st each side of cable (gray squares).

|— Combined —|
repeat 11 sts

Multiple of 11 sts.
The division between patterns is
marked by a slash (/).
Even Rs 2-8 (wrong side): *k1, p4,
k1, / p5*.

Row 1: *k2tog, yo, k3, / p1, sl 2 sts
onto extra ndl and hold in back of
work, k next 2 sts, then k held sts, p1*.
Row 3: *k2, yo, ssk, k1, / p1, k4, p1*.
Row 5: *k3, yo, ssk, / p1, sl 2 sts onto
extra ndl and hold in back of work,
k next 2 sts, then k held sts, p1*.
Row 7: *k1, k2tog, yo, k2, / p1, k4, p1*.
Rep Rs 1-8.

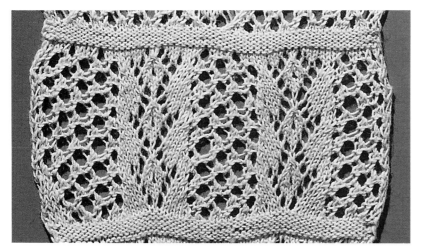

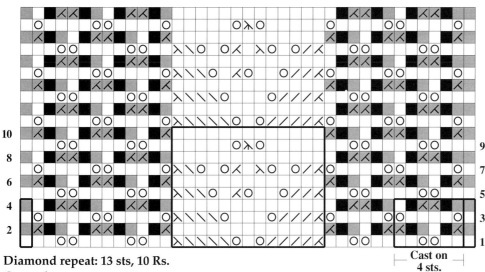

Diamond repeat: 13 sts, 10 Rs.
Ground repeat: 4 sts, 4 Rs.
  Add 2 edge sts: 1 each side.
Combined repeat of 2 ground,
  1 diamond: 21 sts, 20 Rs.
  Add 1 edge st at Rt.

Combined repeat 21 sts

Cast on 4 sts.

Multiple of 21 sts, plus 1.
The division between patterns is
marked by a slash (/).

Row 1: k1, *{k2, yo twice, k2} 2 times,
/ k2tog, k4, yo, k1, yo, k4, ssk*.
Row 2: *p13, / {k2tog, {k1, p1} in yo
twice below, k2tog} 2 times*, k1.

Row 3: k1, *{yo, k4, yo} 2 times,
/ k2tog, k3, {yo, k3} 2 times, ssk*.
Row 4: *p13, / {p1, {k2tog} 2 times,
k1} 2 times*, k1. **Row 5:** k1, *{k2, yo
twice, k2} 2 times, / k2tog, {k2, yo}
2 times, k2tog, k1, yo, k2, ssk*. **Row 6:** Rep
R 2. **Row 7:** k1, *{yo, k4, yo} 2 times,
/ k2tog, {k1, yo} 2 times, ssk, k1, k2tog,
{yo, k1} 2 times, ssk*. **Row 8:** Rep R 4.
Row 9: k1, *{k2, yo twice, k2} 2 times,
/ k5, yo, sl 1-k2tog-psso, yo, k5*.

Row 10: Rep R 2. **Row 11:** k1, *{yo, k4,
yo} 2 times, / k2tog, k4, yo, k1, yo, k4,
ssk*. **Row 12:** Rep R 4. **Row 13:** k1,
*{k2, yo twice, k2} 2 times, / k2tog,
{k3, yo} 2 times, k3, ssk*. **Row 14:** Rep
R 2. **Row 15:** k1, *{yo, k4, yo} 2 times,
/ k2tog, {k2, yo} 2 times, k2tog, k1, yo,
k2, ssk*. **Row 16:** Rep R 4. **Row 17:** k1,
*{k2, yo twice, k2} 2 times, / k2tog,
{k1, yo} 2 times, ssk, k1, k2tog,
{yo, k1} 2 times, ssk*. **Row 18:** Rep

(Pattern 88 continued)
R 2. **Row 19:** k1, *{yo, k4, yo} 2 times, / k5, yo, sl 1-k2tog-psso, yo, k5*.
Row 20: Rep R 4.
Rep Rs 1-20.

Ground pattern when used alone:
Multiple of 4 sts, plus 2.

Row 1: k1, *k2, yo twice, k2*, k1.
Row 2: k1, *k2tog, {k1, p1} in yo twice

below, k2tog*, k1. **Row 3:** k1, *yo, k4, yo*, k1. **Row 4:** k1, *p1, {k2tog} 2 times, k1*, k1.
Rep Rs 1-4.

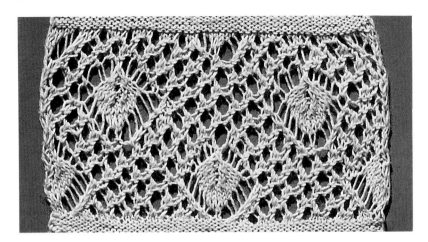

Pattern 89

Repeat: 26 sts, 24 Rs.
Add 2 edge sts: 1 each side.

Cast on 26 sts.

(*Pattern 89 continued*)

Multiple of 26 sts, plus 2.

Even Rs 2-10 and 14-22 have 27 st rep.

⊠ = P 1 st, sl 1 st kwise, return both sts to L ndl. Psso, return st to Rt ndl.

◼ = Sl 2 sts tog kwise, k next st, p2sso.

Row 1: k1, *k2, yo twice, k3, k2tog, yo, k1, yo, ssk, {k2, yo twice, k2} 4 times*, k1. **Row 2:** k1, *{k2tog, (k1, p1) in yo twice below, k2tog} 3 times, k2tog, (k1, p1) in yo twice below, k1, ⊠, yo, p3, yo, p2tog, k2tog, (k1, p1) in yo twice below, k2tog*, k1. **Row 3:** k1, *yo, k3, k2tog, yo, k5, yo, ssk, k3, {yo twice, k4} 3 times, yo*, k1. **Row 4:** k1, *{p1, k2tog twice, k1} 3 times, p1, k2tog, ⊠, yo, p7, yo, p2tog, k2tog, k1*, k1. **Row 5:** k1, *k1, k2tog, yo, k9, yo, ssk, k1, {k2, yo twice, k2} 3 times*, k1. **Row 6:** k1, *{k2tog, (k1, p1) in yo twice below, k2tog} 3 times, ⊠, yo, p11, yo, p2tog*, k1. **Row 7:** k1, *yo, k2, yo, k3, ssk, p1, k2tog, k3, yo, k2, {yo twice, k4} 3 times, yo*, k1. **Row 8:** k1, *{p1, k2tog twice, k1} 3 times, p1, k2tog, k1,

yo, p2, p2tog, k1, ⊠, p2, yo, k1, k2tog, k1*, k1. **Row 9:** k1, *k2, yo twice, k2, yo, k1, ssk, p1, k2tog, k1, yo, {k2, yo twice, k2} 4 times*, k1. **Row 10:** k1, *{k2tog, (k1, p1) in yo twice below, k2tog} 4 times, k1, yo, p2tog, k1, ⊠, yo, k1, k2tog, (k1, p1) in yo twice below, k2tog*, k1. **Row 11:** k1, *yo, k4, yo twice, k2, sl 1-k2tog-psso, k2, {yo twice, k4} 4 times, yo*, k1. **Row 12:** k1, *p1, k2tog twice, (p1, k1) in yo twice below, k4, (k1, p1) in yo twice below, {k2tog twice, (k1, p1) in yo twice below} 2 times, k2tog, ◼, (k1, p1) in yo twice below, k2tog twice, k1*, k1. **Row 13:** k1, *{k2, yo twice, k2} 4 times, k1, k2tog, yo, k1, yo, ssk, k2, yo twice, k2*, k1. **Row 14:** k1, *k2tog, (k1, p1) in yo twice below, k1, ⊠, yo, p3, yo, p2tog, {k2tog, (k1, p1) in yo twice below, k2tog} 4 times*, k1. **Row 15:** k1, *yo, {k4, yo twice} 3 times, k3, k2tog, yo, k5, yo, ssk, k3, yo*, k1. **Row 16:** k1, *p1, k2tog, ⊠, yo, p7, yo, p2tog, {k2tog, (k1, p1) in yo twice below, k2tog} 3 times, k2tog, k1*, k1. **Row 17:** k1, *{k2,

yo twice, k2} 3 times, k1, k2tog, yo, k9, yo, ssk, k1*, k1. **Row 18:** k1, *⊠, yo, p11, yo, p2tog, {k2tog, (k1, p1) in yo twice below, k2tog} 3 times*, k1.

Row 19: k1, *yo, {k4, yo twice} 3 times, k2, yo, k3, ssk, p1, k2tog, k3, yo, k2, yo*, k1. **Row 20:** k1, *p1, k2tog, k1, yo, p2, p2tog, k1, ⊠, p2, yo, k1, {k2tog, (k1, p1) in yo twice below, k2tog} 3 times, k2tog, k1*, k1. **Row 21:** k1, *{k2, yo twice, k2} 4 times, yo, k1, ssk, p1, k2tog, k1, yo, k2, yo twice, k2*, k1.

Row 22: k1, *k2tog, (k1, p1) in yo twice below, k2tog, k1, yo, p2tog, k1, ⊠, yo, k1, {k2tog, (k1, p1) in yo twice below, k2tog} 4 times*, k1. **Row 23:** k1, *yo, {k4, yo twice} 4 times, k2, sl 1-k2tog-psso, k2, yo twice, k4, yo*, k1.

Row 24: k1, *p1, k2tog twice, (k1, p1) in yo twice below, k2tog, ◼, {(k1, p1) in yo twice below, k2tog twice} 2 times, (p1, k1) in yo twice below, k4, (k1, p1) in yo twice below, k2tog twice, k1*, k1.

Rep Rs 1-24.

Note: Rows 16-18 are missing in the sampler, but are included on the chart.

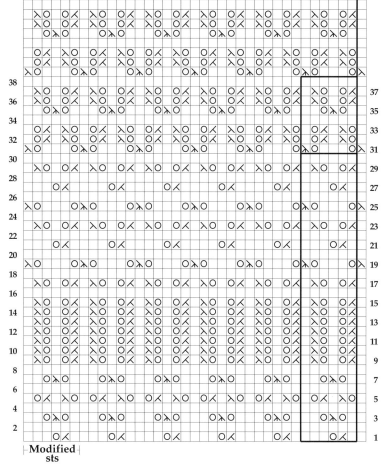

Border repeat: 6 sts, 30 Rs.
Leaf repeat: 6 sts, 8 Rs.
  Add 1 edge st at Rt.
Modified sts at L: Rs 19, 25, 31.

(*Pattern 90 continued*)
Multiple of 6 sts, plus 1.
Even Rs 2-8 and 16-30 (wrong side): P all sts.

⊠ = P 1 st, sl 1 st kwise, return both sts to L ndl. Psso, return st to Rt ndl.

Row 1: k1, *k1, k2tog, yo, k3*.
Row 3: k1, *k1, yo, sl 1-k2tog-psso, yo, k2*. **Row 5:** k1, *yo, ssk, k1, k2tog, yo, k1*. **Row 7:** Rep R 3. **Row 9:** k1, *k2tog, yo, k1, yo, ssk, k1*. **Row 10:** *p1, ⊠, yo, p1, yo, k2tog*, p1. **Row 11:** Rep R 9. **Row 12:** Rep R 10. **Row 13:** Rep R 9. **Row 14:** Rep R 10. **Row 15:** Rep R 9. **Row 17:** Rep R 9. **Row 19:** ssk, *yo, k3, yo, sl 1-k2tog-psso*, end last rep ssk. **Row 21:** Rep R 1. **Row 23:** Rep R 9.

Row 25: Rep R 19. **Row 27:** Rep R 1. **Row 29:** Rep R 9. **Row 31:** Rep R 19. **Row 32:** *p1, yo, p2tog, p1, ⊠, yo*, p1. **Row 33:** k1, *yo, ssk, k1, k2tog, yo, k1*. **Row 34:** Purl. **Row 35:** Rep R 7. **Row 36:** Rep R 10. **Row 37:** Rep R 9. **Row 38:** Purl.
Rep Rs 31-38 for an allover leaf pattern.

Pattern **91**

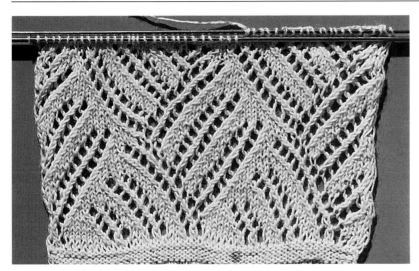

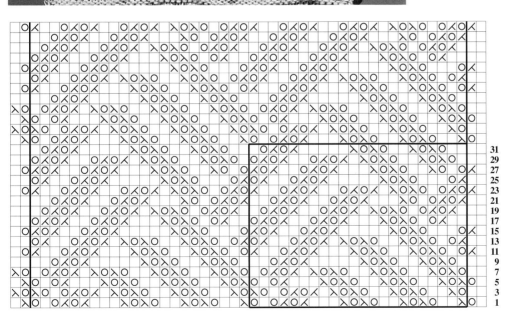

Repeat: 22 sts, 32 Rs.
Add 4 edge sts: 2 each side.
Even Rs: P all sts.

(Pattern 91 continued)
Multiple of 22 sts, plus 4.
Even Rs 2-32 (wrong side): P all sts.

Row 1: k1, yo, *ssk, {k2, yo, ssk, yo, ssk} 2 times, k3, {k2tog, yo} 2 times, k1, yo*, ssk, k1. **Row 3:** k2, *yo, ssk, {k2, yo, ssk, yo, ssk} 2 times, k1, {k2tog, yo} 2 times, k1, yo, ssk*, yo, ssk. **Row 5:** k1, yo, *ssk, yo, ssk, {k2, yo, ssk, yo, ssk} 2 times, k3, k2tog, yo, k1, yo*, ssk, k1. **Row 7:** k2, *{yo, ssk} 2 times, {k2, yo, ssk, yo, ssk} 2 times, k1, {k2tog, yo} 2 times, k1*, yo, ssk. **Row 9:** k2, *{k1, yo, ssk, yo, ssk, k1} 2 times, k4, {k2tog, yo} 2 times, k2*, k2.

Row 11: k1, k2tog, *yo, {k1, yo, ssk, yo, ssk, k1} 2 times, k2, {k2tog, yo} 2 times, k2, k2tog*, yo, k1. **Row 13:** k2, *k2tog, yo, {k1, yo, ssk, yo, ssk, k1} 2 times, {k2tog, yo} 2 times, k2, k2tog, yo*, k2. **Row 15:** k1, k2tog, *yo, k3, {yo, ssk} 2 times, k5, {k2tog, yo} 2 times, k2, k2tog, yo, k2tog*, yo, k1. **Row 17:** k2, *k2, k2tog, yo, k1, {yo, ssk} 2 times, k3, {k2tog, yo} 2 times, k2, {k2tog, yo} 2 times*, k2. **Row 19:** k2, *k1, {k2tog, yo} 2 times, k1, {yo, ssk} 2 times, {k1, k2tog, yo, k2tog, yo, k1} 2 times*, k2. **Row 21:** k2, *{k2tog, yo} 2 times, k1, yo, ssk, k3, {k2tog, yo, k2tog, yo, k2} 2 times*, k2.

Row 23: k1, k2tog, *yo, k2tog, yo, k1, {yo, ssk} 2 times, k1, {k2tog, yo, k2tog, yo, k2} 2 times, k2tog*, yo, k1. **Row 25:** k2, *k2tog, yo, k3, {yo, ssk} 2 times, k5, {k2tog, yo} 2 times, k2, k2tog, yo*, k2. **Row 27:** k1, k2tog, *yo, k1, yo, ssk, k2, {yo, ssk} 2 times, k3, {k2tog, yo} 2 times, k2, k2tog, yo, k2tog*, yo, k1. **Row 29:** k2, *{k1, yo, ssk, yo, ssk, k1} 2 times, {k2tog, yo} 2 times, k2, {k2tog, yo} 2 times*, k2. **Row 31:** k2, *{k2, yo, ssk, yo, ssk} 2 times, k5, {k2tog, yo} 2 times, k1*, k2. Rep Rs 1-32.

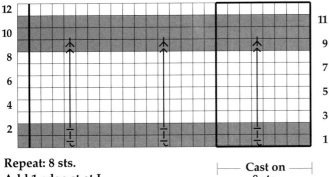

Repeat: 8 sts.
Add 1 edge st at L.
Start R 1 from the p side of the cast on.

Cast on
8 sts.

The hem at the beginning of the sampler

At the beginning of the sampler is a clever and decorative little hem. You can see it in the photo of Pattern 1 on p. 4. It is made in rows of stockinette and reverse stockinette stitches. When the hem is about two-thirds knitted, at intervals along the row, a pair of stitches near the beginning is picked up onto the needle and knitted together with the stitches on the needle, thus forming a narrow pin tuck. The purpose of the hem was probably to prevent the end of the sampler from curling up.

Multiple of 8 sts, plus 1.

Row 1: Purl. **Row 2:** Knit. **Row 3-8:** *k 1 R, p 1 R.* **Row 9:** *p4, with Rt ndl pick up top of purl st directly below from R 2 and place it on L ndl, being careful not to twist it. Do the same with the st below it from R 1. Make a purled double dec (see Symbol 31 in the Glossary of Symbols and Techniques): p the 2 picked-up sts tog, sl next st kwise. Return both sts to L ndl, psso, return to Rt ndl, p3*, p1. **Row 10:** Knit. **Row 11:** Purl. **Row 12:** Purl.
Now start Pattern 1 from the Rt side with R 1.

PART II

A
LACE-
KNITTING
WORKSHOP

CHAPTER 1

Getting Started

A ny kind of beautifully designed and executed lace evokes gasps of admiration from nearly everyone who stops to examine it. It looks so delicate, intricate and complicated, appearing to require extraordinary skill and technical expertise to create it—and often it does. Knitted lace is no exception. It gets its share of admiring gasps, but it looks harder to do than it really is. Mesh patterns can be worked by beginning knitters, and even the most complicated lace patterns can be readily mastered by those who understand the basic principles of lace knitting, can use a chart and are willing to practice a little.

Lace knitting in general, and the patterns in our sampler in particular, do not require advanced knitting techniques or complex stitches. You need only a basic knowledge of stockinette knitting, of making eyelets from both the knit and purl sides of the fabric, and of the various single and double decreases. A comprehensive collection of decreases and eyelet-making techniques can be found in the Glossary of Symbols and Techniques on pp. 193-198, and an explanation of the various basic knitting maneuvers can be found in any manual of knitting techniques (see the Bibliography on p. 205). A few other decorative stitches, namely cables, crossed stitches and wrapped clusters, are incorporated in some of the patterns in the sampler, and instructions for these stitches are included in the Glossary.

Although the techniques of lace knitting are simple, they can produce ingenious and complex structures. This chapter explains the elements of knitted lace and the important lacemaking terms, and gives advice on knitting lace and using lace patterns.

Characteristics of knitted lace

Knitted lace is a plain fabric with a pattern made by repeatedly increasing and decreasing stitches within the fabric. The design of the pattern incorporates three elements: openings, lines and solid areas. Openings are the element that classifies the knitted fabric as lace. Each opening is made by a *yarn over*, also known as "thread forward" and "thread around," which is one of several methods for increasing the number of stitches in a row in any knitted fabric. A yarn over is termed an "open increase" because it makes a space, called an eyelet, in the fabric, which you can see in the photo on p. 110. It is by far the predominant type of increase used in lace designs. The eyelets are usually the most visually dominant part of the design, so their placement and arrangement are important when designing a pattern.

Lines in knitted-lace designs are created by layering or doubling up stitches to decrease the number of stitches in a row. For these decreases, two or three adjacent stitches are knitted together as one, causing them to sit on top of one another. When repeated in the same place in successive rows, decreases give a heavy, linear quality to the design that balances the openness of the eyelets. Like openings, lines are used for outlining and decorating shapes and creating meshes. There are many decrease techniques, each of which causes the stitches to be layered in a different way and creates a different look (see the single and double decreases listed in the Glossary of Symbols and Techniques on p. 195-198).

Facing page: Detail, Pattern 38

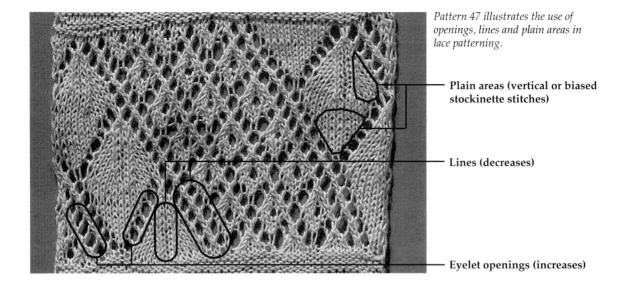

Pattern 47 illustrates the use of openings, lines and plain areas in lace patterning.

Plain areas (vertical or biased stockinette stitches)

Lines (decreases)

Eyelet openings (increases)

Solid, or plain, areas in knitted lace are produced with stockinette stitches and are used to complement the lines and spaces in the design. Sometimes the solid area is so large, however, that it's the lines and spaces that complement the solid shape. The stitches in the plain areas can be vertical or diagonal (biased), and often a mix of the two in different parts of the pattern creates the illusion of three-dimensionality. The stockinette area can be varied with purl stitches, twisted stitches, cables or a second color to add dimension and interest to the pattern. However, in the most basic lace fabrics—the meshes and faggots—there are no solid areas at all. The pattern is composed entirely of lines and spaces, which form a net.

Parallel selvedges

Designing a lace pattern centers around balancing the number of eyelet openings (increases) and layered stitches (decreases). If the fabric is meant to have side selvedges that are parallel, there must be one stitch decreased for every one increased throughout the pattern. Usually this pairing of increase and decrease takes place on the same knitted row, and thus the number of stitches in each row of the repeat remains constant. In some patterns, extra eyelets are inserted in a row, increasing the number of stitches in that row, but their companion decreases are not made until a later row or rows within the repeat. The beginning and end of the repeat will always have the same number of stitches, however, and the selvedges will be parallel. You can see this effect in Pattern 2 (shown at top on the facing page) and also in the leaf shape in Pattern 64.

In fabrics whose selvedges are not meant to be parallel, such as edgings and medallions, several successive rows are knitted with extra increases in each row to widen the fabric, and then the companion decreases are worked over the following several rows to narrow the fabric. Usually, but not always, the extra increases and decreases are worked along the edges of the fabric. For edgings, binding off several stitches at once, rather than decreasing, is often the technique used to narrow the fabric in order to achieve a more dramatic shape. In a shape like a doily, knitted circularly from the center out, stitches are continually increased from the tiny center to the large outer edge.

Basic fabrics

The terms *stockinette* and *plain knitting* or *plain stitches* refer to the most common fabric used for lace knitting. This fabric has a smooth knit, or plain, side and a rough purl side. Nearly always, the knit side is used as the right side of the fabric in lace knitting, as is the case with our sampler. To knit stockinette fabric when working with two needles, knit the stitches on the odd (right-side) rows and purl the stitches on the even (wrong-side) rows. When knitting circularly, knit all the stitches, since all the rounds are necessarily worked from the right side.

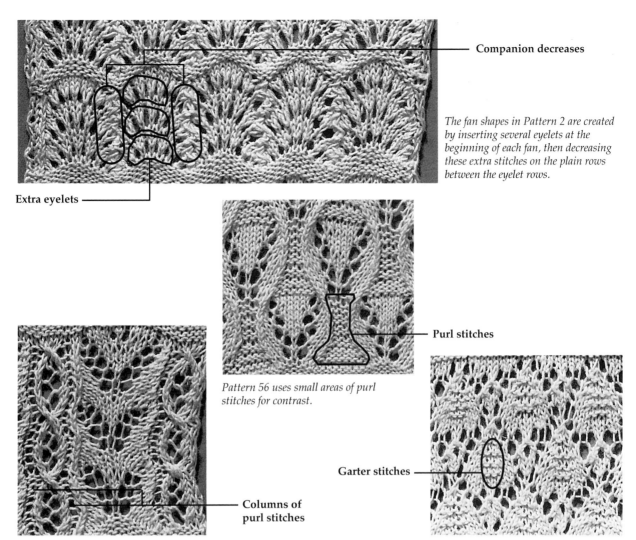

Companion decreases

The fan shapes in Pattern 2 are created by inserting several eyelets at the beginning of each fan, then decreasing these extra stitches on the plain rows between the eyelet rows.

Extra eyelets

Purl stitches

Pattern 56 uses small areas of purl stitches for contrast.

Garter stitches

Columns of purl stitches

In Pattern 24, columns of purl stitches outline the cable.

Pattern 59 uses garter stitch for accent.

Oftentimes a lace pattern will call for purling stitches on the knit side and knitting stitches on the purl side, which is termed *reverse stockinette,* to create small, contrasting areas of purl stitches on the front of the fabric. Pattern 56 (detail shown above right) uses areas of purl stitches in this way. You can also use purl stitches as accents, outlines or a ground pattern. Pattern 24 (above left) illustrates a familiar example: purl stitches outlining a cable panel.

Another basic fabric found in lace knitting is *garter stitch,* a reversible fabric of horizontal ridges. In two-needle knitting both the odd and even rows are knitted, which results in alternating knit and purl rows on both sides. Each horizontal ridge is comprised of one knit row and one purl row. In circular knitting, rounds are alternately knitted and purled.

In this sampler, garter stitch has been used mainly for accent. Pattern 59, for example, has garter stitch within its diamond shapes. Garter stitch is also often used to stabilize the free edge of edgings to prevent the fabric from rolling. There are many variations of garter stitch. Among them, moss stitch and seed stitch appear in the sampler. You can see a garter-stitch variation in Pattern 18.

Ribbing is comprised of alternating columns of knit and purl stitches. To knit it in both flat and circular knitting, you must alternately knit one or more stitches then purl one or more stitches repeatedly across each row. Rib fabrics can have great elasticity, the degree of which depends on the number of adjacent knit and purl stitches. Narrow ribs of one, two or three stitches each are quite elastic; wide ribs maintain the

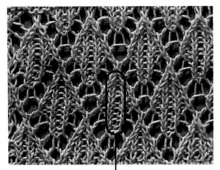

Pattern 36 has a narrow knit-one, purl-one rib within its diamond shapes.

Pattern 81 is an allover pattern of brioche faggoting.

1x1 rib

corrugated appearance but flatten into panels that have little elasticity. You can see in Pattern 36 (detail shown above left) and also in patterns 14 and 44 how plain areas of rib can be used to heighten the effect of the lace portions. If the knit-stitch ribs contain a lace pattern, the plain purl-stitch ribs in between will set off the pattern with striking contrast. You can see this in patterns 37, 41 and 63. Two patterns with wide ribs are patterns 60 and 67.

Brioche is the name for a large group of fabrics of Eastern origin characterized by extra loops of yarn that are taken in with the knitted stitches, giving these fabrics a layered, dimensional quality. Pattern 81 (detail above right) is an example of a brioche fabric. These fabrics are generally thick, soft and very stretchy, even bordering on being unstable if the needles are not the correct size for the yarn. The architecture of these fabrics is fascinating and not easy to discern without careful unraveling.

Brioche fabrics can be based on stockinette, garter or rib stitch, or they can contain elements of all three. In hand knitting, the extra loops are made either by slipping a stitch and making a yarn over (the extra loop) on one row, then knitting these two together as one stitch on the next row; or by knitting into the stitch on the row below, which causes the stitch to become unknitted and the resulting loose loop to be knitted in with the newly made stitch on the needle. In machine knitting, brioche fabrics are known as "tuck knitting" since the extra loops are made by creating tuck loops (unformed stitches) on certain needles, then knitting them off with the stitch on the next row. There are four examples of brioche fabrics in the sampler, only one of which is a lace pattern: Pattern 79, a fisherman rib; Pattern 81, a faggoting pattern (and the one brioche lace pattern); Pattern 82, Tunisian knitting; and Pattern 86, a honeycomb stitch pattern.

Lace patterning

The *motif* is the principal design element of a pattern repeat. Usually it is a geometric or figurative shape such as a diamond, triangle, leaf or flower. An *allover pattern* is a motif pattern that is repeated over a large area of the knitting. Pattern 9 (shown at the top of the facing page) has an allover diamond motif. Motifs can be arranged in many different ways, combined or decorated with another pattern or surrounded by a ground pattern. *Panels*, which are vertical or horizontal bands of repeating patterns, usually set off by a border, can even be used as allovers, as shown in Pattern 51 (facing page, center).

All the patterns in this sampler have been written and charted as allover patterns so that you can easily repeat the pattern horizontally and vertically to knit a large fabric. You don't necessarily have to knit the patterns that way, however. You can lift and combine parts and pieces of patterns to make new ones for panels, insertions, edgings, medallions or single motifs. (For further discussion of allover patterns, see pp. 138-142.)

A *ground*, or background, pattern is a plain or patterned fabric used as a filler for negative areas around motifs and between panels, as a background for a single motif, or as a spot pattern within a large motif. The pattern can be as simple as plain or purled stockinette stitch, garter stitch or rib stitch. Lace-patterned grounds have very small repeats such as tiny diamonds, diagonal stripes of eyelets and decreases, or one of the faggot or eyelet mesh patterns. They are always small and thus can nicely fill in nooks and crannies and still be recognizable as a pattern. Pattern 40 (facing page, bottom) uses a diamond-ground pattern to fill in the areas around the motif. (Diamond grounds are discussed further starting on p. 148.)

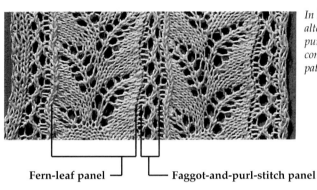

The motif in Pattern 9 is a diamond shape, used in an allover arrangement.

In Pattern 51, a wide fern-leaf panel alternates with a narrow faggot-and-purl-stitch panel, and the two-panel combination is repeated as an allover pattern.

Fern-leaf panel ⌐ ⌐ **Faggot-and-purl-stitch panel**

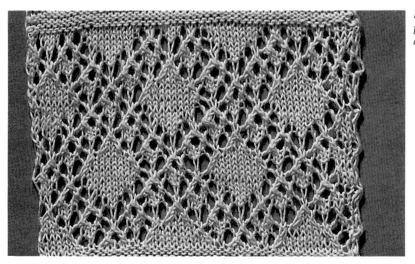

In Pattern 40, a tiny diamond ground pattern surrounds the larger plain diamond motif.

A *mesh* pattern is a lace fabric comprised of eyelets and decreases with very few plain stitches. The resulting fabric has an open, grid-like pattern, which makes it useful as a ground pattern. Some meshes are soft and stretchy, while others are firm and stable. Some are patterned on both the right-side and wrong-side rows (and on all rounds in circular knitting), but several meshes have the wrong side purled without patterning. All faggot patterns make meshes, as do the double-eyelet patterns and the prevalent diagonal stripes of eyelets and decreases. Pattern 88 (shown on p. 114) uses a double-eyelet mesh pattern between panels. The mesh patterns used in the sampler are discussed further starting on p. 148.

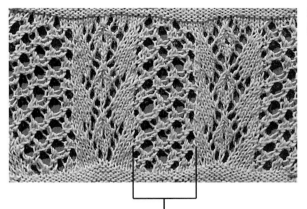

Double-eyelet mesh pattern ⎤

Faggot pattern ⎤

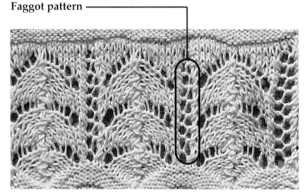

In Pattern 69, one repeat of a faggot pattern is used as a vertical insertion.

Faggot patterns, which are a type of mesh, are also made of eyelets and decreases, but the fabric is composed of alternating open and solid vertical stripes. They are used for decorative vertical insertions or, when knitted as allover patterns, for meshes. Some are patterned on both the right-side and wrong-side rows, while others are purled plain on the wrong-side rows. The faggoting in Pattern 69 (detail shown above) is made over a multiple of four stitches. All the right-side rows are a repeat of "knit two, yarn over, slip one-knit one-pass slipped stitch over (or slip-slip-knit)." All the wrong-side rows are "purl two, yarn over, purl two together." One repeat of this pattern, knitted as a vertical insertion as in Pattern 69, mimics the decorative stitch of the same name used in traditional drawn-thread and deflected-thread needlework and lace work. Originally intended for use as decorative accents, repeating faggots make excellent ground patterns, too. A separate discussion of the various faggots in the sampler can be found on pp. 143-147.

Pattern 88 has a double-eyelet mesh pattern inserted between vertical panels.

Lace used as decoration

A knitted-lace *insertion* is a narrow strip of decorative patterning, like a narrow panel, inserted between areas of other patterning or between two pieces of knitted fabric. The insertion can run either vertically or horizontally, but it is usually only one or two repeats in height (horizontal insertion) or width (vertical insertion) so that it adds a contrasting decorative element to the overall fabric. The faggot in Pattern 69 (shown below, left) is a good example of a vertical insertion. You can knit insertions simultaneously with other patterns, as was done in this sampler, or you can knit them separately and then insert them in seams or between panels. In the latter case the selvedges on the insertion must be firm and stable enough for sewing. Insertions have both selvedges straight and parallel.

An *edging* is a strip of decorative fabric used to embellish a selvedge. Unlike an insertion, it has one free edge, which usually undulates or is scalloped; the other edge, the heading, is straight. Often, the entire edging, or at least its free edge, is knitted in garter stitch or a mixture of knit and purl stitches to keep it from curling and rolling and to give it a bit of visual weight. The sampler contains no edging, but three edgings derived from the sampler's patterns are shown on pp. 157-159.

You can knit an edging simultaneously with the main fabric, knit it onto a completed main fabric by picking up stitches along a selvedge, or knit it separately and sew it onto the main fabric. If you knit the edging separately, the heading must be firm and stable enough for sewing.

A *medallion* is a piece of straight or shaped knitting used to decorate another fabric. Traditionally, the medallion is either sewn on top of woven fabric or stitched into an opening cut in the fabric. You can easily develop medallion patterns by using large motifs or combining a number of small motifs in a pleasing arrangement. Several medallions joined together can become beautiful blocks for coverlets or afghans. You can also knit medallions as single motifs, even as allover patterns, within a larger fabric. (The photo on the facing page shows a medallion design knitted as an allover pattern). A medallion made up of several motifs from the sampler is shown in the photo on p. 160.

Medallion ————————

knitted in a variety of yarns to give you an idea of some of the effects you can achieve. If you have a yarn that's not normally used for lace but that you absolutely love and want to use, there is usually a pattern suitable for it.

Since lace knitting makes a looser fabric than plain stockinette does, the size of the needles must suit not only the yarn but also the proportion of open work (which loosens the fabric) to solid areas (which tighten the fabric). For a given yarn, choose smaller needles to knit an essentially open pattern, and larger needles to knit a fairly solid pattern. To make bigger eyelets when using thick or textured yarns, wrap the yarn twice around the needle instead of once when making yarn overs, then drop one of the loops on the return row and knit normally into the other one.

Stitch and row gauge

I usually measure the gauge over whole repeats of known stitches and rows. I first outline the edges of the repeat(s) with pins, markers or basting stitches. Then I measure the width and height of the marked area and divide these measurements by the number of stitches or rows within the repeat(s). The more repeats you can include in the measurements, the more accurate the gauge will be.

Of course, be sure to measure the gauge after you have blocked and stretched the lace as you plan to for the finished article. Be aware, though, that your freshly blocked piece of lace may change considerably after it has sat around, or been worn or hung for a while. The degree of change depends on the elasticity and resiliency of the yarn as well as the type of pattern worked. Designs patterned every row instead of every other row tend to collapse more readily, since their eyelets have only one strand of yarn instead of two twisted twice, which gives the fabric greater stability. Keep this in mind when planning your knitting.

As for calculating the number of stitches and rows for a given set of garment measurements, I often find it better to calculate by pattern repeats instead of by actual stitches and rows, so that the pattern will break gracefully at the seams. You may have to fudge your measurements a little if the repeat's measurement doesn't fit exactly as needed, but lace is so stretchy that it usually doesn't matter much. However, if I have to fudge with hosiery or some other body-hugging

Hints on knitting lace

Lace knitting involves most of the same elements used in other kinds of knitting. But the open nature of lace and its extensive use of eyelets and decreases call for a few special considerations.

Yarn and needles

Traditionally, lace knitting is worked in very fine cotton, linen, silk or wool thread on thin wire needles. In nontraditional contemporary work, larger thread and needles can be used very successfully, but both must be carefully chosen to suit the design. Smooth, firm thread or yarn shows off an intricate pattern best, while soft and even fuzzy yarns can create a beautifully delicate effect in a simple pattern. The swatches scattered throughout Chapter 2 have been article, I always make the measurement smaller rather than larger, so that the stretchy lace will fit snugly. There's nothing worse than baggy stockings!

Casting on, binding off and handling selvedges

As with most knitting, common sense and experience will tell you what to do with the edges of the knitting. When I knit a garment with lace patterning, I generally knit only one plain stitch at each selvedge, which will be taken into the seam. I don't like more than one selvedge stitch because otherwise the seam becomes too thick and is likely to show between the eyelets from the right side. I knit the edge stitch in the same stitch as the base fabric—garter stitch if the fabric next to the seam is garter stitch, and stockinette if it is stockinette. Unless the yarn is very slippery, I don't slip the selvedge stitch on alternate rows, because that can make the selvedge too tight. I depend on the garment's seams to provide the stability and elasticity needed for the fabric's edges.

For lengthwise seams, I nearly always use mattress stitch (shown in the drawing at right). If the seams need to be decorative, I crochet them, as explained in the shawl project in Chapter 4 (see p. 185).

For knitting items with free edges—that is, edges that will not be joined to another edge or fabric—I often use garter stitch (or a variant) for a border to prevent the knitting from curling and frequently slip the selvedge stitch every other row. Garter stitch is wonderful for borders because it has so much give and will stretch readily when you steam it out.

I don't use any particular cast-on or bind-off just for lace. Because there is usually a border of some kind around the lace, I use whichever cast-on or bind-off is appropriate to the border. (You can find cast-on and bind-off information in the books on general knitting techniques in the Bibliography on p. 205.) Borders at the top and bottom of the knitting, together with their cast-on or bind-off, need to stretch in width as much as the lace fabric they decorate. But when you start knitting, it's hard to know how much stretch to build into a border. Therefore, I often begin without the border and knit it afterward by picking up the stitches at the beginning and knitting it in the other direction. If that isn't suitable, I start the border with an invisible cast-on or waste yarn, leaving a long tail of the main yarn as I start the first row. After the piece is done, when I know how loose or tight the edge needs to be, I use the long tail to bind off the beginning.

Mattress stitch

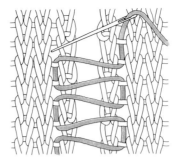

This stitch, done from the right side of the fabric, is used for sewing up lengthwise seams.

Scallops

Be careful about combining patterns when one or more of them has scalloped edges. If the scalloping occurs at the top or bottom of the pattern, plan a buffer zone of garter stitch or some other pattern to absorb the distortion. The lower half of the chevron swatch on p. 122, for example, is filled with diagonal stitches that would make scalloped edges if there was no knitting beneath them. The ridges of garter stitch, however, absorb the scalloping. I purposely put the patterns with the greatest degree of scalloping at the bottom of the swatch, since even garter-stitch buffer zones can absorb only so much.

Seaming fabrics with zigzag sides is less problematic, since what zigs on one selvedge will zag on the other. Consequently, the two fit together like puzzle pieces, as the swatch on p. 129 shows. You can also use this distortion to enhance the effect of another pattern. For example, look at the edges of the garter-stitch ridges in the swatch on p. 136.

Dropped stitches

I don't think anyone would be fooled if I said that handling dropped stitches in lace knitting is easy. If the pattern is fairly simple, you understand it and you have had experience with dropped stitches in other kinds of knitting, picking up and reknitting dropped stitches in a lace pattern can be fairly straightforward.

If a dropped stitch has simply vanished, it has unraveled into the first eyelet below and stopped. This isn't difficult to fix; simply crochet the ladder back up, starting with the cross threads above the eyelet. When the dropped stitch has unraveled into a decrease, things become more difficult, because there are suddenly two—or horrors—three stitches starting to unravel. First, catch the stitches on safety pins to prevent further unraveling. If you can relayer them and then pull the single thread of the dropped stitch through them without getting confused with adjacent plain stitches and eyelets, that's very good! I usually try, using adjacent repeats as a guide for the formation of the stitches and eyelets. If this procedure doesn't work, there's nothing to do but rip out some rows. Take heart though, because usually you don't have to rip all the way back. Sometimes ripping just one or two rows will clarify the layering and construction of the adjacent plain stitches and eyelets in the area below.

Bias

Bias can be a knitter's nemesis in all kinds of pattern knitting. If your swatch wants to bias when it should be straight—that is, if instead of the rectangle it is supposed to be it assumes the shape of a tilted parallelogram—you must find out the cause. I never try to block out a bias tendency because I think it's futile. Every time you wash the garment you have to block it again, and usually the humidity in the air or the movement of the fabric on your body is enough to make it relax, allowing the bias to crawl right back in.

The most obvious cause for a tendency to bias lies with your knitting pattern. Texture patterns with stitches that are crossed, twisted or layered consistently in the same direction will create a torque in the knitted fabric. Only by crossing, twisting or layering in the opposite direction over half the area of the fabric can you rectify the situation. Pattern 85, a lattice pattern of crossed stitches, is a good example of a pattern biased in this way. The stitches cross consistently to the right, which makes the fabric bias to the left (for the photo, the pattern has been blocked upright). To make this pattern more useful, I have included written instructions for the left cross in the Glossary of Symbols and Techniques (see p. 194) so that you can use both crosses in different areas of the fabric.

In lace knitting, bias is caused or created (depending on whether on not you want it) by the position of the eyelet increase in relation to its decrease. A pattern in which a majority of the decreases are to the left of their eyelets, for example, will result in a knitted fabric that biases to the right, as does Pattern 1. Controlling the effect of bias is a useful and important aspect of designing lace patterns. A more complete discussion of this subject can be found starting on p. 129.

Sometimes, however, biasing is not created by the pattern but rather by the twist spun and plied into the yarn. Many cotton yarns are tightly plied and are designed for crochet or tatting, not knitting. Some single-ply and hard-twisted wool yarns designed for weaving will also bias when knitted. If the biasing is not too extreme, you can sometimes get rid of it by choosing a pattern that biases in the opposite direction or by adding areas of purl stitches. Garter stitch, moss stitch and narrow ribs are useful ground patterns for straightening out problem yarns.

CHAPTER 2

Exploring the Sampler Patterns

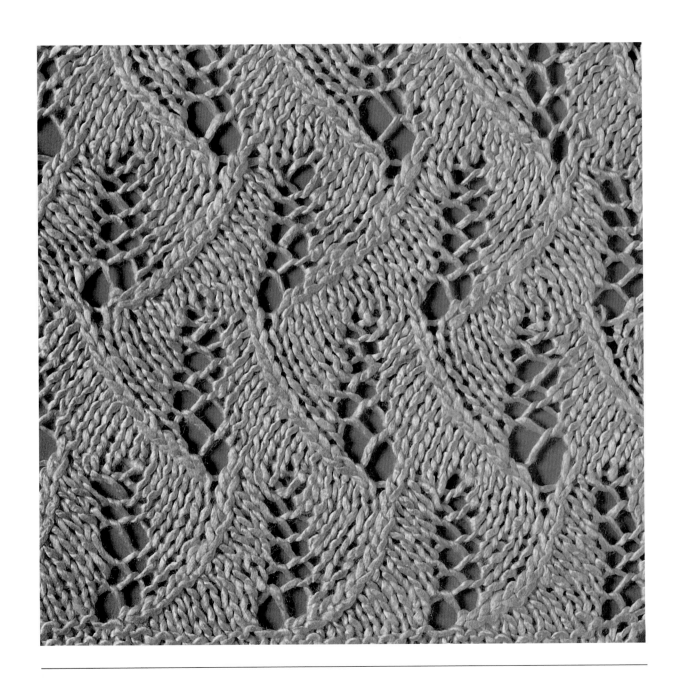

W hen you reach the stage at which you want to incorporate knitted-lace patterns into your knitting projects, develop your own patterns or perhaps modify an existing one, you'll need to know more about lace knitting than just how to follow existing patterns. As I discovered in working with this sampler, it's a great teacher. You can learn much more than just new patterns from it. By studying the sampler you can learn to identify many lace patterning elements and understand how they're built and combined. This gives you the freedom to enlarge or reduce the elements and recombine them into new charted patterns. Even if you don't plan to design your own patterns now, this chapter will help you understand what actually happens when you knit a lace design.

Balancing eyelets and decreases

As I explained in Chapter 1, the element that distinguishes lace knitting from other knitting is the spaces, or eyelets, created by yarn-over increases. And where there are increases, there must be an equal number of decreases to maintain the stitch count within the pattern's repeat. The eyelets form the skeleton of the pattern, while the decreases are its backbone. The relationship between these two elements is the single most important factor in a knitted lace design. A good way to begin exploring the sampler's patterns is by examining the ways that eyelets and decreases can be paired.

There are two basic ways to pair eyelets and decreases. You can pair each eyelet in a row with a decrease in the same row, or you can pair an eyelet in one row with a decrease in a different row within the repeat.

Facing page: Detail, Pattern 54

Eyelets paired with decreases in the same row

When each eyelet in a row has a decrease in the same row throughout the repeat, every row in the pattern repeat will have the same number of stitches. One eyelet can be paired with a single decrease, or two eyelets with a double decrease. The eyelet and its decrease can be adjacent, or they can be separated by one or more stitches. The arrangement used determines the way the pattern's plain stitches lie.

If all the eyelets are paired with adjacent decreases, as in the detail of Pattern 4 at the top of p. 120 for example, the diagonal linear elements of the design made by the decreases will be adjacent to the eyelets. The columns of plain stitches that form the solid pattern areas will be aligned vertically, parallel to the selvedges, giving the pattern a flat, two-dimensional effect. Most of the patterns in the sampler are of this type. Two other examples from the beginning of the sampler are patterns 5 and 7.

If an eyelet and its decrease are separated by one or more stitches, as in the detail of Pattern 16 on p. 120, for example, the stitches between the eyelet and its decrease will lean, or bias, toward the decrease. On the chart, these leaning stitches are marked with a slanted line (/ or \, Symbol 4 in the Glossary of Symbols and Techniques on p. 193), so that you know at a glance that they are biased, the direction in which they lean, and which eyelet and decrease belong together—the eyelet on one side of the diagonal stitches belongs to the decrease on the other side. When repeated above each other on successive rows, the resulting columns of leaning stitches will reflect light differently from the other stitches, giving the pattern's design a three-dimensional element. Notice in Pattern 16 that the columns of plain stitches between two sets of eyelets, as well as the garter stitches between two sets of decreases, are still vertical. Usually, patterns of this type make wavy or scalloped selvedges at either the

Pairing eyelets and decreases

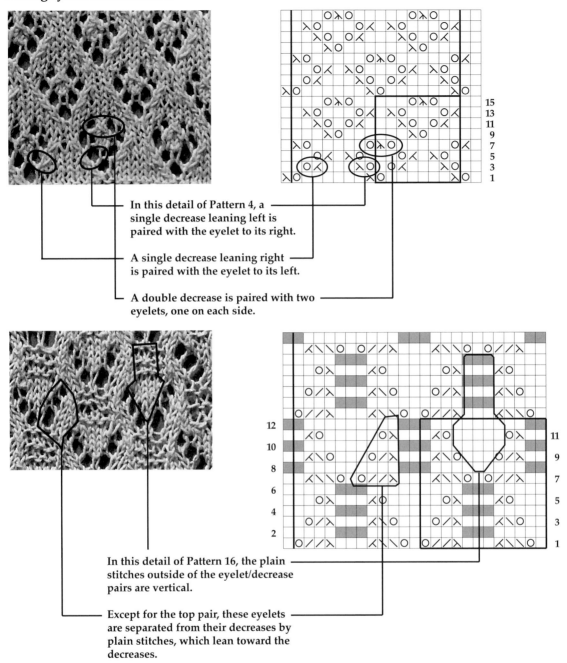

In this detail of Pattern 4, a single decrease leaning left is paired with the eyelet to its right.

A single decrease leaning right is paired with the eyelet to its left.

A double decrease is paired with two eyelets, one on each side.

In this detail of Pattern 16, the plain stitches outside of the eyelet/decrease pairs are vertical.

Except for the top pair, these eyelets are separated from their decreases by plain stitches, which lean toward the decreases.

cast-on edge or the side edges of the fabric. Two other such examples from the beginning of the sampler are patterns 6 and 15.

In complicated charts that contain a lot of symbols, the mixtures of eyelets and decreases can seem confusing. If you can't tell which eyelet belongs to which decrease on any given row, start reading the row from either edge of the chart and enclose the first eyelet and decrease (or two eyelets with a double decrease) within a circle to indicate that they are paired. Then circle the next eyelet and decrease. Work across the row until each eyelet is matched with its decrease.

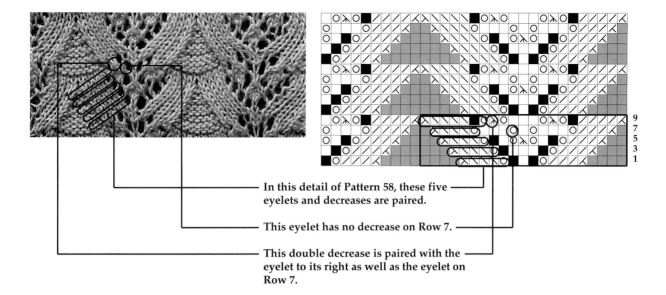

In this detail of Pattern 58, these five eyelets and decreases are paired.

This eyelet has no decrease on Row 7.

This double decrease is paired with the eyelet to its right as well as the eyelet on Row 7.

A comprehensive discussion of the patterning effects that can be achieved by positioning eyelets and decreases in various ways can be found in the following section on chevrons.

Eyelets paired with decreases in different rows

When an eyelet in one row is paired with a decrease in a different row, the rows within the repeat will vary in their numbers of stitches, but the repeat will always start and end with an identical number of stitches. This method of pairing eyelets and decreases is a way to add fullness to certain areas of the pattern or to emphasize a shape by giving it extra stitches or a greater decrease. In addition, this method of balancing eyelets and decreases causes at least some of the stitches in the plain knitted areas to bias. In Chapter 1 you saw Pattern 2 (p. 111), where eyelets without decreases are inserted on one or several rows to expand the fabric. Their corresponding decreases are on subsequent rows, to narrow the fabric. In the detail of Pattern 58 above, a pair of eyelets without their decreases is inserted in the middle of Row 7 in order to provide enough stitches to form the two upper diamonds. The decreases for these two eyelets can be found in Row 9, which has four eyelets and six decreases.

Further discussion of the effects of this type of pairing of eyelets and decreases, including other examples from the sampler, can be found in the section on patterns with black squares (starting on p. 142).

Chevrons

The chevron shape, with its two symmetrical "arms" of eyelets, is probably the most versatile patterning element in lace knitting. Almost two-thirds of the patterns in the sampler use it as the building block for their motifs. When you learn to recognize this pattern shape and understand how it can be used in its many forms, you'll be delighted at how simple seemingly complex patterns really are once you break them down into their basic motif units and examine their architecture.

The chevron is a bilaterally symmetrical V-shape of diagonally placed eyelets that step by one stitch every row of patterning. The decreases for the two arms are on the same rows as their companion eyelets and are in mirror image, that is, one arm has decreases to the left of their eyelets and the other arm has decreases to the right of their eyelets. This balances the bias tendencies inherent in the increase-decrease relationship. The key to the chevron's patterning versatility is that you can place the decreases in many ways and thereby change the look of the plain stitches within and around the chevron. The chevron swatch on p. 122 and its charts throughout this section show two chevrons of eyelets for each of the seven styles of decrease placement: the chevron with its point, or pivot eyelet, at the bottom and the same chevron with its point at the top. The points are often omitted when the chevron shapes are combined or repeated, but I've included them here so you'll know how to handle them in your own patterns.

This chevron swatch shows some of the many different ways of pairing eyelets and decreases. Charts for each chevron accompany the text. Above and below each chevron are two rows knitted plain that are not shown on the charts. Each "window" is separated by three garter stitches across the width and six rows of garter stitch (three ridges). The selvedges are three garter stitches.

Chevron eyelets with adjacent decreases

The style of chevron used most often in this sampler and, indeed, throughout lace-knitting literature has its decreases adjacent to the diagonal lines of eyelets. It is easy to chart this kind of patterning and to anticipate accurately from the chart what the knitted piece will look like. There are no bias stitches to consider, and the fabric is simply stockinette stitch punctuated by eyelets with adjacent lines of decreases.

The decreases can point in the same direction in which the arms of the chevron are moving—a left decrease for arms moving left and a right decrease for arms moving right, as in chevrons 1a, 1b and 1c (shown below). In this arrangement, the leaning decreased stitch lies on top of the vertical plain stitch, as you can see from the corresponding chevrons in the swatch on p. 122. The decreases, as well as the stitches from the wrong-side, unpatterned rows, show as a visible, continuous line of diagonal stitches adjacent to the line of eyelets of the chevron, creating a "hard" line of decreases.

The decreases can also point in the direction opposite the movement of the arms—that is, a right decrease for left-moving arms and a left decrease for right-moving arms, as in chevrons 2a and 2b. The leaning decreased stitch lies underneath the vertical plain stitch and is partially hidden by it. Only the stitches from the wrong-side, unpatterned rows show as diagonal, thus creating a "soft" line of decreases. For V-shaped chevrons, such as 1a and 2a, put the decreases to the outside of the eyelets. For inverted-V chevrons, such as 1b, 1c and 2b, put the decreases to the inside of the eyelets.

The sampler contains many examples of ways to use chevron type 1. They are discussed below.

Diagonal outlines

The simplest way to use chevron eyelets with adjacent decreases is for outlining shapes, and there are plenty of examples in the sampler. In patterns 9, 11, 36, 68 and 70, the chevrons divide the fabric into allover diamond shapes, each pattern having a different stitch pattern within its diamonds. When you want to try out textured patterns, you can use these diagonal outlines to divide your fabric into diamond shapes of whatever size you like, then put a different texture pattern within each one.

Pattern 26 is a diamond shape similar to the aforementioned, but it has doubled eyelets—two patterning rows knitted alike in succession throughout most of the repeat—which elongate the diamond. The diamonds in patterns 18 and 73 were elongated differently: The row at the widest point of the diamond was knitted several times in succession. Pattern 5 consists of diamonds within diamonds. Patterns 66 and 75 are tilted rectangles; they provide a welcome relief to the prevalent diamonds. Pattern 43 uses a pair of nested chevrons to outline a leaf shape for the flower shape made of small diamonds. The nested chevrons look very heart shaped and could stand on their own as a pattern.

Chevrons with decreases adjacent to eyelets

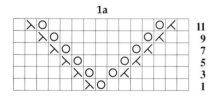

1a

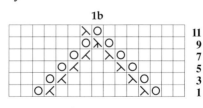

1b

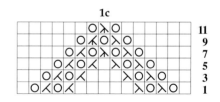

1c

Decreases pointing in the same direction as the arms of the chevron are moving create a "hard" line.

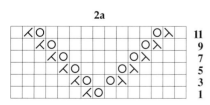

2a

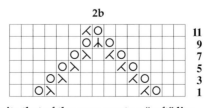

2b

Decreases pointing in the direction opposite that of the arms create a "soft" line.

Diagonal lines running in the same direction

By using one arm of the chevron alone, you can create a great variety of asymmetrical patterns. In flat knitting, repeatedly using only one arm of the chevron will always produce a fabric that has bias selvedges. Pattern 1 is a good example of this. If the knitting is circular, the pattern will spiral up the tube. From the bottom to the top of the fabric, the bias will be from left to right, because our knitter consistently put each decrease to the left of its eyelet, which makes the fabric bias to the right. Similar examples are found in patterns 3, 21, 39, 55, 62 and 75.

This biasing characteristic doesn't mean that you can't normally use the patterns containing just one arm of a chevron, but it does mean that you must mirror the arm in half the pattern area in order to keep the selvedges going straight up. The knitted swatches on p. 130 and p. 134 illustrate ways to mirror patterns 55 and 75 to compensate for their bias tendencies. The patterns in the sampler that illustrate other ways of mirroring are discussed below.

Diagonal lines in mirror image

Patterns 29 and 48, both large-diamond patterns, fill half the diamond with single diagonal lines of decreases plus their adjacent eyelets, and they mirror these lines along a vertical axis on the other half of the diamond. The diagonal lines in the bottom half of Pattern 66, a lozenge pattern, are mirrored in the top half. Because each half of the pattern has a predominance of either left-placed or right-placed decreases, the side selvedges tend to zigzag.

Horizontal zigzags

Nested chevrons like Chevron 1c are wonderful devices for borders around other patterns. The decreases for the bottom chevrons in the nest become outlines for the plain stitches below the zigzag. You can see this in Pattern 35, where the zigzag appears as a single line of decreases with an eyelet on each side. Pattern 17 has two zigzags of the same type as in Pattern 35, with the bottom-most decreases outlining the tops of the diamonds below. You can make the zigzag chevrons of different thicknesses, too, by inserting plain stitches between the layers of eyelets, as in patterns 13, 15 and 74. The zigzags in pattern 74 are thick enough to incorporate additional patterning in the form of eyelets.

Vertical zigzags

Vertical zigzags are made in much the same way as horizontal ones, but the left and right arms of the nested chevrons are alternated vertically instead of horizontally. It is easy to see this in Pattern 77, where multiple arms of the chevron sashay left and right,

appearing as single columns of eyelets with plain stitches between. In this pattern the plain stitches are visually dominant. By contrast, in Pattern 87, which has a smaller version of the same single columns of eyelets, it is the eyelets that are visually dominant, rather than the plain stitches between them. Pattern 65 has three adjacent columns of eyelets, forming two zigzag lines of decreases between them. These two decrease columns are easy to see, but can you find the decreases for the third column of eyelets? (It's not difficult if you refer to the chart.)

Lattices

Patterns 20 and 91 both appear to have woven lines, which are actually sets of intersecting diagonal lines of eyelets and decreases. In Pattern 91 you could enhance the effect by adding another pair of eyelets to the top of each set of lines.

One-stitch diagonal stripes used as fillers

Diagonal lines composed entirely of an eyelet and its paired decrease are useful for filling areas of the fabric around some other pattern. There are plenty of these stripes in the previous examples, used in fairly large pattern areas. But because they consist of only two stitches — an eyelet and a decrease — you can use these stripes to fill quite small areas, too. In patterns 12 and 46, one-stitch diagonal lines fill the bottom half of a diamond shape that has a solidly filled upper half. In Pattern 10, they fill the space between vertical columns of plain diamonds. In Pattern 49, arrowhead shapes float on a background of diagonal lines. Patterns 46 and 49 will probably produce fabrics with bias selvedges since their diagonal stripes are not mirrored. You could alleviate this by turning the stripes in the opposite direction on alternate repeats, either vertically or horizontally.

Chevron eyelets with adjacent decreases crossing over the eyelets

The style of eyelet/decrease combination shown in the charts for chevrons 3a and 3b (on the facing page) is not often seen in lace knitting — I have found only three examples in the sampler: in patterns 25, 39 and 90 — but it is an important one to understand. If you examine the outline of the eyelets in most of the other chevrons in the chevron swatch, you'll see that each eyelet is separated from the next by a pair of twisted threads, created by the top of the yarn over and the bottom loop of the knitted stitches above it. (In chevrons 12 and 13 there is only one thread — the top of the yarn over — separating the eyelets, because the chevron is patterned every row.) The eyelets in

Chevrons with decreases adjacent to and crossing over eyelets

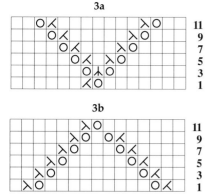

3a

3b

Decreases are placed on the inside of the V-shaped chevron and on the outside of the inverted-V chevron.

Chevron 3, on the other hand, are separated by a whole stitch, not by threads, making the eyelet smaller and giving the whole pattern a heavier look.

Compare the charts for chevrons 3a and 3b with the other charts. In the other chevron patterns, the lines of decreases are placed so that each decrease will cause the stitches of the previous row to pull away from the eyelets as the chevron shape progresses upward, thus opening the eyelet and giving it a large shape. Here, the placement of the decreases causes the stitches of the previous row to pull toward the eyelet.

The effect of this kind of decrease upon its adjacent eyelet is not evident from first glance at a chart, unless you know from experience what the effect will be. The principle is that if the pull of the decreases is in the same direction that the eyelets are stepping, the eyelets will be separated by threads. If the pull of the decreases is opposite the direction the eyelets are stepping, the eyelets will be separated by stitches. Note that it doesn't make any difference whether the decreases are pointing left or right; what matters is their position in relation to the direction the eyelets are moving.

You can try out this variation on all the designs of the chevron swatch by using the decreases as charted for each chevron but putting them on the other side of the eyelets. There will be a different effect with each change—some good and some not so good. When might you use this arrangement? I use it when knitting alphabets or outlines of eyelets. It's the best way I know to make diagonals that have the same style as vertical eyelets spaced every four rows and horizontal eyelets made of knit-two-together, yarn overs.

Pattern 25 is an unusual two-eyelet pattern in a vertical zigzag. The double decreases are midway between the eyelet pair, with three bias stitches between the decrease and each of the eyelets. Since the line of decreases follows the same zigzag path, the bias stitches between the zigs of one eyelet line and the zags of the other cross over these eyelets. The effect is a mixture of open eyelets and these heavier eyelets. You can see this pattern used in the long-socks project in Chapter 4.

Rows 1 through 8 at the beginning of Pattern 90 have this type of heavier eyelet. Pattern 39 uses the right half of Chevron 3a (or the left half of Chevron 3b). Each eyelet/decrease pair is separated by one stitch. Since all the decreases are to the left of their eyelets, the side selvedges bias to the right.

Chevron eyelets with decreases separated and parallel

For chevrons 4 and 5, whose charts are shown on p. 126, the decreases can be in any of the arrangements shown for chevrons 1 or 2, but separated from the eyelets by one or more stitches. The number of spacing stitches between the eyelet and the decrease is usually consistent throughout the repeat. The spacing stitches on each row are pulled toward the decrease, biasing in its direction. This makes the columns of spacing stitches lie diagonally, parallel to the lines of eyelets, and thus adds a new dimension to the solid areas of the design. In chevrons 4 and 5, there is only one stitch (although it could be any number) between each eyelet and its decrease. The lower edge under the chevron will scallop slightly.

The decreases in Chevron 4, like those in Chevron 2, are soft decreases, where the decreased stitches lie underneath the plain stitches and virtually disappear. But because of the diagonal stitch between each eyelet and its decrease, the effect is of one column of diagonal stitches against the eyelets. Compare the similar effect in chevrons 4a and 4b with chevrons 1a and 1b, respectively.

The decreases in Chevron 5, like those in Chevron 1, are hard decreases, where the decreased stitches lie on top of the plain stitches, creating prominent diagonal lines. Each line of decreases, together with the diagonal stitch between each decrease and eyelet, creates the effect of two columns of parallel diagonal stitches against the eyelets.

Patterns 25, 56, 57 and 60 all have a waving, ribbon-like appearance created by spacing the eyelets from their decreases with two, three or four stitches. In

Chevrons with eyelets and decreases separated and parallel

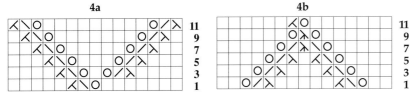

The decreased stitch lies underneath the plain stitch, making a soft line.

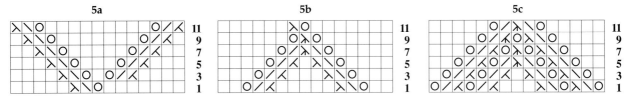

The decreased stitch lies on top of the plain stitch, making a hard line.

Pattern 56 the knitter has also elongated the chevron by knitting each pattern row twice, providing more length for the ribbon to wave with twisting reality. In patterns 57 and 60, the ribbon is more flattened, but its effect is heightened by the textured and patterned stitches around it.

In patterns 58 and 65, the ribbon has been broken into pieces for a different effect. In Pattern 58, the pieces fly outward in a sideways direction, while in Pattern 65, they are dovetailed to make a drooping leaf pattern.

These are all clever and effective patterns in my opinion, with a nice combination of textures. Their tiny lace motifs coupled with purl stitches provide a nice background for the ribbon-like bias stitches weaving and waving through the fabric. Incidentally, when you knit Pattern 57, instead of making the purled decreases of the chevron on the right-side rows as shown on the chart, try making them on the wrong-side rows. It's a lot easier to make these decreases knitwise than purlwise.

Chevron eyelets with decreases in vertical columns

For chevrons 6 and 7 (charts, top of facing page), the decreases are collected into straight lines under the highest point of the chevron. On each row, all the stitches between the eyelet and its decrease will bias toward the decrease. The biasing will also affect the lower edge of the pattern, causing it to wave up and down in scallops, with the lowest point of the scallop underneath the vertical lines of decreases. The rows of garter stitches on the chevron swatch just below these

two sets of patterns reveal their tendency for scalloping. The top and side selvedges will be straight. These chevrons make excellent decorative edgings for lower borders and hemlines. They also make good tops for leaf shapes, and the variations shown in chevrons 9 and 11 can be used for ferns. It's quite remarkable how one motif can be used for so many different effects.

Take a moment to compare the right sides of the charts for chevrons 1a, 5a and 6a. The right-leaning decreases are all identical except for their placement. In chevrons 1a and 5a, the decreases make a hard line, but in 6a the same decreases create a soft line. The reason for this difference is their placement. The decreases in chevrons 1a and 5a are lined up on the diagonal, creating a diagonally moving column of stitches that lies on top of the plain stitches below them. In Chevron 6a, lining up the same decreases in a vertical column creates a soft line. Compare chevrons 1b, 5b and 6b; 2a, 4a and 7a; and 2b, 4b and 7b to see the opposing effects of the same kind of decrease.

In chevrons 6a and 6b, the decreased stitches lie on top of the plain stitches, giving such a soft edge to the vertical line that it virtually disappears. What is more noticeable is the column of plain stitches next to it. In Chevron 6c, the two decreases are combined into a double decrease, which can slant either left or right, or left and right alternately.

In chevrons 7a and 7b, the decreased stitches lie underneath the vertical plain stitches, giving hard edges to the lines of decreases and creating the appearance of two vertical columns on each side in 7a, or three vertical columns in the center of 7b. In

Chevrons with decreases in vertical columns

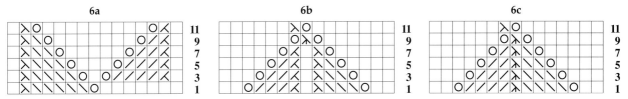

The decreased stitch lies on top of the plain stitch, making soft lines when lined up vertically.

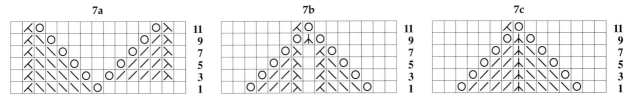

The decreased stitch lies underneath the plain stitch, making hard lines when lined up vertically.

Chevron 7c, the two decreases are combined into a vertical double decrease, which gives the appearance of a single column of plain stitches up the center. Compare this effect to that of Chevron 6b.

Patterns 16, 32, 33, 34 and 69 use the style of chevrons 6 and 7 to make the classic horseshoe shape. In Pattern 16, the single stitch between the decreases has been widened to three, and these are knitted in garter stitch. Pattern 32 has the chevron arranged as a half-drop, with the right side dropped three grid rows.

Patterns 38, 45, 46, 47, 59 and 89 use the chevron to make leaves. In Pattern 38, the center stitch between the decrease is purled, and the first row of each motif is repeated several times to elongate the leaf (see the photo on p. 108). Patterns 45, 47 and 89 illustrate plain leaf-type diamonds, while patterns 46 and 59 include another pattern in the plain stitches under each chevron. If you look carefully at Pattern 88, you'll see that its chevron has been split in the middle and a fairly wide eyelet-ground pattern inserted between the halves. The narrow space between one chevron and the next sports a small diamond shape.

Combination decreases with purl stitches

Chevron 8 (chart at right) is a combination of chevrons 5a and 7a that shows how to change effectively the width of bias columns of stitches to retain a hard-edge outline. The purl background helps to show off the texture of the bias stitches. You can see a similar example in the ribbon-like bias stitches of Pattern 56.

Chevron with a combination of decrease styles

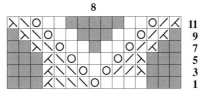

Hard-edge vertical and diagonal decreases are combined to make a continuous line.

Two-eyelet chevron

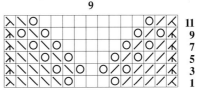

Two eyelets are coupled with a double decrease.

Two-eyelet chevron

Instead of single diagonal rows of eyelets, Chevron 9 (chart above), which is a variation of Chevron 6a, incorporates two eyelets separated by one plain stitch. The lines of decreases reflect this change by becoming double decreases instead of single decreases, and they pull the single stitch between the eyelets and all the other intervening stitches into the bias. You can alter any of chevrons 6 or 7 in this manner (these motifs make good fern-type leaf patterns).

Expanded chevrons

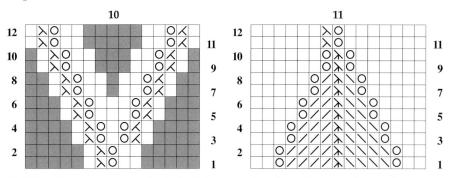

Knitting the pattern row on both the knit row and again on the returning purl row creates a faggoted chevron. This expands the pattern without elongating it.

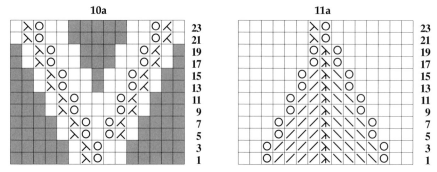

Knitting the same pattern row twice in succession on odd rows and purling the even rows plain elongates a faggoted chevron.

Patterns 51 and 61 incorporate this technique, with the chevrons arranged in vertical panels in both. They are essentially alike, with Pattern 51 arranged as a half-drop and Pattern 61 as a stacked motif. (Pattern arrangements are discussed starting on p. 138.)

Two other patterns with dominating pairs of eyelets are patterns 25 and 78. These two differ from Chevron 9 in that each eyelet has its own decrease on opposite sides of the eyelet pair, pulling the intervening bias stitches on each side of the eyelets in opposite directions.

Faggoted chevrons: Expanding the pattern

Some ways to expand and elongate a pattern were mentioned earlier in the section on diagonal outlines (p. 123). Chevrons 10 and 11 illustrate another way to expand a pattern, but without elongating it. Instead, the pattern is made into a faggoted version of the original.

Chevron 10 (charts above left) is a faggoted version of Chevron 1a, and Chevron 11 (charts above right) is a faggoted version of Chevron 6c. You can make any of

the chevrons become faggoted simply by knitting the same pattern row twice in succession—on both the knit row and the returning purl row. You can also elongate a faggoted chevron: Knit a row in pattern and purl the return row as usual without patterning, then knit and purl the same two rows again. You can see this effect in patterns 26 and 56. Charts 10A and 11a are the elongated versions of chevrons 10 and 11, respectively. There wasn't room to include these styles in the chevron swatch on p. 122.

Pattern 24 is a classic fern pattern. One motif of either chevron 6a or 7a (depending on how you like your decreases) is arranged in vertical panels with a faggoted cable pattern in the panels between. In Pattern 54, which was used for the swatch shown on the facing page, the left and right halves of chevron 7a or 7b have been separated, with one half repeated across the fabric first, then the other half knitted in the rows above it, creating an allover pattern. Since the two halves of the chevron are separated vertically, the bottom selvedge no longer scallops, but instead, the two side selvedges swing in and out. Because of these zigzag selvedges, it would be easiest to knit garments

The thick, softly twisted, one-ply pure silk roving used for this swatch was too soft for lots of leggy eyelets. Instead it called for a pattern of mostly stockinette stitches, with bias stitches to reflect light in various directions. Pattern 54 was the solution (see p. 118 for an enlarged detail of this swatch).

Condensed chevrons

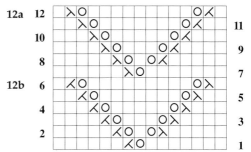

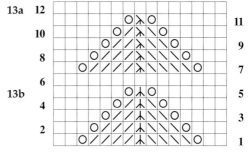

Knitting the pattern on both the knit and the purl rows condenses the chevron.

as tubes on circular needles. For flat knitting, fit the zigs and zags together at the side seams like puzzle pieces. For jackets and cardigans, use cut-and-sew techniques for the front opening.

Chevrons patterned every row: Condensing the pattern

Chevrons 12 and 13 (charts at right) show the effect of patterning a chevron on both the knit and purl rows, instead of just the knit rows, with the purl rows plain, as in chevrons 1 through 9. Whatever the chevron's effect, it will be emphasized dramatically when the chevron is condensed in this way. Because each chevron is now only half as tall, there is room for two examples in each window of the knitted swatch. Chevron 12a is Chevron 1a condensed, and Chevron 12b is Chevron 2a condensed. Chevron 13a is Chevron 6c condensed, and Chevron 13b is Chevron 7c condensed. Chevrons 13a and 13b are both without the very top eyelet, as you can see from the chart. Note in the chevron swatch (p. 122) that all the eyelets in these chevrons are separated from each other by only one thread, instead of two threads twisted as in chevrons 1 through 9. You can see Pattern 55, which has chevrons like those in Chevron 12a, used in the left swatch on p. 130. The yarn used for this swatch, a

4-ply wool/acrylic blend with much bounce and elasticity, enhances the tendency for lines of decreases to become embossed in every-row patterns like this one. The diagonal lines of decreases stand as high as the braid of the cable, and the zigzag of the vertical bars in the faggoting makes a neat braid effect.

Bias effects in lace patterning

Some of the most beautiful lace patterns make extensive use of bias. In lace knitting, bias refers to plain stitches that lie on the diagonal, as opposed to plain stitches that are vertical. You encountered diagonal stitches in several of the chevrons of the swatch on p. 122, such as chevrons 5, 6 and 7. Bias stitches create two distinctive effects in knitted fabric. First, the diagonal stitches add a dimensional quality to the pattern design by creating shapes that seem to leap out of the fabric. Second, they affect the outline of the fabric's selvedges, causing some or all sides to scallop and zigzag. Since these two effects are interactive, understanding how to create bias stitches and control their effects is an important aspect of lace knitting and lace design.

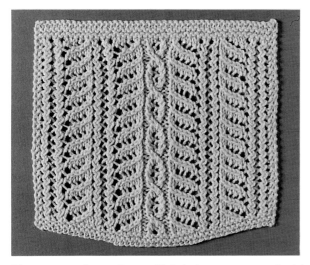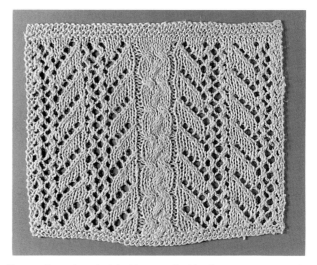

These two swatches use Pattern 55. In both, two repeats on the right side are mirrored on the left side around cables from patterns 22 and 24, making the entire pattern symmetrical and compensating for the biasing. In the left swatch, both right-side and wrong-side rows are patterned, embossing the lines of decreases. In the right swatch, the wrong-side rows are worked plain, elongating the pattern and flattening and smoothing its surface texture.

You're probably familiar with shaping knitted fabric by adding stitches to widen it and decreasing stitches to narrow it. The three edgings and one medallion on pp. 157-161 are examples of this method of shaping fabric. It is a straightforward approach, and the charts fairly represent what the knitted shapes will look like. But the outline of the knitting can also be shaped with bias stitches within the pattern's design, although the resulting contours are not always evident from a first glance at the chart.

If you compare the swatches on the gridded panel shown on pp. 132-133 to their corresponding charts, you'll see that the outlines of their shapes don't match. The reason is that these shapes are motifs for allover patterns. Unlike edgings and medallions with widened and narrowed shaping, motifs for allovers have consistent numbers of stitches that allow the pattern to fit into a rectangular chart, so that it can be repeated in height and width and combined with other patterns to knit a whole fabric. Rectangular charts naturally do not allow for shaped selvedges. Furthermore, in cases of extreme bias, as in Bias Swatch 4 (p. 133), the lines of eyelets and decreases are aligned differently in the swatch than they are on the chart. The chart symbols are positioned so that the knitter knows when and where to make the eyelets and decreases; the charts can't indicate how the eyelets and decreases might realign in the knitted fabric or how the diagonal stitches affect the shape of the fabric's edges.

If this sounds pretty hopeless and you feel betrayed by the charts, take heart. The effect of bias in a lace fabric is predictable once you are aware of the effects that various eyelet/decrease arrangements will have. The bias swatches and charts on pp. 132-133 are discussed in detail on the following pages; they'll give you a package of bias effects to work from. The sampler has many examples of their application.

In the sampler, much of the effect of bias around the edges of the patterns is lost, because each pattern has knitting above and below it that absorbs some of the shaping. In addition, for its photos the sampler has been blocked into as straight a strip as possible. To really see the effect of bias in the sampler patterns and bias swatches discussed below, I recommend that you knit individual little swatches, each with its own cast-on and bound-off edges.

Swatches 1 and 1a: Eyelets with adjacent decreases

As you know, lace patterning relies on increases and decreases working together. If you knit a plain, unshaped fabric in stockinette stitch, the columns of stitches (the vertical grain) will all have the same number of rows and be parallel to the side selvedges and perpendicular to the top and bottom edges. In short, the fabric will be a perfect rectangle with a straight grain. Because it is composed of eyelets and decreases that push and pull on the surrounding stitches, lace patterning will create bias in the stockinette fabric, causing some or all of the stitches to lie on the diagonal and, in turn, affecting the shape of the edges of the fabric. The lower half of Bias Swatch 1 (p. 132) is an example—a stockinette fabric with a pair of diagonal lines of eyelets and decreases. Note that the fabric leans slightly to the right.

Every eyelet increase causes the fabric to grow in width by one stitch, pushing the stitches between itself and the selvedge outward by one stitch. At the same time, every companion decrease causes the fabric to shrink in width by one stitch, pulling the stitches between itself and the selvedge inward by one stitch. When the decrease is to the left of the eyelet increase, as in Bias Swatch 1, the fabric will grow toward the right and shrink from the left, and the selvedges will lean from left to right. When the decrease is to the right of the eyelet, the fabric will lean from right to left. It doesn't matter whether the style of decrease is left-leaning (as in a slip-slip-knit decrease) or right-leaning (as in a knit-two-together decrease). The determining factor is the position of the decrease relative to its eyelet.

If you make a single eyelet with a decrease to its left in the middle of a stockinette fabric, the bias will be so slight that it won't even show. But if you make the same eyelet/decrease maneuver every few stitches on all the right-side rows, as in Bias Swatch 1, the accumulated effect will become visible and cause the fabric to lean toward the right. The lower half of Bias Swatch 1 has two eyelet/decrease pairs in every right-side row, and it consequently leans slightly to the right. The upper half has six or more pairs every right-side row, and so it leans more dramatically to the right. Note that the top and bottom edges of both halves are not affected by the biasing; they remain parallel to the horizontal grid lines. That's because this pattern, with adjacent eyelets and decreases, contains no diagonal stitches (signaled by /// or \\\ symbols) that make the edges change their angle. The whole fabric is evenly biased.

This kind of bias, where the side selvedges lean and the top and bottom edges are straight, will occur in all patterns where the decreases are adjacent to their eyelets and are consistently to one side or the other. Examples in the sampler include patterns 1, 3, 21, 31, 39, 55, 62 and 75. You can use these patterns just as they are for fabrics with biased selvedges or for circular knitting. In the latter case, the jog in the knitting where one round ends and the next begins will spiral up the tube. If you were to insert vertical panels of another pattern within the bias pattern, you would make very dramatic spiral patterning.

You can compensate for the leaning tendencies inherent in lace patterning simply by positioning half the decreases in the pattern repeat to the left of their eyelets and half to their right. This is called "balancing" the pattern. Most of the patterns in the sampler are already balanced in this way. You can check them by counting the eyelets with decreases to their left, and those with decreases to their right, within the repeat box. Two eyelets with a double decrease between them are already balanced, so you can leave them out of your count. If the numbers are the same, or nearly so, the pattern is balanced.

You can balance any pattern that isn't already balanced simply by mirroring the pattern over half the fabric area. The two swatches on the facing page illustrate a simple way to mirror an unbalanced pattern on a vertical axis. The knitted swatches on p. 134 illustrate more complex mirroring. An easy way to chart a pattern's mirror image is to trace the chart symbols on tracing paper, then turn over the tracing paper and copy the symbols as they appear through the back. You'll have a chance to try this yourself in Chapter 3.

You can use any unbalanced pattern, such as Pattern 1 in the museum sampler, to make a fabric with zigzag selvedges. Knit enough repeats of the pattern in width and height to bring out the bias tendency in the selvedges (the zig). Then mirror the pattern so that the eyelets and decreases are reversed relative to each other and knit an equal number of repeats. The fabric will lean in the opposite direction, forming the zag.

You can see an example of this kind of mirroring in Pattern 66 of the museum sampler. In the lower half of the repeat, all the decreases are to the left of their eyelets, and in the sampler photo, this portion of the pattern biases to the right. In the second half of the repeat, where the eyelet/decrease orientation is reversed, the fabric biases to the left. Pattern 77 is similar on a smaller scale. If you wanted zigzag selvedges with this pattern, you could place the lines of eyelets and decreases closer together to accumulate a greater degree of bias per area of fabric and make the shaping more pronounced.

Bias Swatch 1a illustrates what happens to the bias when the pattern is mirrored on a vertical axis. The side selvedges are now straight, but the top and bottom edges are biased. You can see why this occurs if you mentally rotate the top half of Bias Swatch 1 so that the left selvedge is vertical. The right selvedge will also be vertical, but the top and bottom edges will slant up to the right, just as they do in the right side of Bias

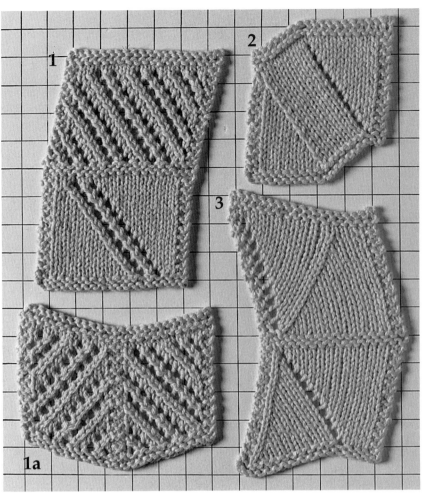

The swatches here and on the facing page illustrate the bias effects that result from various positionings of eyelets and decreases. In swatches 1 and 1a, the decreases are consistently to one side of and adjacent to their eyelets, resulting in evenly biased fabric. In Swatch 2, the eyelets and decreases are separated but parallel, making a dramatically biased section within the evenly biased fabric. Swatch 3 shows the even more dramatic effect of bias stitches when the eyelets or decreases are lined up in a column.

Charts for bias swatches

For all charts:
Even Rs: P all sts.
2 garter sts at each selvedge.
2 ridges of garter st at bottom, center, top.

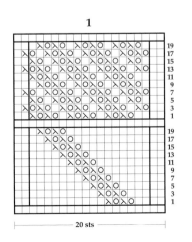

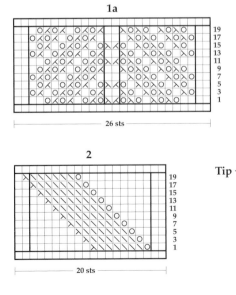

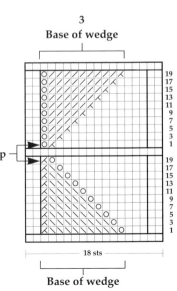

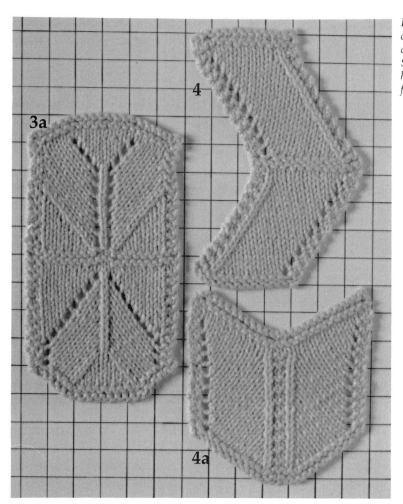

In Swatch 3a, the eyelet/decrease shapes of swatches 2 and 3 are mirrored and combined to make a pair of chevrons. Swatches 4 and 4a are vertical and horizontal mirror images of straight fabric knitted on the bias.

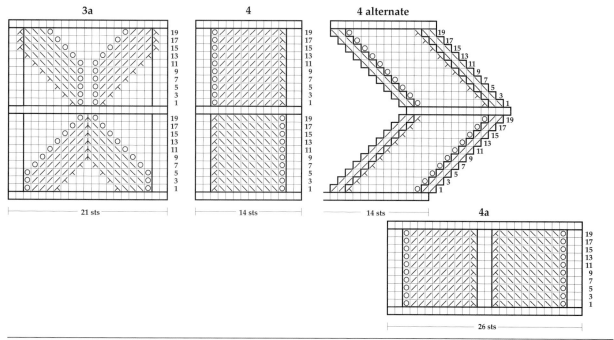

Bias effects in lace patterning   133

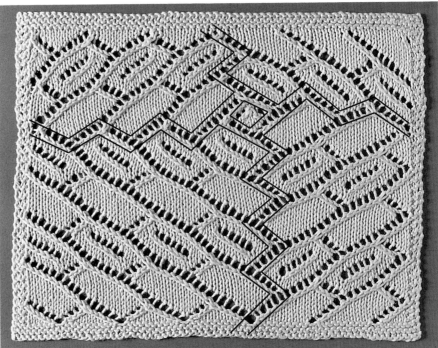

These swatches illustrate two ways to mirror and balance an unbalanced pattern. The original design from Pattern 75 is in the lower left quadrant of both swatches and is mirrored on a vertical axis in the lower right. The entire bottom portion is then mirrored on a horizontal axis in the upper part. The pivot lines in the swatch at top are straight and break the motifs at the axes. The pivot lines in the swatch above conform to the motif's outline, resulting in a zigzag pivot line with the motifs in a half-drop arrangement.

Swatch 1a. The bias doesn't go away when you mirror a bias pattern on a vertical axis, but its orientation changes. We'll examine this further later on.

Swatch 2: Diagonal eyelets and decreases, separated and parallel

Now we can add another element to bias—the diagonal stitches. If you push apart a diagonal line of eyelets and decreases so that there are some plain stitches between them, these in-between plain stitches will slant, becoming diagonal stitches, while the plain stitches outside of the decreases and eyelets will be vertical. As you know, the diagonal stitches that lie between an eyelet and its decrease always slant away from the eyelet and toward the decrease and are indicated on the chart by the symbols /// or \\\. What the chart doesn't show is the effect the diagonal stitches have on the selvedges, which is quite dramatic.

First, note that the side selvedges of Bias Swatch 2 on p. 132 lean slightly to the right, because the decreases are consistently to the left of their eyelets, as in Bias Swatch 1. Second, note that the top and bottom edges are no longer horizontal where they abut the diagonal plain stitches. Cast-on and bound-off edges are always perpendicular to the columns of stitches they abut, whether the stitches are vertical or diagonal. In effect, the center panel of parallel diagonal stitches has pushed the right side of the swatch higher than the left. However, as with Bias Swatch 1a, if you mirror this pattern on a vertical axis and place the mirror image on the left side of Chart 2, the new motif will be rotated so that the side selvedges are vertical and the lower and upper edges are scalloped.

Chevrons 5b and 5c in the chevron swatch on p. 122 and patterns 58 and 65 of the museum sampler have the same kind of eyelet/decrease arrangement, mirrored on a vertical axis. Patterns 56 and 57 are mirrored on both vertical and horizontal axes. Pattern 60 is mirrored on a horizontal axis, and Pattern 25 is an interesting variation. In all these patterns, the contour of the top and bottom edges is affected by the diagonal stitches adjacent to them.

We now have three factors to work with in bias patterning: the biasing of the side selvedges, created by the consistent position of the eyelets relative to their decreases; the diagonal stance of plain stitches between the eyelets and their decreases, creating dramatically biased panels within the evenly biased fabric; and the scalloping of the top and bottom edges that abut the diagonal panel stitches. Of these three factors, only the second can be indicated on a chart.

Swatches 3 and 3a: Eyelets and decreases forming a wedge

Lining up either the decreases or the eyelets in a vertical column concentrates the bias effect along that line and makes it more pronounced. You can see in Bias Swatch 3 on p. 132 that the leaning of the side selvedges is greater than in either bias swatch 1 or 2, even though Swatch 3 has only one eyelet/decrease pair per row. In the lower half this swatch, the decreases are lined up vertically, their eyelets diagonally; in the upper half, the eyelets are vertical, the decreases diagonal. In both halves, the diagonal stitches between the eyelets and the decreases form a triangle shape or a wedge, which also affects the contour of the upper and lower edges of the swatch, just as in Swatch 2. The only part of this swatch that remains straight is the horizontal ridges of garter stitch separating the upper and lower halves. This is because where the eyelets and decreases of each wedge come to a point and meet, there are no diagonal stitches adjacent to the ridges.

If you separate the upper and lower halves and mirror each on a vertical axis along their left selvedges, both wedges will make deeply biased scalloped triangles within a wing-shaped, less biased fabric like Swatch 1a (or an upside-down wing shape for the upper half). For each of the triangles, the highest point of the scallop will be at the place where the eyelets meet the base of the wedges; the lowest point will be where the decreases meet the base of the wedges.

Swatch 3a is a mirrored combination of swatches 2 and 3, one of several possible combinations. The wing shape of Swatch 3 (when mirrored) is reduced to a minimum by allowing the chevrons of eyelets in the lower half, or decreases in the upper half, to proceed all the way to the side selvedges and lining them up vertically for a few rows to counterbalance the pull of the central decreases (lower half) or eyelets (upper half).

In the museum sampler, there are a number of examples of wedges consisting of vertical decreases with diagonal eyelets. Those mirrored on a vertical axis include patterns 33, 34, 45, 46, 47, 59, 69 and 89, all of which have a triangle shape that forms scallops wherever it touches the lower edge. You can see this effect especially well in the knitted swatch on p. 200, which uses Pattern 33. Since the pattern is used in the lower border, there is no fabric below it to absorb the scalloping. You can also see this effect in the lower edge of the chevron swatch below chevrons 11 and 13 on p. 122. Since there is no bias at the tip of a wedge, balanced patterns that don't create biased edges are appropriate choices for above a scalloped border. In Pattern 32 the wedges are in a half-drop arrangement

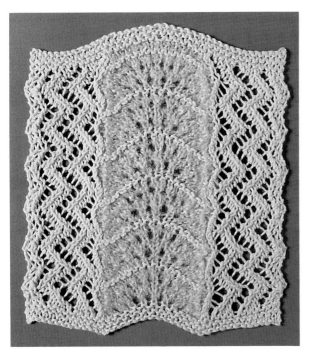

This swatch of Pattern 52 is knitted as three separate panels with two different yarns, then stitched together. A ridge of garter stitch is added to the top of each fan repeat. When the panels were assembled, the garter-stitch ridge was coordinated with the shaped edge of the zigzag ground to help pull it into shape.

(see "Arrangements for allover patterns" starting on p. 138), which will result in a syncopated scallop at the lower edge. In patterns 24, 51, 61 and 88, the position of the two halves of the wedge are reversed. In these patterns, the wedges are arranged as vertical panels with another pattern between them.

Pattern 54, which you can see in the knitted swatch on p. 129, is an example of mirrored wedges with the two halves of the triangle separated and placed one above the other. If you mentally remove the lower wedge from Bias Swatch 3 (which is the same wedge as in Pattern 54), and rotate it so its lower edge is horizontal, then repeat it horizontally, you can see why this repeating shape creates zigzag side selvedges instead of scalloped upper and lower edges. Look closely at the lower edge of Pattern 54 on p. 129 and you can easily pick out the first row of wedges.

There are two patterns with wedges consisting of vertical eyelets and diagonal decreases. Pattern 78 is mirrored on a vertical axis. It has a delightful little motif of twin eyelet columns surrounded by biased stitches and the quilted effect of the diagonal decreases. Pattern 6 is the counterpart of Pattern 54. It is the upper wedge of Bias Swatch 3, rotated so its upper

edge is horizontal, then repeated horizontally. The alternate rows are the wedge's mirror image, the same as in Pattern 54, creating the same zigzag selvedges with straight upper and lower edges.

Swatches 4 and 4a: Eyelets and decreases separated and in vertical columns

In bias swatches 3 and 3a, either the eyelets or the decreases were lined up in a vertical column, while their companion decreases or eyelets were lined up diagonally. The degree of biasing in the selvedges was greater than when both sets were on the diagonal, as in swatches 1, 1a and 2. In bias swatches 4 and 4a on p. 133, both the eyelets and the decreases are in vertical columns, and the biasing is even more pronounced, as you can see from their selvedges. Bias Swatch 4 illustrates the zigzag bias effect when the pattern is mirrored on a horizontal axis, and Bias Swatch 4a shows the scalloping effect when it is mirrored on a vertical axis.

Patterns 15 and 38 of the sampler, which have eyelets and decreases that are separated and vertical, are both mirrored on a vertical axis. In Pattern 15, the chevrons above and below the bias section fit around the bias effect, so that no biasing appears in the upper and lower edges. If you knit the pattern without the chevrons (knitting only rows 23 through 36), the result will look like a repeating pattern of Swatch 4a. In Pattern 38 (detail photo, p. 108), the elongated leaf motif containing the vertical eyelets and decreases is arranged as a tessellated pattern, so that the bias of each motif fits against the bias of the motifs surrounding it. The only part of the selvedges that will exhibit any bias effect is the lower edge, which is adjacent to the diagonal stitches. The upper edge will also scallop if you stop the pattern at row 10 or 28 in the repeat.

The zigzag ground of Pattern 52 is the sole example of this arrangement of eyelets and decreases mirrored on a horizontal axis. It is a miniature version of Bias Swatch 4 repeated in width and height. You can see a knitted swatch of Pattern 52, including the fan in the center, in the photo above left. In the same way as Bias Swatch 4, this little ground pattern when knitted does not resemble its charted pattern. If it is released from the confines of the fan pattern on both sides and knitted with only three selvedge stitches as shown on the chart of Pattern 52, it will make very nice zigzag selvedges. For the same reasons as in patterns 6 and 54 mentioned in connection with Swatch 3, the upper and lower edges will exhibit no bias, even though there are diagonal stitches against these edges. To understand the reason for this apparent anomaly, we must examine the two swatches and their charts.

If you look closely at the garter-stitch selvedges in the lower half of Swatch 4, their stitches appear to be diagonal, while the stockinette columns between the eyelets and decreases appear vertical, the opposite of what the chart indicates they should be. This is because the pattern is mirrored in the upper half, which changes the orientation of the swatch as a whole. If you mentally take just the lower half and rotate it so that the left selvedge is vertical, then it will look like the right half of Swatch 4a, which follows the principles of bias already examined. Taking the mirror image of a pattern with diagonal stitches and placing it above or below the original pattern on a horizontal axis will change the orientation of the whole and cause an apparent rotation in the alignment of the plain and diagonal stitches, as you have already seen in patterns 6, 52 and 54. Now let's look at Bias Swatch 4 from a different viewpoint.

Chart 4 alternate will knit into a swatch identical to Bias Swatch 4. This is a more realistic way to chart Swatch 4, because this swatch is actually a shaped fabric, like the edgings and medallion, with increases on one edge and decreases on the other. But the shaping is hidden within the rectangular chart.

It's easy to convert Chart 4 into Chart 4 alternate. Starting with the second row from the bottom and working up, push each grid row by one grid square in the direction of the eyelet (one increased stitch at right and one decreased stitch at left), stairstepping the rows. At the halfway point, push the rows in the opposite direction, because from this point up, the eyelets and decreases are on opposite sides of the chart. You must also transpose the symbols on the biased and the plain squares, because by stairstepping the chart, you have removed the bias from the center portion of the fabric and put it into the selvedges. Try knitting a few repeats in width of Chart 4 alternate, including the four selvedge stitches in the repeat. You'll see that these four stitches are diagonal, while the center stitches between the eyelets and decreases are vertical.

You could put a balanced lace pattern in place of the plain stitches of Chart 4 alternate. The knitted fabric would be patterned and also diagonally shaped. The one pattern in the sampler that illustrates this idea is the diamond ground of Pattern 64. If you knitted just the central ground section from the chart for Pattern 64, you would have a fabric that looks like the bottom quarter of the swatch in the photo above right. The pattern is a tiny, allover diamond with strong diagonal

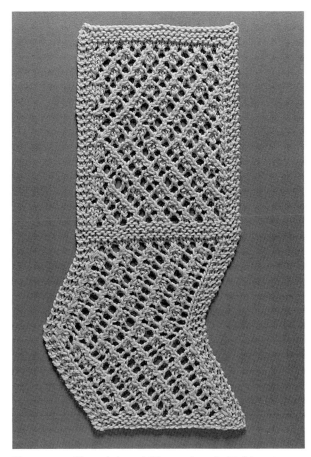

The upper and lower halves of this swatch are knitted from two different charts that have the same tiny diamond ground pattern. The lower half is from the chart for Pattern 64, which has shaped selvedges built into the chart. The upper half is from the chart for Pattern 19, an identical pattern, but charted with straight selvedges.

lines of decreases in a diagonally shaped fabric that leans to the left. Both the selvedge shaping and the diamond pattern are built right into the chart, but the chart is not stairstepped because the diamond pattern must fit against the vertical leaf panels of Pattern 64. In the photo above, the second quarter from the bottom is the same chart mirrored, so that the shaping and diagonal pattern lines move to the right. The tiny diamond pattern is in fact a duplicate of Pattern 19, which is *not* charted as a shaped fabric. The top half of the swatch shows Pattern 19 as knitted from its chart, with straight selvedges, and its mirror image.

You can convert the chart for the diamond of Pattern 64 by stairstepping it, just as we converted Chart 4 to Chart 4 alternate. Doing so will enable you to see both the pattern and the shaping along the edges. Push each row of symbols to the left (because the eyelet is at the left end of the line) by one square beyond the row

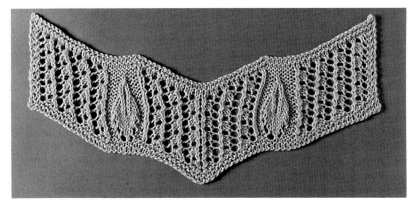

For this swatch, Pattern 64 was used to shape a piece of knitting into what could conceivably be part of a garment shape. The ground pattern from Pattern 64 on the left side abuts its mirror image on the right, throwing the two sides upward into wing shapes. The leaf panels, which do not have bias shaping, remain straight, creating a jog in the silhouette of the wing shapes. The chart for this swatch is shown below.

| Ground | Leaf | Ground | Ground, mirrored | Leaf | Ground, mirrored |

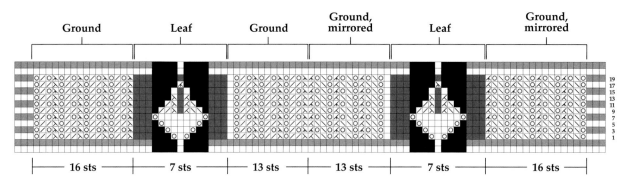

| 16 sts | 7 sts | 13 sts | 13 sts | 7 sts | 16 sts |

below, just as in the upper part of Chart 4 alternate. Remove the bias symbols. Now you have a diagonal chart, filled with Pattern 19, with an eyelet along the left edge to widen the fabric and a decrease along the right edge to narrow it. In order to fit the leaf pattern into the ground, you would have to push the stairsteps back together again into a rectangular chart. The leaf pattern itself is a balanced pattern, but when it is placed within the biased diamond ground it will appear as a diagonal panel because of the diagonal shaping of the diamond ground around it. The pattern would look beautiful knitted circularly so the leaf panel spirals up the tube.

The swatch in the photo above shows what Pattern 64, including the leaf panel, looks like when it is released from the confines of the sampler and knitted in mirror image on a vertical axis. Remember that when the mirror image is attached at the side, the diagonal selvedges are rotated to vertical. The resulting wing shape has a jog in the edges above and below the leaf panel because the leaf, unlike the surrounding ground, is not knitted on the bias.

Drawing the chart as a shaped fabric is a helpful way to understand how a balanced pattern is charted into a bias-knit fabric. But, as shown with patterns 52 and 64, you must keep the chart in its rectangular form if you plan to combine it with another pattern.

You have now come full circle through the effects of bias. You started with plain stockinette fabric, progressed through the bias effects within a pattern that also affect the shaping of the selvedges, and ended with bias that affects the selvedge shaping but not the pattern within. You'll find that these principles can be applied to other kinds of pattern knitting as well.

Arrangements for allover patterns

Whole books have been written on the subject of allover patterns. There is an entire vocabulary to describe in detail just how a pattern motif relates to its neighbors and to the other elements in the design. Fortunately we don't have to know all the professional terms to understand some of the basics and be able to design beautiful lace patterns for knitting.

What follows is a brief description of a few of the allover pattern arrangements found in the sampler. These arrangements can serve as guidelines when you develop your own patterns, and the information is equally useful for color knitting or any other kind of pattern design. My terminology is descriptive and easy to remember. As you read through the following pages, you may find that you already know much of it without realizing it. If you'd like to pursue this subject, see the books listed in the Bibliography on p. 205.

By understanding how motifs can be grouped, you can start to arrange your own patterns and make combinations and variations of those you see here. One of the easiest ways to vary these arrangements is to make panels. Select any group of motifs along a vertical, horizontal or diagonal plane and then alternate them with another pattern or surround them with a ground pattern. In the museum sampler, you can see examples of vertical arrangements in patterns 24 and 33, of horizontal arrangements in patterns 15 and 35, and of diagonal arrangements in patterns 47 and 62.

I have used triangle and diamond motifs in the drawings in this section because they are prevalent throughout the sampler, but the motif can be any shape. The circles represent eyelets while the dark dashes represent their decreases, shown as both edge decreases and central decreases. All the arrangements are gridded, so you can easily see how the motifs are combined.

Stacked motifs

In a stacked arrangement the motifs are placed one above the other and one next to the other on the same plane. The drawings at right show triangles and diamonds in stacked arrangements. The negative spaces between the motifs can be in plain stockinette stitch, a mixture of knit and purl stitches, another motif or a ground pattern. Some of the larger motifs are shown in the sampler as two or more repeats in width, but only one repeat in height. Imagine them with several repeats in height and width as I point them out.

The patterns in the sampler with stacked triangle motifs include Pattern 34 with a ground pattern in the negative space and patterns 33 and 69 with stockinette stitches. In the latter two, the motifs are arranged in vertical columns or panels with another pattern between them. In patterns 24 and 61, the triangles are arranged as in patterns 33 and 69, but with the left and

Stacked motifs

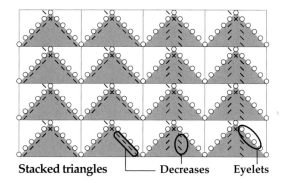

Stacked triangles — Decreases — Eyelets

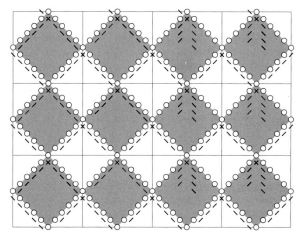

Stacked diamonds

right halves reversed. Pattern 14 is interesting in that it repeats only half the usual isosceles triangle rather than a full one.

Some patterns that are arranged as stacked diamond motifs include Pattern 5, which is a group of nine small diamonds treated as one motif, with the negative spaces in stockinette stitch; Pattern 48, which is similar but has a ground pattern in the negative spaces; and the smaller patterns 44 and 49. In Pattern 10, the columns of diamonds are pushed apart slightly to make room for a larger ground pattern with its own little motif. In patterns 18 and 73, the diamond is elongated by a repetition of the center row several times, and in Pattern 63, only the left half of the diamond is used.

Alternating stacked diamonds

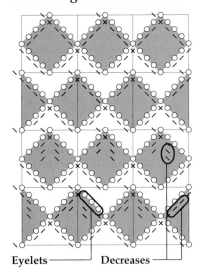

Eyelets ——————— Decreases ——————

Alternating adjacent (tessellated) diamonds

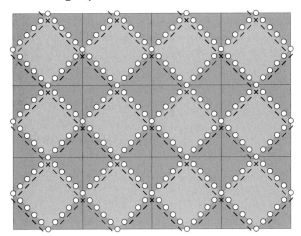

Alternating stacked motifs

If you shift stacked diamonds to the left or right by half a motif on alternate rows, the negative space between the rows of diamonds becomes a zigzag shape, as shown in the drawing at left. As with stacked motifs, the negative space of alternating stacked motifs can be filled with stockinette stitch or another pattern. There are two examples of this arrangement in the sampler, patterns 7 and 17. Both patterns have a diamond motif made up of four little diamonds. The negative space in Pattern 7 is filled with stockinette stitch, while that in Pattern 17 is a ground pattern.

Alternating adjacent motifs, or tessellated patterns

The negative spaces between the stacked diamonds in the drawing on p. 139 make spaces that are the same size as the motif itself. If you fill these negative spaces with the same diamond motif, you create an allover alternating pattern, in which the bottom half of one diamond is adjacent to the top half of its neighbors. There is no negative space in this kind of arrangement, as shown in the drawing at left. Instead, the motifs fit together like mosaic tiles, which is why they are called "tessellated." This is a popular patterning method, and there are lots of examples of it in the sampler. Patterns 9, 11, 12, 26, 36, 45, 46, 59, 68 and 70 all make a continuous lattice of eyelets throughout the fabric. The diamonds within are filled with a variety of interesting textures. The large scale of Pattern 29 allows it to be filled with two designs. Patterns 4 and 78 are a little different in that the lattice effect is formed by decreases instead of eyelets. Pattern 38 is another elongated pattern, so its lattice of eyelets includes verticals as well as diagonals.

An interesting motif that is not a diamond but fits in a diamond outline is Pattern 91. Notice that it has an asymmetrical pattern, which is flopped on alternate rows of motifs.

Alternating spaced motifs

In another common arrangement, alternating adjacent motifs are spaced apart from each other, resulting in alternating spaced motifs, shown in the drawing at left on the facing page. You can insert another pattern, or stockinette stitch, between the motifs. There are several such arrangements in the sampler: Patterns 3, 42 and 76 are patterned diamonds surrounded by stockinette stitches, whereas patterns 20, 40, 53 and 89

Alternating spaced diamonds

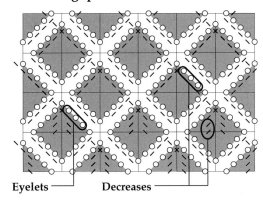

Eyelets —————— Decreases ——————

are plain diamonds surrounded by fancy ground patterns. The very wide spacing of the diamonds in Pattern 89 makes them look like they are floating in the ground.

Lopped triangles

As their name suggests, lopped triangles (shown at right) are triangles with their tops cut off. Because both the top and bottom now have flat surfaces, you can fit together the new trapezoid shape in some interesting ways. The sampler includes examples of stacked, alternating and staggered lopped triangles.

Pattern 58 is the sole example in the sampler of stacked lopped triangles. The lopped triangle is knitted in stockinette, and the negative triangular spaces between are just big enough for three tiny diamonds.

The sampler contains three examples of alternating lopped triangles: patterns 16, 56 and 57. Notice how the upper edge of one triangle overlaps the corners of the two triangles above it. This characteristic combined with spaced decreases creates the ribbon effect of these patterns. In Pattern 56, the ribbon effect is even three-dimensional.

Pattern 65 in the sampler is an example of staggered lopped triangles. It is made by sliding a pair of stacked triangles so that the start of the left decreases of the upper triangle is almost directly above the ending of the same decreases in the lower triangle. The leaf effect of this pattern is attained by pushing apart columns of staggered triangles and inserting a ground pattern between them.

Lopped triangles

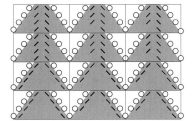

Stacked lopped triangles

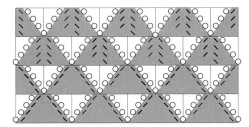

Alternating lopped triangles

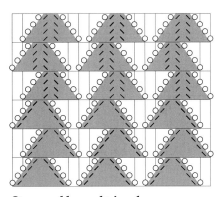

Staggered lopped triangles

Half-drop triangles

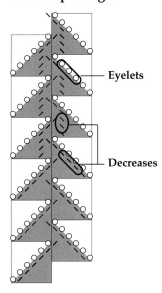

Eyelets

Decreases

Inverted triangles, alternated

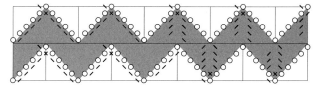

Half-drop triangles

In two patterns in the sampler, the triangle motif is divided in half lengthwise, and one side is dropped by half the motif's length, as shown above. The term *half-drop* describes this arrangement and applies to the arrangement of whole motifs too; alternating adjacent diamonds and alternating spaced diamonds are also half-drop arrangements. In Pattern 32, the columns of divided triangles are pushed together as closely as possible so that the outlining eyelets almost overlap and appear to branch left and right between the columns of motifs. The central decrease for the two halves forms an undulating line up the center. In Pattern 51, the two halves are pushed apart by an insertion of faggoting, making the double lines of eyelets between the two columns appear as an alternating fern pattern.

Inverted triangles, alternated

The zigzag effect of half-drop diamonds can be produced horizontally as well as vertically. Using triangle motifs, mirror them on either side of a horizontal line, then alternate them as shown in the drawing above right. In Pattern 13, this horizontal line is between rows 15 and 17 on the chart. In Pattern 15, it is mirrored on either side of Row 11, and in Pattern 35, between rows 17 and 19.

Patterns with black squares: Increasing and decreasing on different rows

Sometimes a pattern motif has to be very dimensional, or at least somewhat raised in relief from the fabric surface, to be effective. And occasionally a pattern needs eyelets in certain places to open up the fabric but hasn't enough stitches in the right spots on the same row to make the accompanying decreases. These are only two of several reasons why the number of stitches per row may not be consistent throughout a pattern's repeat.

Making charts for these patterns presents something of a dilemma, because an allover pattern needs to be charted within a four-sided box where all the grid rows have the same number of squares. Since each square represents one stitch, some of the grid rows will have unused squares for the rows in the repeat with fewer stitches. The solution is to black out these unused squares and skip over them when knitting the pattern.

When you chart a pattern of this type, it's best to place the black squares so as to keep the design's main features visually intact on the grid, for example, by placing the black squares along lines of eyelets or decreases. Grouping them together at one side of the grid may be easier, but it can destroy the flow of the pattern's elements from one row to the next. Look at the charts of patterns 2 and 52 of the museum sampler to see two solutions for charting the same motif.

Patterns 2 and 52 have a fan motif whose stitch count varies from row to row. You'll probably recognize it as part of the well-known Shetland patterns "Old Shale" and "Feather and Fan." On the first row of the repeat, eight eyelets are made, an increase of eight stitches, with a plain stitch between each one. A single decrease only is made at each edge of the panel on the first row. The remaining six stitches are decreased gradually—one decrease at each edge of the following three rows—in order to force the rows gradually into a gentle upward curve. The center panel of the swatch on p. 136 is based on this motif. The decorative ridge of garter stitch, added to every other repeat of the fan pattern, emphasizes the fan shape. Although it adds an extra two rows, I ignored them in the total row count and simply skipped over them when sewing together the panels.

Pattern 64 and the swatch on p. 138 both contain a leaf motif that is very dimensional when surrounded by purl stitches. I used the same leaf motif to create a scalloped edge for the edging on p. 159 as the leaf will flare outward when freed from the restraints of the purl-stitch background. To create the bottom of the leaf, increase eight stitches over four right-side rows. To shape the upper part, decrease two stitches at a time in the center of the leaf over the next three right-side rows and then decrease the final two stitches several rows later, to create the top of the leaf's petiole.

Patterns 50, 58, 59 and 65 are typical patterns that need an extra eyelet or two in strategic locations in order to have enough stitches to outline a motif such as a small diamond (58) or the tips of a pair of leaves (50), or to place a point precisely in a line of decreases (65). In Pattern 59, four extra eyelets are carefully placed to allow the arrowhead motif room to expand at the bottom.

Pattern 46 also has black squares, not because the rows vary in their numbers of stitches, but to make the pattern more understandable visually. The black squares serve to place the first, central eyelet, located at the bottom of each diamond, between the two decreases of the diamond below it.

Another stitch pattern that calls for increases and decreases on different rows is the double-eyelet mesh found in patterns 83, 88 and 89. These patterns are discussed in the section on the eyelet ground patterns and meshes on p. 148.

Faggot patterns

Faggots are a type of mesh pattern characterized by one or two adjacent vertical columns of eyelets separated by one or two adjacent columns of decreases. If there are any plain stitches in the pattern, they are used to make decreases on the next row. The term *faggot* stems from needlework techniques in existence before the development of lace knitting, principally the deflected-thread and drawn-thread laces and embroideries of western Europe, where narrow insertions of twisted and gathered threads resembling herringbone stitch were used at seams and between larger patterns. In lace knitting, faggots are commonly used as vertical insertions of one or two repeats in paneled patterns, or sometimes as allover ground patterns dressed up with some purl stitches or a floating motif.

The six faggot patterns in this sampler conveniently fall into three categories described below, with two patterns in each category. Other faggot patterns can be found in knitting pattern books. In order to make the faggots easier to identify and their construction easier to decipher, I've shown the faggoting patterns in the swatches in this section as enlarged details of allover repeats, even though they aren't all used this way in the sampler. The decreases and eyelets are so close together that unless you can see them up close their construction can be a real puzzle.

Faggots patterned every row

Faggots patterned every row make firm, stable, open fabrics. Between the eyelets are a pair of twisted threads, since each eyelet is composed of a yarn over with a plain stitch knitted into it on the next row. The decreases are made from the plain stitches of the previous row. This holds the eyelets open and makes the vertical bars of layered stitches very firm, stable and slightly raised. The two swatches on p. 144 are knitted of a crisp, smooth, cabled mercerized cotton, which highlights the relief texture of the vertical bars.

1a. *This faggot, one of the two most commonly used in the sampler, is patterned every row. There are two vertical bars of decreases between the eyelets.*

1b. *Similar in effect to Faggot 1a, this faggot has only one vertical bar of decreases between the eyelets. The chart for Faggot 1c shows a variation.*

Faggot 1a

Multiple of 4 sts.

Row 1: *k2, yo, ssk*.
Row 2: *p2, yo, p2tog*.

Faggot 1b

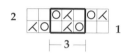

Multiple of 3 sts, plus 4.

Row 1: k2, *yo, k2tog, k1*, yo, k2tog.
Row 2: p2, *yo, p2tog, p1*, yo, p2tog.

Faggot 1c

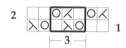

Multiple of 3 sts, plus 4.

Row 1: k2, *yo, ssk, k1*, yo, ssk.
Row 2: p2, *yo, p2tog, p1*, yo, p2tog.

Faggot 1a (above left) is one of the two most commonly used faggots in the sampler. It is found in Pattern 27 as an allover repeat, in patterns 24 and 37 within a cable, and in Pattern 69 as a vertical insertion. In Pattern 63, the faggot pattern has been used as a vertical and even a diagonal insertion. This pattern is worth careful scrutiny to understand how it has been done. I made a complete study of the pattern in the swatch on the facing page, mirroring the diagonal faggot on a vertical axis around the central vertical faggot, then extending the three faggots above and below the diamond.

Faggot 1b (above right) is used in Pattern 50 as an allover repeat. The two extra stitches at each side of the repeat complete the faggot at the edges.

A common variation of this faggot is to make the decrease on Row 1 a slip 1-knit 1-pass slipped stitch over (or slip-slip-knit), as in the chart for Faggot 1c, instead of knit-two together. The vertical bar of decreases will be a little wider and more flattened.

Brioche-type faggots patterned every row

The faggots shown in the photos on p. 146 belong to the brioche family. They make soft, unstable fabrics with eyelets that tend to collapse. They make nice insertions, but they should not be used as allover patterns when a firm, open fabric is desired. Unlike faggots 1a and 1b, there are no plain stitches in these patterns. Thus, one stitch in every decrease is a yarn over, which makes the stitch behave in an unstable fashion, slipping and sliding behind its companion stitch. Between each eyelet there is only one thread, which crosses its neighbor but does not twist with it. For these swatches I used a soft matte cotton whose slight "stickiness" helps to prevent the yarn overs from slipping and working themselves into the formed stitches of the decrease, thus abolishing the eyelets.

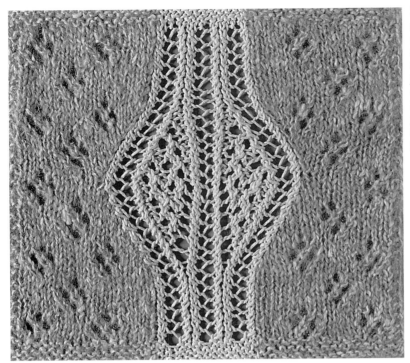

This swatch examines the intriguing diagonal faggot pattern from Pattern 63, which is Faggot 1a on p. 144. It is used at the left side of the center panel and mirrored on the right side. The same faggot is used vertically in the center of the swatch. Within the diamond is Faggot 3a (p. 147). The fuzzy yarn used for the side panels hides detail, so I chose the simple spot motif from Pattern 35 for decoration.

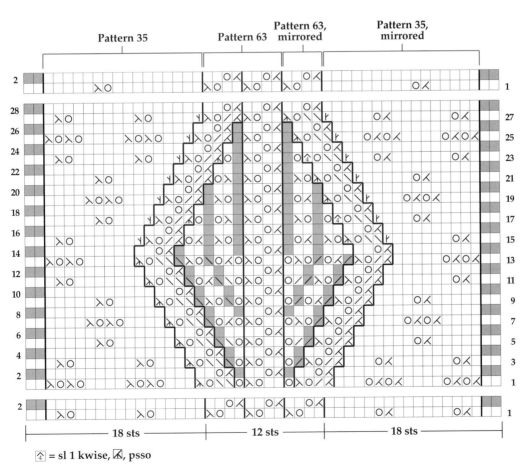

⬆ = sl 1 kwise, ⟋, psso

2a. This faggot pattern creates a soft and stretchy fabric. It has one vertical bar of decreases between the eyelets.

2b. This fabric is in the brioche family. One repeat makes a nice insertion, but the fabric tends to collapse when the pattern is knitted as an allover.

Faggot 2a

Multiple of 2 sts, plus 2.

Row 1: k1, *yo, ssk*, k1.
Row 2: p1, *yo, p2tog*, p1.

Faggot 2b

Multiple of 2 sts, plus 2.

Row 1: k1, *yo, ssk*, k1.
Row 2: p1, *yo, k2tog*, p1.

Faggot 2a (above left) is used in Pattern 55 as an insertion. Faggot 2b (above right) makes a brioche fabric based on garter stitch. The only difference between these two patterns is the decrease in Row 2: In Faggot 2a it is purled and in Faggot 2b it is knitted. This slight variation completely alters the fabric structure, however, and in Faggot 2b makes the two faces of the fabric very different. The rough side is created on the odd rows and the smooth side on the even rows. In the photo, the rough side is shown. Faggot 2b can be seen in Pattern 81 as an allover repeat.

Faggots patterned every other row

For faggots patterned every other row, you make all the yarn overs and decreases on the right-side rows and purl the wrong-side rows plain. This means that the stitches of each decrease will be comprised of plain stitches, and each eyelet will be made by a yarn over with a plain stitch on the following row. The eyelets are thus separated by a pair of twisted threads, just as for faggots 1a and 1b.

These are firm, stable fabrics. The eyelets can take on different shapes, depending on the kind of decrease you use. Even though the yarn I used for the swatches shown on the facing page is limp and has practically no body, the pattern creates such a firm fabric that the swatches have both stability and drape, and they show off the shapes of the eyelets well.

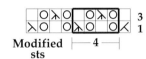

3a. *This pattern is Faggot 2a with a plain row inserted between every pattern row. This elongates the pattern, completely changing the fabric structure and resulting in very round eyelets. The chart for Faggot 3b shows a variation.*

3c. *This faggot, patterned every other row, has a double decrease instead of a single decrease. Its eyelets are triangular rather than round. The variation shown in the chart for Faggot 3d will result in square eyelets.*

Faggot 3a

Multiple of 2 sts, plus 2.
Even Rs 2 and 4 (wrong side): P all sts.

Row 1: k1, *yo, ssk*, k1.
Row 3: k1, *k2tog, yo*, k1.

Faggot 3b

Multiple of 2 sts, plus 2.
Even Rs 2 and 4 (wrong side): P all sts.

Row 1: k1, *yo, k2tog*, k1.
Row 3: k1, *ssk, yo*, k1.

Faggot 3c

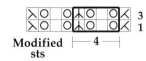
Modified sts

Multiple of 4 sts plus 1.
Even Rs 2 and 4 (wrong side): P all sts.

Row 1: k2tog, *yo, k1, yo, sl 1-k2tog-psso*, end last rep ssk.
Row 3: k1, *yo, sl 1-k2tog-psso, yo, k1*.

Faggot 3d

Modified sts

Multiple of 4 sts, plus 1.
Even Rs 2 and 4 (wrong side): P all sts.
⋏ = s2tog kwise, k next st, pss2o.

Row 1: k2tog, *yo, k1, yo, ⋏*, end last rep ssk.
Row 3: Rep R 1.

Faggot 3a (above left) has a chart like that of Faggot 2a, but purling the wrong-side rows completely changes the fabric. The zigzag of the vertical bar of Faggot 2a is still apparent. The very round eyelets hold themselves open with two strands of yarn twisted around each other. Faggot 3a is one of the two most popular faggots in the sampler. You can see it in patterns 28, 53, 61 and 63 as a ground pattern and in patterns 14, 37, 41 and 51 as an insertion. A variation of this pattern (Faggot 3b) is to reverse the two decreases. This puts the eyelet stitch on top of the plain stitch instead of under it.

Faggot 3c (above right) is used in Pattern 67 as an insertion and in Pattern 76 as a ground. This faggot is different from all the other faggots in the sampler in that it has a double decrease instead of a single decrease. Thus the vertical bars between the eyelets are composed alternately of a decrease and a plain stitch. Because the decrease is double, with the two side stitches layered over the middle stitch, the vertical bars

are straight and do not zigzag. The eyelets are triangular, not their normal round shape, because of the alternating placement of the decreases on the two pattern rows.

Faggot 3d is an interesting variation. Vertical double decreases (Symbol 30 in the Glossary of Symbols and Techniques, p. 193) are placed one above the other, and the alternate vertical bars are made from a single plain stitch throughout. The resulting eyelets will be perfectly square.

Eyelet spot and mesh patterns

Tiny motifs floating within a larger fabric or pattern are known as "spot patterns." The museum sampler contains three eyelet spot patterns that float in fabrics of stockinette stitch. One is a trefoil of three eyelets, and the other two are quatrefoils of four eyelets. These little patterns are used in the sampler to fill the center of a diamond (Pattern 44), as motifs for a horizontal zigzag pattern (Pattern 35), and to decorate diagonal panels (Pattern 62). Although used in the sampler as accents, spot patterns are also useful as unobtrusive fillers for large plain areas of fabric, where you want a little decoration but nothing to draw attention away from the primary motifs. The sweater and the shawl projects on pp. 173-177 and pp. 185-189 and the swatch on p. 145 make use of them.

There are also several single-eyelet and double-eyelet meshes that can function in the same way as a faggot mesh. You can use them as horizontal or vertical insertions or as an allover background pattern to support a motif design. Making variations in the meshes is easy: You can knit them in either stockinette or garter stitch, and you can alternate their eyelets on successive rows or place them one above the other.

Pattern 31 is a single-eyelet mesh with its eyelets one above the other. It consists of two stockinette rows, with the eyelets and decreases in the first stockinette row, alternated with one ridge of garter stitch.

Pattern 23 is a double-eyelet mesh with its eyelets one above the other. It is knitted entirely in garter stitch. The eyelets and decreases are made in the first row, followed by three more knitted rows before the next row of eyelets.

Pattern 83 is also a double-eyelet mesh made in garter stitch. It differs from Pattern 23 in that it is patterned every ridge instead of every other ridge, its eyelets are alternated rather than one being positioned above the other, and the eyelets and companion decreases are on different rows. The double eyelet is put in on the first row, then a pair of single decreases is knitted on the second row. The process is repeated for the next two rows, with the eyelets in the alternate position. In Pattern 88, this mesh is used in alternating vertical panels, and in Pattern 89 it is used as an allover fabric with floating leaf motifs.

Patterns 21 and 39 are both single-eyelet meshes with the eyelets in diagonal columns, and the columns are separated by a decrease and one or two plain stitches, which give the mesh a diagonal linear quality. The decreases cause the fabric to bias because they are consistently placed to the left of their eyelets. To compensate for the biasing, just flip over the chart and mirror the mesh elsewhere in the design, as discussed in the section on chevrons (see p. 124).

Diamond ground patterns

Our knitter certainly has made full use of the diamond shape in this sampler. In addition to large and decorative diamonds, there are scattered throughout the sampler a number of small diamonds used as accents, fillers and allover repeats. In this section I have grouped these useful little diamonds and extracted their basic repeats.

There are a total of seven small diamonds in three sizes in the museum sampler. Some of the diamonds have a central eyelet, and they vary in their arrangement of decreases. You could transform any of the diamonds by using a variation for one of the others. You can also vary the size by patterning on both the right-side and wrong-side rows for a smaller diamond, or only on the right-side rows for a larger diamond. The patterns in the sampler where each diamond can be found are given with the charts for the diamond patterns shown on the facing page so you can compare how they are combined and used.

In the sampler, none of the diamonds appears as a single unit as shown here. To work out arrangements of multiples, copy the eyelet/decrease configuration for one motif onto graph paper. Then lay a piece of tracing paper over the new grid and trace the eyelets, decreases and shading. The shading represents the solid area of the diamond, framed by eyelets. You can then move the tracing paper around the graph-paper diamond, trying out different ways for the diamonds to share eyelets. Examine the positioning and direction of the decreases, too, to see how you might combine two overlapping single decreases into a double decrease. In all the grids, the double decrease at the top faces left, providing the opportunity to make all the decreases of the upper right quadrant face to the left also, as with diamonds 1b, 3a and 3c. When knitted, the effect will be of diamonds lying within a series of right-to-left diagonal parallel lines, as in patterns 5 and 19. To make left-to-right diagonal parallel line, flip the tracing paper over and copy the symbols from the back of the tracing.

One of the diamond patterns in the sampler, Pattern 64, is a special case. It is knitted on the bias and was discussed in the section on bias (see pp. 137-138).

Diamond ground patterns

The shaded squares represent the solid area of the diamond, framed by eyelets.

1a

Grid sts = 7; grid rows = 4.

This diamond without a center eyelet is used in patterns 4, 34, 42 and 58. Patterns 34 and 58 delete the bottom pivot eyelet.

1b

Grid sts = 7; grid rows = 4.

This diamond pattern without a center eyelet is used in patterns 19 and 64.

2a

Grid sts = 7; grid rows = 5.

This diamond without a center eyelet is used in patterns 7, 22, 30 and 90, which all delete the bottom pivot eyelet. In Pattern 90, the second and fourth rows are knitted twice. Pattern 22 has a reversed double decrease and is knitted in garter stitch.

2b

Grid sts = 7; grid rows = 5.

This diamond, with a high center eyelet, is used in patterns 8, 33, 40, 43 and 59, which all delete the bottom pivot eyelet. In the chart for Pattern 33, the diamond is version 3b (shown below) to make it fit into a rectangular repeat with the adjacent horseshoe panel.

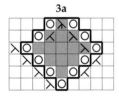

3a

Grid sts = 9; grid rows = 6.

This diamond, with no center eyelet, is used in Pattern 5.

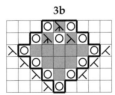

3b

Grid sts = 9; grid rows = 6.

This diamond, which has a high center eyelet, is used in patterns 33 and 57. In Pattern 33 (and in 2b above), the bottom pivot eyelet is deleted. Pattern 57 has three diamonds in a trefoil with the central overlapped eyelet deleted.

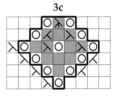

3c

Grid sts = 9; grid rows = 6.

This diamond, with a low center eyelet, is used in Pattern 47.

CHAPTER 3

Charting
Lace
Patterns

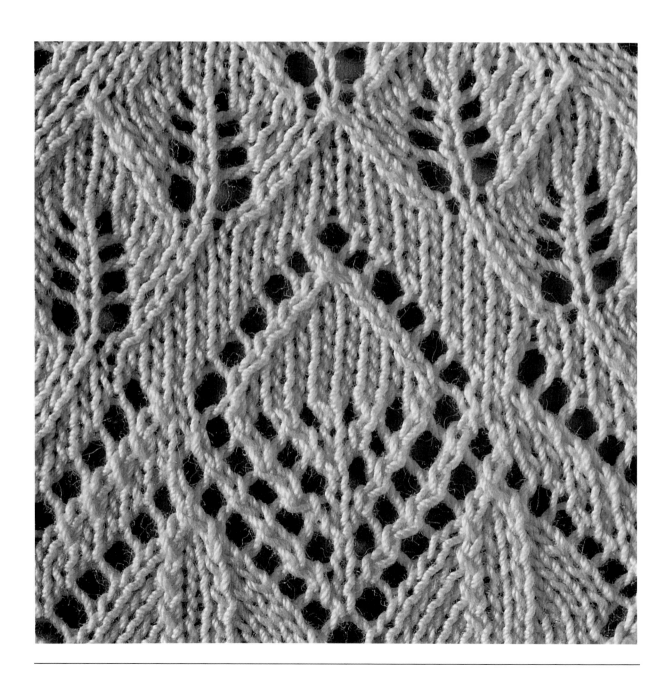

In the previous chapter, I virtually took apart the sampler, examining the construction of its patterns and their underlying principles. In this chapter, to encourage you to expand your lace-knitting horizons, I'll approach lace knitting from the standpoints of pattern design, translation and documentation. These are all practical ways for you to put your lacemaking skills and knowledge of its principles to work. I'll show you how to design a pattern from scratch, combine parts of patterns to make new patterns, chart a pattern from written knitting instructions and chart a pattern from a photograph of a piece of knitted lace. The sampler is our resource. For each of these exercises you'll need to have at hand the equipment described in the sidebar on p. 156.

Charting a pattern from scratch

A good way to gain a real understanding of lace knitting is to jump right in — design a lace pattern and then knit it. Patterns with parallel selvedges are the simplest. Those with nonparallel selvedges are a little more complicated because of the added shaping. We'll design both.

Charting patterns with parallel selvedges

We'll start with a diamond motif, since diamonds are an easy shape to understand and can be combined and modified in many ways. We'll use the chevron swatch on p. 122 and its charted patterns to build the diamond.

1. Copy the first four rows of Chevron 1a (p. 123) in the center of a blank sheet of graph paper, as shown on p. 152. Above these rows, chart the last five rows of Chevron 1b to complete the diamond motif. Decorate the exact center of the diamond with an eyelet and put a left-slanting decrease to its left. Note that every eyelet of the diamond has a companion decrease, with a double decrease for the two eyelets near the top. With a colored pencil, lightly color in the diamond shape within the eyelet border, both the plain squares and those with decrease symbols. Leave the eyelet squares uncolored. The colored squares within the outline of eyelets represent the solid parts of the knitted diamond — stockinette stitches and lines of decreases.

Before you can chart a second diamond you have to decide on a pattern arrangement. Look at the drawings for allover patterns on p. 139. Stacked diamonds will provide space between the diamond motifs to put a second pattern. Trace the eyelets and decreases of your first diamond onto a piece of tracing paper. Shade the solid areas lightly so you can still see through the paper. With this tracing, you can try out different arrangements and also quickly check your work later on.

Facing page: Detail, medallion, p. 160.

Charting an allover diamond pattern from scratch

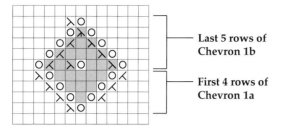

— Last 5 rows of Chevron 1b

— First 4 rows of Chevron 1a

1. Chart a diamond using chevrons 1a and 1b. Add a decorative eyelet to the center, with a decrease to its left. Shaded squares represent solid stitches of the diamond, outlined by eyelets.

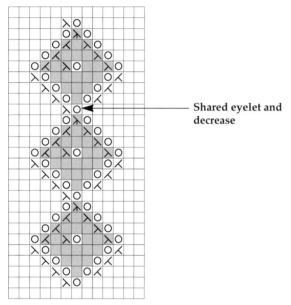

— Shared eyelet and decrease

2. Chart a second and third diamond so they share the overlapping eyelet and decrease at the top and bottom points.

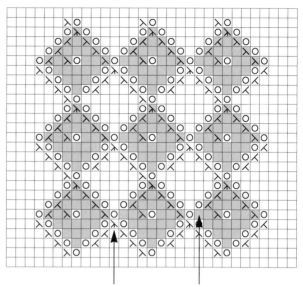

Two single decreases combine into a double decrease.

The shared eyelet cannot have two decreases. This one is deleted.

3. Add two more columns of three diamonds, having them share their outermost overlapping eyelets.

2. Lay the tracing above your first diamond so that the bottom eyelet of the tracing overlaps the top eyelet of the graphed diamond. The companion decreases will also overlap. Chart a second diamond on your grid in this position. Chart a third diamond either above or below the first two, also sharing an eyelet and decrease at the point. Shade these diamonds as you did the first. You will have a column of three diamonds in the center of your page, as in the chart above.

3. You'll need some more columns of three diamonds. To start the next column, lay the tracing to the right of the bottom diamond so that the tracing's leftmost eyelet overlaps the rightmost eyelet of the bottom diamond. This eyelet now has two decreases, one on

each side. You have to choose which decrease to erase. Below this eyelet, two decreases overlap and are flanked by an eyelet on each side. These decreases will be changed to a double decrease, so you have to choose the kind of double decrease to substitute. By deleting the decrease to the right of the single eyelet and changing the overlapped decreases to a left double decrease (Symbol 26 in the Glossary of Symbols and Techniques on p. 198), you'll create an unbroken diagonal line of decreases from one diamond to the next, as in the diamonds of patterns 5, 36 and 47 of the museum sampler. Chart this new diamond, then two more above it, each time correcting the decreases on your grid (but not those on the tracing).

Chart another column of three diamonds to the left, making the same corrections. Double-check your chart row by row to be sure all the eyelets and decreases are paired. Shade the solid part of the diamonds. You can see the value of adding color as your chart becomes more complicated.

You now have an arrangement of nine stacked diamonds, as shown in the chart above. The eyelets form a diagonal lattice that crisscrosses the grid at even intervals.

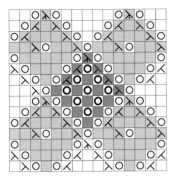

4. On tracing paper, chart a checkerboard of eyelets in the blank area between diamonds (dark circles). Shade blank and symboled squares except eyelets (dark shading).

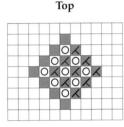

Top	Top

One-stitch diagonal stripes traveling right

One-stitch diagonal stripes traveling left

Reposition the tracing over a clean area of graph paper. Add right decreases to the right of the eyelets.

Flip the tracing over to mirror the pattern.

Next time, you can draw this pattern much more quickly by first charting all the eyelets, then using the tracing to position their decreases. Varying the eyelet lattice is easy. For example, syncopate the eyelets by alternating wide and narrow spacing to make large and small diamonds, as in Pattern 29 of the museum sampler. Pattern 47 has a diagonal panel of small diamonds plus a panel of large diamonds made by erasing some of the lattice lines. Whatever size diamond you create, you can follow the same procedure for putting in the decreases—make a tracing of one motif with all its decreases and then make the necessary changes to the decreases as you overlap parts of the pattern. At the end of each stage of charting, double-check that all the eyelets and decreases are paired.

4. Between the nine diamonds are four blank diamonds identical to those you just drew except for the central decorative eyelet. If you were to give a central eyelet to each of the four, you would no longer have an arrangement of stacked diamonds, but rather one of alternating adjacent diamonds (see p. 140), like those in Pattern 9. For variety, why not put a different pattern in the blank diamond-shaped areas? You'll need two more colored pencils.

An open, linear ground pattern would make a nice contrast to the quite solid diamonds. One used throughout the sampler is the one-stitch diagonal stripe pattern, which you can see in patterns 1 and 3 of the museum sampler. An advantage of this ground pattern is that it will fit into small spaces. Its disadvantage is that the fabric will bias to the right because all its decreases are to the left of their eyelets. To counteract the biasing, you can flip over the pattern and mirror it in different areas of your design, as has been done in various ways in patterns 20 and 29. To keep it simple, put right-traveling stripes in the two lower diamonds and left-traveling stripes in the upper ones.

Design the stripes on tracing paper first. Lay a clean area of tracing paper over one of the blank diamonds. On the tracing paper, chart a checkerboard of eyelets in the blank area of the diamond, positioning the topmost eyelet just under the double decrease at the top of the diamond. You'll have five rows with eyelets: The first and fifth rows have one eyelet, the second and fourth rows have two eyelets, and the third row has three eyelets. The darker circles in the chart at top left indicate these eyelets. You can see that the eyelets form diagonal rows. With a different colored pencil, shade all the diamond's plain or symboled squares not occupied by an eyelet.

Move the tracing to a clean area of graph paper, aligning the eyelets over grid squares. On the tracing, chart a right decrease to the right of each eyelet, as shown in the small chart at far left. Write the word "top" above so you'll know which way to orient the tracing on the grid. This diamond will go in the lower row of empty diamonds. To mirror the right-traveling stripes for the two empty diamonds of the upper row, flip over the tracing paper. As viewed through the back of the tracing, the diamonds now have left-traveling stripes, as shown in the small chart at near left.

Position the tracing of the right-traveling stripes over one of the two empty diamonds in the bottom row of your nine-diamond pattern. The three decreases along the upper right side of the tracing overlap the left decreases of the diamonds already in place. When you add the traced stripes to your pattern, you'll have to

Completing the chart

Original nine diamonds

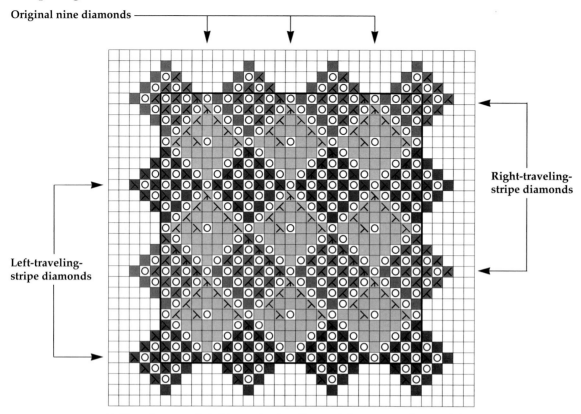

Right-traveling-stripe diamonds

Left-traveling-stripe diamonds

5. Chart the one-stitch diagonal-stripe diamonds between and around the original nine diamonds. Change overlapping single decreases to double decreases. Outline the original nine diamonds.

change these three decreases to left double decreases. The four colored squares without symbols along the lower left of the traced stripes are plain stitches.

5. Chart the new eyelets and decreases of the right-traveling stripes into the two empty diamonds of the lower row, making the necessary changes to the three decreases. Shade these striped diamonds the same as on the tracing. When this pattern is knitted, the right decreases will force each diagonal row of colored squares into a single-stitch line traveling to the right. Chart the eyelets and decreases of the left-traveling stripes onto your chart just as they appear through the back of the tracing, changing the two overlapping decreases on the left upper edge to right double decreases. Shade the left-traveling stripes with a third color.

This ground pattern was mirrored on a horizontal axis. By putting left-traveling stripes in the two empty diamonds at the left and right-traveling stripes in the two empty diamonds at the right (or vice versa) you

could instead have mirrored it on a vertical axis. Here, the purpose of mirroring is to have an equal amount of both kinds of stripes to balance their bias tendencies.

To complete the pattern, add twelve more striped diamonds around the outside of the original nine diamonds, continuing the left-traveling and right-traveling stripes on alternate rows of diamonds, as shown in the chart above. Shade them in lightly because you will erase part of them in a moment.

Box the original nine diamonds with an outline placed outside and adjacent to their outermost eyelets. All the squares within the outline should have either an eyelet or a colored square.

6. The pattern is finished except for the repeat box, row numbers and selvedges. To complete the top and bottom edges, erase all the symbols and shading above the top of the outline and below the bottom of the outline.

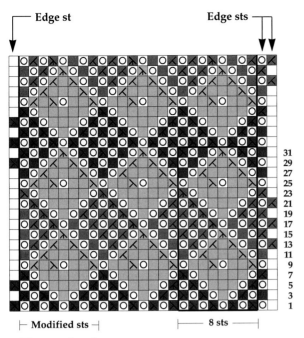

Edge st   Edge sts

31
29
27
25
23
21
19
17
15
13
11
9
7
5
3
1

├─ Modified sts ─┤   ├──── 8 sts ────┤

6. The completed pattern.

To complete the selvedges at each side, retain one column of squares beyond the outline on each side so that when the pattern is knitted, the outermost eyelets of the original diamonds will have a plain stitch to their outsides. Erase everything outside these columns. In the column at the left, outside the outline, find the eyelets whose companion decreases are *within* the outline and erase both symbols. You'll find some at the edge of the right-traveling stripes. Be careful—if the decrease you are about to erase is a double decrease, then there is another eyelet paired with it within the outline. Change the double decrease to a single decrease (there are none in this pattern). Next, erase the eyelets in this outer column whose decreases had been to their left, but have already been erased. Do the same with the decreases in this column whose eyelets had been to their left, but have been erased. This leftmost column now contains only plain stitches plus any decreases that belong to eyelets within the outline. Check your work against the chart above.

In the column at the right, outside the outline, erase no-longer-needed symbols in the same way: Erase eyelets as well as their decreases if the decreases are within the outline. Erase eyelets in this right column that no longer have decreases, and erase decreases that no longer have eyelets. This column now resembles the left column, containing only plain stitches and

decreases that belong to eyelets within the outline. Recheck every row of the grid to be sure all the remaining eyelets and decreases are still paired.

Next, indicate which block of pattern is the repeat. Each diamond is eight stitches wide, including a shared eyelet. As close to the right side as possible, find a width of eight stitches that does not include a column of squares where you have erased a symbol or changed a double decrease to a single decrease. In this pattern you cannot include these columns in the repeat box because symbols were deleted from both the outside column at the right and the one next to it. So the repeat box will begin with the third column from the right side and extend eight squares to the left. In height it will extend 16 squares. Draw a heavy line around this repeat box.

To mark off the selvedge stitches at the right, extend the heavy line at the right side of the repeat box up to the top of the grid. Erase the leftover outline between the first two columns. To mark off the selvedge stitches at the left, count groups of eight squares from right to left and draw a heavy vertical line between the last group and the remaining squares to their left. In this case the line corresponds to the original outline you drew around the diamonds. Because you erased some of the decreases in the column just inside the outline, mark this repeat of eight squares "modified."

Last, number the grid rows with odd numbers on the right if you plan to knit the right-side rows in pattern and purl the wrong-side rows plain. Alternatively, if you wish to pattern the even rows, put odd numbers at the right on alternate rows and even numbers at the left on the in-between rows.

Now that you've done all this work, you can sit back and enjoy knitting a swatch. If you'd like to chart another design, how about making some variations to this pattern? Pattern 36 in the museum sampler has the same diamond knitted in ribbing, and Pattern 26 has a similar diamond whose upper half is purled and lower half is knitted. The diamond in Pattern 18 is knitted in a type of moss stitch. Or you can go back to the chevron swatch and choose a different top half for the diamond, maybe the fashioned decreases of chevrons 4b or 5b or the central decreases of chevrons 6 or 7. Or you can arrange the diamonds as alternating stacked motifs; you will have even more space to fill with another pattern. The sampler is filled with parts and pieces of designs and effects that you can combine in new and different ways.

Tools needed for making charts

Graph paper with five or six squares per inch is a good size. For large designs you can use eight squares per inch. An 8½-in. by 11-in. pad of blue or green quadrille is perfect—inexpensive and easy on the eyes. Avoid graph paper with heavier lines every five or ten squares because the lines are distracting.

Transparent tape for joining sheets of graph paper in case the design runs off the page.

A **ruler** marked in inches for quickly counting squares (depending on the gauge of your paper, an inch equals five or six squares) and for drawing straight lines around your design.

A **pencil** with No. 2 lead and a **pencil sharpener**, if necessary. I prefer an automatic pencil of 0.5 diameter with HB (the standard) lead, as the point is always sharp. Don't use either a hard lead (No. 3), which is too difficult to see and to erase, or a very soft lead (No. 1), which smears.

A **white plastic eraser** that comes in a holder and looks like a pencil. This type of eraser allows you to clean just one square or a block of squares without injuring the paper surface. The leavings make tidy little rolls that are easy to clean up. If you need to buy one, get a refill at the same time; you're likely to do considerable erasing.

Colored pencils or **crayons**, half a dozen or so different colors in light or medium shades. The erasable types are best; if yours are not, just color lightly. These are for filling in the squares of motifs to differentiate the parts of the design, which is especially helpful while you are learning or planning a complex design.

Tracing paper. A small pad is fine, or you can tear up a large sheet into smaller pieces. A little goes a long way, since you can erase your old pencil marks and reuse the paper.

A **pair of short knitting needles** and appropriate **yarn,** to try things out. The needles should be of a comfortably large diameter. You want stitches that are big enough so that you can pull out the needle completely to unravel rows quickly, and loops that are large enough to pick up again quickly and easily. You may have to knit a row and undo it several times in succession.

The following are optional: a **pocket calculator,** in case of memory lapse for the multiplication tables; a **magnifying glass,** for studying eyelets and decreases in photographs or finely worked pieces; and **reading glasses,** if your eyes bother you after staring at grids for a long time.

Charting shapes with nonparallel selvedges

Now that you've learned the basics of charting from scratch, you're ready to tackle shapes with nonparallel selvedges, which is simply a fancy way of referring to edgings, medallions and anything else that might have shaped edges. The process is essentially the same as in the previous example, where you lifted patterning motifs from the sampler and recombined them in a new way.

The main principle to understand is that to widen the fabric there must be more increases than decreases per row, and to narrow the fabric there must be more decreases than increases. In lace knitting you place extra eyelets or decreases either within the pattern or adjacent to it to accomplish this shaping. The three edgings and a medallion that you'll chart in this section illustrate three different ways to shape lace-knitted pieces—adding eyelets and decreases, binding off, and expanding or contracting the shaping inherent in a pattern motif. Using some of the leaf and ground

patterns in the sampler, the shapes we'll chart also illustrate how to lift and combine motifs from other patterns to make new patterns. Although there are certainly more than three ways to shape a knitted fabric, these methods will get you started designing patterns and understanding how to control shapes.

Each leaf and ground motif used for the edging and medallion patterns is first shown exactly as it was traced from its parent pattern. When you isolate a motif this way, make sure that the eyelets and decreases within the motif are balanced before you begin to work with it. In the finished charts the individual motifs are differentiated by shades of gray to show how the motifs have been fitted together, so you can see how the added stitches, such as the heading and left selvedge on the edgings, work with the motifs.

The edging and medallion swatches are knitted in stockinette stitch. If your swatches tend to curl, work the selvedge stitches in garter stitch.

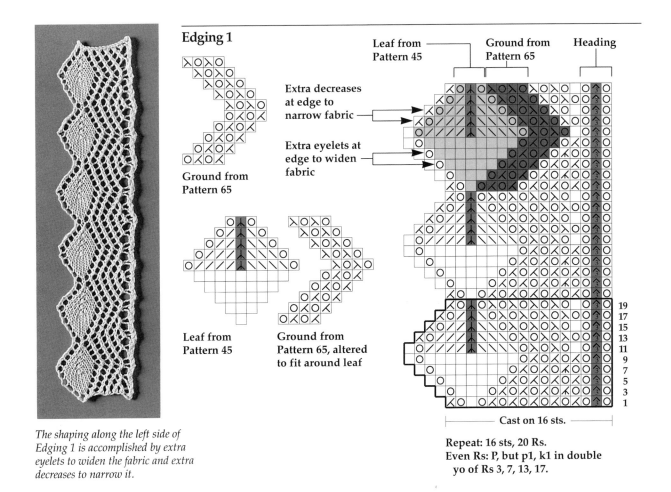

Edging 1

Leaf from Pattern 45   **Ground from Pattern 65**   **Heading**

Extra decreases at edge to narrow fabric →

Extra eyelets at edge to widen fabric →

Ground from Pattern 65

Leaf from Pattern 45   **Ground from Pattern 65, altered to fit around leaf**

The shaping along the left side of Edging 1 is accomplished by extra eyelets to widen the fabric and extra decreases to narrow it.

Cast on 16 sts.

Repeat: 16 sts, 20 Rs.
Even Rs: P, but p1, k1 in double yo of Rs 3, 7, 13, 17.

The division between pattern sections is marked by a slash (/).
Even Rs 2-20 (wrong side): P all sts, but {p1, k1} into double yo twice of Rs 3, 7, 13, 17.

◿ = ssk, return st to L ndl, pnso, return st to Rt ndl.

▲ = P2 tog, then sl 1 st kwise. Return both sts to L ndl, psso, return to Rt ndl.

Cast on 16 sts.
Row 1: yo, p3tog, yo, / {k2tog, yo} 5 times, / k1, yo, k2tog. **Row 3:** yo, p3tog, yo, / yo, ◿, yo, {k2tog, yo} 3 times, / k3, yo, k1. **Row 5:** yo, p3tog, yo, / k2tog, yo} 4 times, / k5, yo, k1. **Row 7:** yo, p3tog, yo, / yo, ◿, yo, {k2tog, yo} 2 times, / k7, yo, k1. **Row 9:** yo, p3tog, yo, / k2tog, yo} 3 times, / k9, yo, k1. **Row 11:** yo,

p3tog, yo, / k1, {yo, ssk} 2 times, / yo, k4, ▲, k4, yo, k1. **Row 13:** yo, p3tog, yo, / {yo, ssk} 3 times, / yo, k3, ▲, k3, yo, k2tog. **Row 15:** yo, p3tog, yo, / k1, {yo, ssk} 3 times, / yo, k2, ▲, k2, yo, k2tog. **Row 17:** yo, p3tog, yo, / {yo, ssk} 4 times, / yo, k1, ▲, k1, yo, k2tog. **Row 19:** yo, p3tog, yo, / k1, {yo, ssk} 4 times, / yo, ▲, yo, k2tog.
Rep Rs 1-20.

Edging 1

Edging 1 uses the leaf from Pattern 45 and the ground from Pattern 65. The shaping occurs entirely along the left edge. The eyelets added to the lower left side of the leaf cause the edging to widen. The decreases added to the left edge of the upper half cause the piece to narrow. The central double decrease in the upper half of the leaf is balanced by the eyelet to either side and therefore does not contribute to the narrowing.

The ground pattern in the center follows the contours of the leaf shape, although the original ground did not. I altered it by moving the upper half of the original ground pattern to the right by one stitch (one square). Additional eyelets and decreases were then added at the right, following the established diagonal lines of eyelets and decreases, to make a straight side for the heading.

The heading consists of two eyelets with a double decrease between them. This creates a double eyelet wherever the eyelets from the ground pattern are adjacent to the heading.

Edging 2

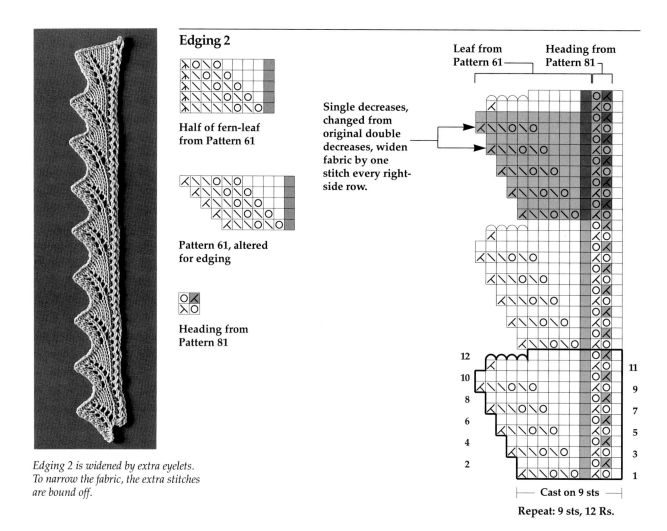

Half of fern-leaf from Pattern 61

Pattern 61, altered for edging

Heading from Pattern 81

Leaf from Pattern 61 ⎯⎯   Heading from Pattern 81 ⎤

Single decreases, changed from original double decreases, widen fabric by one stitch every right-side row.

Cast on 9 sts

Repeat: 9 sts, 12 Rs.

Edging 2 is widened by extra eyelets. To narrow the fabric, the extra stitches are bound off.

The division between pattern sections is marked by a slash (/).

Cast on 9 sts.
Row 1: k1, yo, k2tog, p1, / yo, k1, yo, k2, k2tog. **Row 2:** p6, / k1, yo, k2tog, p1.

Row 3: k1, yo, k2tog, p1, / k1, yo, k1, yo, k2, k2tog. **Row 4:** p7, / k1, yo, k2tog, p1. **Row 5:** k1, yo, k2tog, p1, / k2, yo, k1, yo, k2, k2tog. **Row 6:** p8, / k1, yo, k2tog, p1. **Row 7:** k1, yo, k2tog, p1, / k3, yo, k1, yo, k2, k2tog. **Row 8:** p9, / k1, yo,

k2tog, p1. **Row 9:** k1, yo, k2tog, p1, / k4, yo, k1, yo, k2, k2tog. **Row 10:** p10, / k1, yo, k2tog, p1. **Row 11:** k1, yo, k2tog, p1, / k8, k2tog. **Row 12:** bind off 4, p5, / k1, yo, k2tog, p1. Rep Rs 1-12.

Edging 2

Edging 2 uses only the left half of the fern-leaf motif in Pattern 61. No ground pattern is needed (although you could add one) because the pattern shape already has a straight edge for the heading on the right side. In the original motif, the double decrease in each row balances the two eyelets. Changing the double decrease to a single decrease thus causes the fabric to widen by one stitch each right-side grid row. The decrease has also been repositioned so that there is a consistent number of stitches between it and the eyelets.

The fabric is narrowed all at once, by binding off all but one of the extra stitches at the end of the repeat. One decrease is put in the row before the bind-off to round off the point. An easy way to alter this pattern and make a wider edging is to omit the edge decrease altogether. Then the fabric will widen by two stitches every right-side grid row, and there will be more stitches to bind off at the end of the repeat.

The heading of this edging is one repeat in width of the faggot in Pattern 81. You could easily substitute one repeat in width of any other faggot pattern.

Edging 3

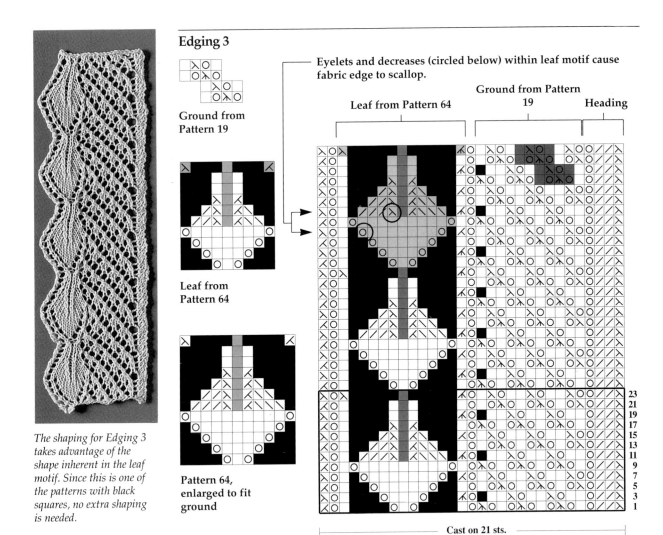

Ground from Pattern 19

Leaf from Pattern 64

Pattern 64, enlarged to fit ground

Eyelets and decreases (circled below) within leaf motif cause fabric edge to scallop.

Ground from Pattern 19

Leaf from Pattern 64

Heading

The shaping for Edging 3 takes advantage of the shape inherent in the leaf motif. Since this is one of the patterns with black squares, no extra shaping is needed.

Cast on 21 sts.

Repeat: 21 sts, 24 Rs.
Even Rs: P, but p1, k1 in double yo of Rs 7, 15, 23, and k single st in center of leaf, Rs 11-23 (gray squares).

The division between pattern sections is marked by a slash (/).

⟋ = ssk, return st to L ndl, pnso, return st to Rt ndl.

Cast on 21 sts.
Row 1: ssk, k2, yo, / k1, {yo, sl 1-k2tog-psso, yo, k1} 3 times, / yo, k1, yo, / k1, yo, k2tog. **Row 2:** Purl. **Row 3:** ssk, k2, yo, / k2, {yo, ssk, k2} 2 times, yo, ⟋, / yo, k3, yo, / k1, yo, ssk. **Row 4:** Purl. **Row 5:** ssk, k2, yo, / ssk, yo, k1, {yo, sl 1-k2tog-psso, yo, k1} 2 times, yo, k1, / yo, k5, yo, / k1, yo, k2tog. **Row 6:** Purl. **Row 7:** ssk, k2, yo, / yo, ssk, {k2, yo, ssk} 2 times, k1, yo, k2tog, / yo, k7, yo, / k1, yo, ssk. **Row 8:** p25, k1, p3. **Row 9:** ssk, k2, yo, / k1, {yo, sl 1-k2tog-psso, yo, k1} 3 times, / yo, k9, yo, / k1, yo, k2tog. **Row 10:** Purl. **Row 11:** ssk, k2, yo, / k2, {yo, ssk, k2} 2 times, yo, ⟋, / k3, k2tog, p1, ssk, k3, / k1, yo, ssk. **Row 12:** p7, k1, p20. **Row 13:** ssk, k2, yo, / ssk, yo, k1, {yo, sl 1-k2tog-psso, yo, k1} 2 times, yo, k1, / k2, k2tog, p1, ssk, k2, / k1, yo, k2tog. **Row 14:** p6, k1, p20. **Row 15:** ssk, k2, yo, / yo, ssk, {k2, yo, ssk} 2 times, k1, yo, k2tog, / k1, k2tog, p1, ssk, k1, / k1, yo, ssk. **Row 16:** p5, k1, p15, k1, p3. **Row 17:** ssk, k2, yo, / k1, {yo, sl 1-k2tog-psso, yo, k1} 3 times, / k2tog, p1, ssk, / k1, yo, k2tog. **Row 18:** p4, k1, p18. **Row 19:** ssk, k2, yo, / k2, {yo, ssk, k2} 2 times, yo, ⟋, / k1, p1, k1, / k1, yo, ssk. **Row 20:** p4, k1, p17. **Row 21:** ssk, k2, yo, / ssk, yo, k1, {yo, sl 1-k2tog-psso, yo, k1} 2 times, yo, k1, / k1, p1, k1, / k1, yo, k2tog. **Row 22:** p4, k1, p18. **Row 23:** ssk, k2, yo, / yo, ssk, {k2, yo, ssk} 2 times, k1, yo, ⟋, / p1, / ssk, yo, ssk. **Row 24:** p3, k1, p13, k1, p3. Repeat Rs 1-24.

Edging 3

Edging 3 uses the leaf from Pattern 64 and the ground from Pattern 19. The shaping occurs within the leaf form—this is one of the patterns with black squares, in which the number of stitches in a row varies. Because the scalloped form of the leaf is already very pronounced, no additional shaping is needed.

The leaf motif was enlarged by two grid rows and two stitches to make it fit a multiple of the ground repeat. To each side, one column each of plain stitches and eyelets were added to outline the leaf. On the left edge, the column of decreases that balance the adjacent eyelets makes a firm edge that resists curling. On the right side, the extra eyelet and its decrease are not balanced every row in order to give some shaping to the ground and help it contract and expand against the leaf. In Row 1, the extra eyelet is balanced by the double decrease of the ground to its right. In Row 3, in order to have two plain ground stitches next to the extra eyelet instead of three, a double decrease is made to its left, thus reducing the ground stitches by one. The missing ground stitch is put back in Row 5, where the extra eyelet has no decrease at all. In Row 7 the eyelet is balanced by a single decrease.

Medallion

The medallion uses the leaves from patterns 12, 47 and 78. The leaf from Pattern 47 was made smaller so that three leaves in a trefoil would create a negative space just the right size for the leaf from Pattern 12. The shaping of the medallion was accomplished by the same method used for Edging 1. In the lower half, the second border of eyelets widens the piece; in the upper half, the outside decreases of the leaves are extra, narrowing the fabric.

Medallions are very useful shapes. They can be knit as allover patterns (as in Pattern 29), as motifs within other patterns, or as isolated shapes floating in a plain or patterned ground. You can knit them by themselves, as is the case with the medallion in the photo at right, and attach them to other fabrics. This was often done with lace curtains in the Victorian era. If you make lots of separate medallions, you can join them together as blocks for bedcovers.

You can make this medallion into a flat, star-shaped mat, as for a doily, by knitting five repeats in a circle. After Row 50, where decreasing begins, knit the upper half of each of the five repeats separately on two needles. If you added a ground pattern between the points of

the upper half, you could knit the entire star circularly. You can also use the medallion as a single motif in a larger fabric or repeat it as an allover pattern using one of the allover arrangements shown on pp. 139-142. For another medallion, you could extract the whole motif of Pattern 29.

The medallion is shaped by extra eyelets on both sides of its lower half and extra decreases on both sides of its upper half.

Medallion

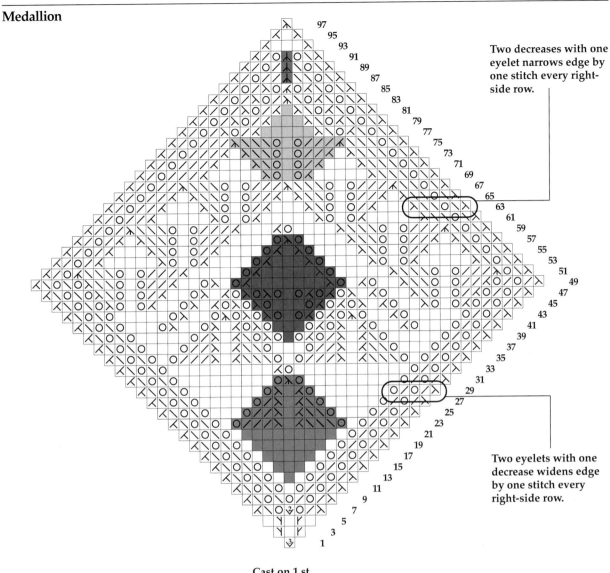

97
95
93
91
89
87
85
83
81
79
77
75
73
71
69
67
65
63
61
59
57
55
53
51
49
47
45
43
41
39
37
35
33
31
29
27
25
23
21
19
17
15
13
11
9
7
5
3
1

Two decreases with one
eyelet narrows edge by
one stitch every right-
side row.

Two eyelets with one
decrease widens edge
by one stitch every
right-side row.

Cast on 1 st.
Repeat: 49 sts, 98 Rs at greatest
  width and height
Even Rs: P all sts.

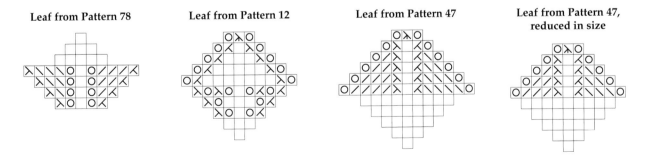

Leaf from Pattern 78   Leaf from Pattern 12   Leaf from Pattern 47   Leaf from Pattern 47,
                                                                          reduced in size

(Medallion pattern continued)
Even Rs 2-98 (wrong side): P all sts.

⊠ = ssk, return st to L ndl, pnso, return st to R ndl.

⊠ = P2tog, then sl 1 st kwise. Return both sts to L ndl, psso, return to R ndl.

Cast on 1 st.
Row 1: p1, k1, p1 into st. **Row 3:** k1 into back of 1st st in R below, k the next 3 sts on the ndl, k1 into the back of the last st in R below. **Row 5:** k1, k1 into back of 2nd st in R below, k the next 3 sts on the ndl, k1 into the back of the next-to-last st in R below, k1. **Row 7:** ssk, k1, yo, k1 into front, then k1 into back of same st, yo, k1, k2tog. **Row 9:** ssk, {k1, yo} 3 times, k1, k2tog. **Row 11:** ssk, {k1, yo} 4 times, k1, k2tog. **Row 13:** ssk, {k1, yo} 2 times, k3, {yo, k1} 2 times, k2tog. **Row 15:** ssk, {k1, yo} 2 times, k5, {yo, k1} 2 times, k2tog. **Row 17:** ssk, {k1, yo} 2 times, k7, {yo, k1} 2 times, k2tog. **Row 19:** ssk, {k1, yo} 2 times, k9, {yo, k1} 2 times, k2tog. **Row 21:** ssk, {k1, yo} 2 times, k11, {yo, k1} 2 times, k2tog. **Row 23:** ssk, {k1, yo} 3 times, k3, k2tog, k1, ssk, k3, {yo, k1} 3 times, k2tog. **Row 25:** ssk, {k1, yo} 2 times, k3, yo, k2, k2tog, k1, ssk, k2, yo, k3, {yo, k1} 2 times, k2tog. **Row 27:** ssk, {k1, yo} 2 times, k5, yo, k1, k2tog, k1, ssk, k1, yo, k5, {yo, k1} 2 times, k2tog. **Row 29:** ssk, {k1, yo} 2 times, k7, yo, k2tog, k1, ssk, yo, k7, {yo, k1} 2 times, k2tog. **Row 31:** ssk, {k1, yo} 2 times, k9, yo, sl 1-k2tog-psso, yo, k9, {yo, k1} 2 times, k2tog. **Row 33:** ssk, {k1, yo} 2 times, k11, yo, k2tog, k10, {yo, k1} 2 times, k2tog. **Row 35:** ssk, {k1, yo} 3 times, {k3, k2tog, k1, ssk, k3, yo, k1, yo} 2 times, k1, yo, k1, k2tog.

Row 37: ssk, {k1, yo} 2 times, {k3, yo, k2, k2tog, k1, ssk, k2, yo} 2 times, k3, {yo, k1} 2 times, k2tog. **Row 39:** ssk, {k1, yo} 2 times, k5, yo, k1, k2tog, k1, ssk, k1, yo, k2tog, yo, k1, yo, ssk, yo, k1, k2tog, k1, ssk, k1, yo, k5, {yo, k1} 2 times, k2tog. **Row 41:** ssk, {k1, yo} 2 times, k2, {k1, yo, k2tog, k1} 2 times, ssk, yo, k2tog, yo, k3, yo, ssk, yo, k2tog, {k1, ssk, yo, k1} 2 times, k2, {yo, k1} 2 times, k2tog. **Row 43:** ssk, {k1, yo} 2 times, k5, yo, k2tog, k2, yo, sl 1-k2tog-psso, yo, {k2tog, yo} 2 times, k1, {yo, ssk} 2 times, yo, sl 1-k2tog-psso, yo, k2, ssk, yo, k5, {yo, k1} 2 times, k2tog. **Row 45:** ssk, {k1, yo} 2 times, k2tog, yo, k1, yo, ssk, k2, yo, k2tog, k1, ssk, yo, {k2tog, yo} 2 times, k3, {yo, ssk} 2 times, yo, k2tog, k1, ssk, yo, k2, k2tog, yo, k1, yo, ssk, {yo, k1} 2 times, k2tog. **Row 47:** ssk, {k1, yo} 2 times, k2tog, k1, yo, k1, yo, k1, ssk, k2, yo, k2tog, k1, ssk, yo, {k2tog, yo} 2 times, k1, {yo, ssk} 2 times, yo, k2tog, k1, ssk, yo, k1, yo, k1, ssk, {yo, k1} 2 times, k2tog. **Row 49:** ssk, {k1, yo} 2 times, k2tog, k2, yo, k1, yo, k2, ssk, k2, yo, k2tog, k1, yo, ssk, k7, k2tog, yo, k1, ssk, yo, k2, k2tog, k2, yo, k1, yo, k2, ssk, {yo, k1} 2 times, k2tog. **Row 51:** ssk, k1, yo, sl 1-k2tog-psso, k3, yo, k1, yo, k3, ssk, k5, yo, ssk, k5, k2tog, yo, k5, k2tog, k3, yo, k1, yo, k3, ⊠, yo, k1, k2tog.
Row 53: ssk, k1, yo, k1, ssk, k5, k2tog, yo, k1, yo, ssk, k4, yo, ssk, k3, k2tog, yo, k4, k2tog, yo, k1, yo, ssk, k5, k2tog, k1, yo, k1, k2tog. **Row 55:** ssk, k1, yo, k1, ssk, k3, k2tog, {k1, yo} 2 times, k1, ssk, k4, yo, ssk, k1, k2tog, yo, k4, k2tog, {k1, yo} 2 times, k1, ssk, k3, k2tog, k1, yo, k1, k2tog. **Row 57:** ssk, k1, yo, k1, ssk, k1, k2tog, k2, yo, k1, yo, k2, ssk, k4, yo, sl 1-

k2tog-psso, yo, k4, k2tog, k2, yo, k1, yo, k2, ssk, k1, k2tog, k1, yo, k1, k2tog. **Row 59:** ssk, k1, yo, k1, ⊠, k3, yo, k1, yo, k3, ssk, k4, yo, {k2tog, k3} 2 times, yo, k1, yo, k3, sl 1-k2tog-psso, k1, yo, k1, k2tog. **Row 61:** ssk, k1, yo, k2, ssk, k5, {k2tog, yo, k1, yo, ssk, k5} 2 times, k2tog, k2, yo, k1, k2tog. **Row 63:** ssk, k1, yo, k2, ssk, k3, {k2tog, k1, yo, k1, yo, k1, ssk, k3} 2 times, k2tog, k2, yo, k1, k2tog. **Row 65:** ssk, k1, {yo, k2, ssk, k1, k2tog, k2, yo, k1} 3 times, k2tog. **Row 67:** ssk, k1, yo, k2, ⊠, {k3, yo, k1, yo, k3, sl 1-k2tog-psso} 2 times, k2, yo, k1, k2tog. **Row 69:** ssk, k1, yo, k3, ssk, k5, k2tog, yo, k1, yo, ssk, k5, k2tog, k3, yo, k1, k2tog. **Row 71:** ssk, k1, yo, k3, ssk, k3, k2tog, {k1, yo} 2 times, k1, ssk, k3, k2tog, k3, yo, k1, k2tog. **Row 73:** ssk, k1, yo, k3, ssk, k1, k2tog, k2, {yo, k1} 2 times, k1, ssk, k1, k2tog, k3, yo, k1, k2tog. **Row 75:** ssk, k1, yo, k3, ⊠, k3, {yo, k1} 2 times, k2, sl 1-k2tog-psso, k3, yo, k1, k2tog. **Row 77:** ssk, k1, yo, k1, k2tog, yo, k1, ssk, k5, k2tog, k1, yo, ssk, k1, yo, k1, k2tog. **Row 79:** ssk, k1, yo, k1, k2tog, yo, k1, ssk, k3, k2tog, k1, yo, ssk, k1, yo, k1, k2tog. **Row 81:** ssk, k1, yo, k1, k2tog, yo, k1, ssk, k1, k2tog, k1, yo, ssk, k1, yo, k1, k2tog. **Row 83:** ssk, k1, yo, k1, k2tog, yo, k1, sl 1-k2tog-psso, k1, yo, ssk, k1, yo, k1, k2tog. **Row 85:** ssk, k1, yo, k1, k2tog, yo, ⊠, yo, ssk, k1, yo, k1, k2tog. **Row 87:** ssk, k1, yo, k2, ⊠, k2, yo, k1, k2tog. **Row 89:** ssk, k1, yo, k1, ⊠, k1, yo, k1, k2tog. **Row 91:** ssk, k1, yo, ⊠, yo, k1, k2tog. **Row 93:** ssk, k3, k2tog. **Row 95:** ssk, k1, k2tog. **Row 97:** sl 1-k2tog-psso.
Rep Rs 1-98.

Charting from written instructions

One of the best reasons to understand chartmaking for knitted lace is that it enables you to convert written instructions to visual form. For many knitters, lines and lines — even pages — of type full of abbreviations, brackets, asterisks and numbers are thoroughly daunting. Fortunately, you don't have to let long written instructions kill your desire to knit lace. You can convert these instructions to charts.

I love to scout publications from the Victorian Era for knitted lace. Many of the patterns have lengthy written instructions, often with errors. One reason for the errors is that many patterns were carelessly translated or copied from other sources. Oftentimes those sources were the charted patterns in French and German publications. The charted patterns were written out and published in magazines and booklets for British and American gentlewomen. Who knows whether these ladies might have preferred the charts, had not the publishers turned these beautiful patterns into wordy puzzles, thus establishing the tradition of written-out knitting patterns? But there are some beauties among them, especially the figurative patterns. The time you spend charting the pattern is worthwhile, because in the process you'll find and correct many of the errors.

Your first attempts at charting from written instructions should be with patterns that create parallel selvedges, such as allover patterns, a decorative insertion, a rectangular table mat or lace curtains knitted straight from beginning to end. Coping with shaped edges, such as those for edgings, a circular doily, or a lace collar, can be confusing until you have some practice.

The pattern from the sampler that I'll walk you through is for an allover. Its written instructions are at right. After you have finished charting it, knit a swatch to check your chart. Then find the sampler pattern that looks like your swatch and compare the charts. Two other patterns that you might try charting on your own are patterns 16 and 58. They're a little more complicated, but nonetheless are typical patterns. Photocopy the written instructions to help yourself avoid the temptation to look at their charts.

Charting from written instructions

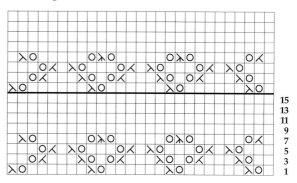

Written instructions
Multiple of 8 sts, plus 3
Even Rs 2-16 (wrong side): P all sts.

Row 1: k1, yo, *ssk, k6, yo*, ssk.
Row 3: k2, *yo, ssk, k3, k2tog, yo, k1*, k1.
Row 5: k2, *k1, yo, ssk, k1, k2tog, yo, k2*, k1.
Row 7: k1, k2tog, *yo, k5, yo, sl 1-k2tog-psso*, end last rep ssk, k1.
Row 9: k2, *k3, yo, ssk, k3*, k1.
Row 11: k2, *k1, k2tog, yo, k1, yo, ssk, k2*, k1.
Row 13: k2, *k2tog, yo, k3, yo, ssk, k1*, k1.
Row 15: k2, *k2, yo, sl 1-k2tog-psso, yo, k3*, k1.
Rep Rs 1-16.

At the beginning of written pattern instructions there is usually a statement about the stitch multiple, perhaps indicating some extra stitches for the selvedges. If there is no such statement, count the number of stitches within asterisks (or whatever denotes the repeat) in the first or last row of the repeat, plus the stitches outside the asterisks. See how many rows are in the repeat and whether the wrong-side rows are purled plain or are patterned.

1. On graph paper, draw a box containing the number of squares for at least three repeats in width, plus edge stitches, and two repeats in height. I chart this number of repeats because it allows me to see how they join together. In addition, three repeats in width accommodate any modified edge stitches at both sides and still give me a complete, unmodified repeat in the middle.

For the example, the box will be 27 squares wide (eight stitches times three repeats plus three edge stitches), as in the chart on p. 163. There are 16 rows in the repeat, but because the even rows are purled, you don't need to include them. That gives you a box 16 squares high (eight rows times two repeats).

2. Number the rows for one repeat—right-side rows numbered along the right side, wrong-side rows along the left.

In the example, the numbers will be odd numbers at the right side only, because the odd-numbered rows are right-side patterned rows. The even-numbered, wrong-side rows are purled, so they're omitted. Number the rows 1 through 15. Then draw a horizontal line across the box above Row 15 to divide the box into two repeats in height. You don't have to number the second repeat unless you want to. The vertical lines for the selvedges will be put in later.

3. Fill in the symbols exactly as the instructions tell you. Fill in right-side rows from right to left, wrong-side rows from left to right. On wrong-side rows, chart the symbols as the stitches will appear from the right side. In other words, if the instructions for a wrong-side row indicate to purl a stitch, chart it as a knit stitch; likewise, chart a knit stitch as a purl stitch. The direction of the decreases must be charted as the decreases appear on the front of the fabric. Use the Glossary of Symbols and Techniques (pp. 193-198) to cross-reference the instructions with their symbols. When you finish each row, double-check to see that the number of eyelets and decreases is balanced.

In the example there are only right-side rows, so fill in all of them from right to left. Fill in the edge stitch first, then the stitches for the repeat three times, and finally the edge stitches at the left. The chart on p. 163 shows the first four rows filled in.

Here are some hints in case you encounter problems filling in a chart. If the number of stitches in a gridded row is not what it should be, it is probably for one of four reasons. First, you may have skipped an abbreviation, read one twice, misplaced a bracket or an asterisk, or miscounted. These are the most common errors, so check carefully. Second, you may have misinterpreted an abbreviation or instruction. Instructions from older books often use words, symbols or abbreviations we aren't accustomed to or that now have a different meaning. Third, some rows of the pattern may be intended to have more stitches than others. In such cases there will often be several rows in succession with more or fewer stitches because of an extra eyelet or decrease. The companion decrease or eyelet will turn up in the row in which the stitch count changes again. Fourth, there may be an error in the instructions.

After checking the first two possibilities, check whether every eyelet in the row has a companion decrease, and vice versa. If not, circle the extra one and finish charting the repeat. Then count up all the eyelets and decreases throughout the repeat and make sure the numbers match. If they do, the companion for the extra eyelet or decrease is in a different row. If your eyelet-decrease count does not match, it's usually because of an error.

If you still have trouble finding the problem, pick up yarn and needles, cast on stitches for the number of squares on your grid, and knit to the point in question. The problem spot often becomes obvious when you actually see the formation of the lines of decreases and eyelets. Many times the error is in the edge stitches— a forgotten decrease, for example—so check these carefully as you knit. If the pattern looks great when you knit it, the inconsistency may be due to the third reason—that some rows are meant to have more stitches. Finish knitting the repeat so you can see the whole pattern. If it still looks good, widen your box to accommodate the row with the greatest number of stitches. Blacken unneeded squares in the rows with fewer stitches, positioning them so that the decreases and eyelets are aligned as much as possible the way they appear in the knitting. Double-check that all the eyelets and decreases balance between the beginning and end of the repeat.

4. Draw a box around one repeat in width and height. Position this box as close to the right side as you can, without including any modified stitches for the right selvedge. The number of edge stitches to the right of the box does not have to correspond with the edge-stitch count given in the written instructions, nor do the first and the last stitch in your box have to correspond with the first and the last stitch in the repeat in the written instructions. Mark off edge stitches for the right side by extending the line for the right side of the repeat box up to the top of the chart. Count across the center and left repeats and draw another vertical line between the left repeat and any remaining stitches for the left selvedge. If the left repeat includes some modified stitches for the selvedge, write "modified" below that repeat.

Sometimes, especially in large patterns, the right selvedge has so many modified stitches that there is room on the chart for only two repeats in width with a great many edge stitches left over. In these cases it is best to move the repeat box into the middle of the chart with room for one repeat at each side marked "modified."

In the example, the first column of squares at the right has no symbols, and the second column has a modified decrease on Row 7. Mark off these two columns as edge stitches. The repeat box will start with the third column. Draw a box around eight squares in width and height. Count off eight squares for the middle repeat and eight more for the left repeat. There is one square left over, which will be the left edge stitch. Mark off this column with a vertical line. Check whether there are any modified stitches in the left repeat. In the example there is one on Row 7. Write "modified st" under the left repeat.

5. Knit a swatch to check your chart. Cast on the number of squares in the width of the chart and check each square row by row as you knit. Feel free to make modifications, especially in the types of decreases. If you have charted an old pattern, you probably will want to modify decreases. Today we are more sophisticated at layering stitches for the exact effect we want than were the knitters of even 50 years ago.

Charting from a knitted piece

Charting from a knitted piece, or a photograph of it, is an adventure. It begins with the quest for beautiful knitting, for you never know what you will encounter or what technical nuance you will discover. Setting off on this adventure, equipped as we are with a knowledge of pattern building, will show how far we knitters have come from the "words writ in stone" of the Victorian Era pattern booklets.

The adventure begins for me when I go to museums, antique shows or secondhand shops. I nearly always take my camera in case I see an intriguing piece of old knitting that I want to try to reproduce in whole or part. If you'd like to do this too, first make sure that photography is allowed. Most museums will allow photography without flash, so load your camera with high-speed film. Then, with the piece in the best light possible, get as close as you can. If it is a light-colored lace piece and you are allowed to handle it, lay it on a dark background so the eyelets will show up to best advantage. As much as is safe, stretch the piece to open the eyelets, for they are the first key to the pattern. The lines of decreases are the second key; they usually show up best if the light is at an angle.

You need one shot that shows the whole piece, or at least one selvedge, especially if that selvedge is scalloped, indicating a bias pattern; one shot that shows several repeats in width and height, so you can see how the motifs are arranged and the repeats joined together; and a close-up shot of one or two repeats so that every stitch is clear. If possible, photograph both sides—the wrong side can often clarify what the pattern is doing on the right side. If you're able to take all these pictures, you can thank your luck and good fortune. Sometimes you can't get any closer than the wall of glass separating you from the beautiful baby clothes on the equally beautiful bedcover that is part of a period room in a museum, but do the best you can.

When I charted the patterns in this sampler, I worked from 8-in. by 10-in. black-and-white enlargements of the fronts and backs of the sampler patterns, two or three patterns per photo. The photographs enlarged each pattern to more than twice its actual size. Thus the task of charting was much easier than if I had worked from the sampler itself, which has such minuscule stitches that I would have had to use constant magnification under strong light. An old textile like this one can be quite frail and should not be handled or exposed to light excessively. If I had any doubts about a pattern's chart, I looked at the sampler under magnification just long enough to check the pattern.

As with your first attempts at translating written instructions, choose a piece that has an allover pattern or a piece with parallel selvedges, such as an insertion or a panel from a larger piece of knitting. If you are working from a photograph, enclose it in a transparent sheet protector. You can mark on this with a colored marker to clarify decreases, eyelets or whatever. If you have only a photograph of the front of the fabric to work from, you may have to do some guessing, since some of the design in the photograph may be out of focus and you won't have the wrong side to refer to. Be prepared to satisfy yourself with reproducing the general look of the pattern, and regard the details as your own creative improvements. Keep yarn and needles handy to try out various alternatives, and remember, this is an adventure.

To work from an actual piece, you need a magnifying glass, pins to stretch out portions of the design and to use as markers, and a board covered with a dark cloth to serve as a contrasting background and pin stabilizer. Wrap the parts of the piece you are not looking at in cloth so that they stay clean, protected and safely out of the way.

General procedures

I don't enjoy counting stitches any more than I enjoy reading wordy knitting patterns, and so the methods I use to decipher a knitted fabric avoid stitch counting until absolutely necessary. I may have to peer at a decrease for several minutes to figure out how it is layered, but that's less dizzying than counting stitches.

First determine whether all the wrong-side rows are purled without patterning or whether they contain eyelets and decreases and are part of the pattern. The easiest way to do this is to look at a diagonal line of eyelets. When one thread separates them, both right-side and wrong-side rows are patterned; when there are two threads twisted twice, the wrong-side rows are plain. In the case of faggots, when the two threads between eyelets are twisted once, both rows are pattern rows; when they are twisted twice, the purl rows are plain.

Look also at the diagonal lines of decreases. When there is a vertical stitch separating each decrease and the angle of the diagonal is steep (about 66°), the decreases are on the right-side rows only. When the decreases are very close together and march in a straight line at a less steep angle (about 33°), they are on both right-side and wrong-side rows.

Start charting by positioning the eyelets on the graph for two or three repeats in width. Eyelets form the skeleton of the pattern and are usually highly visible and easy to count. Then put in the decreases either adjacent to the eyelets or, if there are bias stitches, on the other side of the bias stitches. When there are bias stitches, you will know that the decrease at one side of the sloping stitches and the eyelet at the other side are paired. If you are unsure what kind of decrease it is or exactly which square it belongs in, just place a mark in the approximate position to indicate that it is a decrease. As you progress, you'll be able to clarify the decreases.

Working with several repeats on the grid enables you to see the pattern clearly and allows you to mark alternative ideas on different repeats until you can knit the pattern and find out the answers for sure. It also gives you enough pattern for dealing with the selvedges later on.

Use the sampler and its charts, as well as the chevron swatch and its charts in Chapter 2, as resources of patterning techniques. You can save time by finding a section of the sampler or the chevron swatch that looks similar to what you're charting, because you can examine its chart to see how the pattern was achieved.

When you are satisfied that all the eyelets and decreases are in place, check that they balance in each row or, if you suspect that some rows have more stitches than others, in each repeat. Copy one whole repeat at least twice in height and three times in width, checking that the join between the repeats conforms to the piece you are working on.

Put in any other texture stitches, such as purled stitches, crossed stitches and so on. Then add stitches for selvedges, modify those already charted, or both. Draw a box around one repeat.

Knit a swatch and make corrections or modifications where needed. At this time you can determine the exact type of decreases used or modify them so they are layered in the best possible way for the pattern.

A sample case: Pattern 15

To put this procedure to work, we'll chart Pattern 15 from its photograph (shown above). Gather your charting materials, including a magnifying glass.

First make some observations about the pattern as a whole. You can see that it is patterned on the right-side rows only, because all the eyelets are separated from each other by a pair of threads twisted twice; the decreases on all the chevron shapes have a steep angle, and they alternate with vertical stitches along the tops of the chevrons. For comparison, look at the two swatches on p. 134, which are patterned on both right-side and wrong-side rows.

Note also that there are bias stitches in the center section, which means that an eyelet is separated from its decrease. If you pick any eyelet in this section and follow the adjacent row (not column) of stitches downward to the companion decrease, you'll see that they are not on the same horizontal plane, which is characteristic of all bias knitting. You can see also that this entire center section is made up of one pattern row repeated over several rows, because both the eyelets and the decreases are lined up vertically and are parallel. Finally, note that the chevrons as a group are similar to the one-stitch, diagonal-striped grounds found throughout the sampler, but that these are a little wider. If necessary, you can compare these chevrons to those in Pattern 17 from the sampler, which has similar chevrons, or to Pattern 13, whose chevrons look just like those in Pattern 15.

Charting Pattern 15 from its photograph

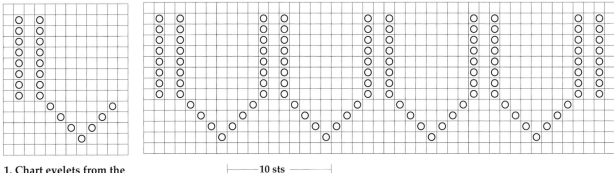

1. Chart eyelets from the center section and from one lower chevron.

2. Chart several columns of eyelet pairs and chevrons. Mark one repeat.

|—— 10 sts ——|

1. Start your chart by placing on the grid the eyelets of the center section, which is the easiest. There are eight pairs of eyelets in a vertical column—all of them except the bottom pair are separated by one plain stitch. The pair at the bottom is separated by a double decrease from the top of the chevron below. Pull out your magnifying glass and have a look. In some repeats the pair at the top of the columns is slightly hidden, due to the distortion of bias stitches changing to vertical stitches in that area. The photograph shows four columns, so if one column isn't very clear, look at another. Draw a column of eight pairs of eyelets on your grid. If you were working from a photograph in a sheet protector, you could color in the eyelets you've already charted, so that later you wouldn't count one of them again by mistake.

Next count the diagonal eyelets in the V that connects the bottom of one column of eyelet pairs to the bottom of the neighboring column of eyelet pairs. There are seven eyelets in the V; the fourth one is a pivot eyelet at the bottom. Put these on the grid, as shown in the chart above left.

2. Repeat the columns and V's three or four times. Count squares to determine the stitch repeat and mark it somewhere on the grid. It doesn't matter where yet; from one pivot eyelet to the next is a logical place.

Normally you would continue to install eyelets on the grid. But until we put in the centered pairs of decreases between the eyelet columns, we don't know exactly where to start the V-shape of the eyelets above, which begins just above the decreases. So, marking the decreases between the columns of eyelets is the next step.

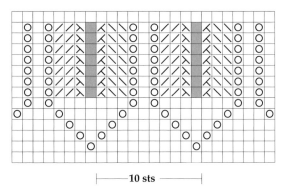

|—— 10 sts ——|

3. Chart the column of purl stitches, then the pair of decreases centered between the columns of eyelets. Mark the stitches between each eyelet and decrease with a bias symbol.

3. There are two columns of centered decreases that appear to be adjacent. We know that they are single decreases, not double, because one decrease is coupled with one of the eyelets in each pair. However, we cannot center a pair of adjacent decreases on our grid because there is an odd number of squares between the eyelet columns. Yet we know they are centered because they are poised directly above the pivot eyelet below. If you examine the pivot eyelet with a magnifying glass, you'll see that one column of stitches rises from it then disappears between the pairs of decreases. It reappears at the top of the decrease column as a pivot stitch for the chevron of eyelets that we haven't yet charted. Thus what appears to be a loose connection between the pairs of decreases may in fact be a purl stitch. Looking at the photo of the reverse side of the sampler on p. 3 confirms this— there is a column of knit stitches at exactly the spot in question. If you had only a photo of the front side to work with, you would have to confirm your guess later on by knitting a swatch.

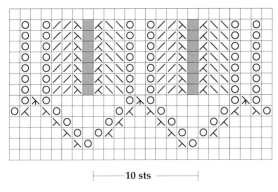

4. Add the decreases for the chevron of eyelets.

├──── 10 sts ────┤

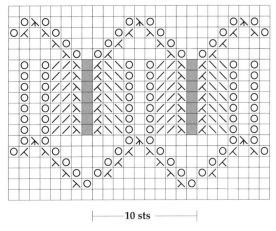

├──── 10 sts ────┤

5. Chart the chevrons centered above the columns of eyelets.

Put a column of seven gray squares (purl stitches) midway between the columns of eyelets, starting on the same row as the top pair of eyelets. There are only seven purl stitches, not eight, because the decrease for the bottom pair of eyelets is a double decrease between them, not single decreases at each side as in the pairs above. To each side of the purl stitches place the single decreases and two bias marks to show which decrease and eyelet are paired and that these stitches slant, as shown in the lower chart at right on the facing page. To determine in which direction each decrease is pointing, refer to the chevron swatch on p. 122, which is helpful for quick identification of eyelet/decrease relationships. Chevrons 6b and 7b both show eyelets along the edges of the chevron, and between them, a pair of decreases pointing opposite the direction of the bias, just as in our pattern.

4. Now you can add to the chart the decreases for the chevron of eyelets. You already know where the double decrease goes, and you can see that it points to the left. Put in the proper symbol between the eighth pair of eyelets at the bottom of the column, as in the chart at left, above. Add the decreases for each arm of the chevron, referring to the chevron swatch on p. 122 if you are unsure which direction they face. Chevron 1b looks just like the one we are working with, but without the top eyelet. Its chart (p. 123) even shows the left double decrease, in case you can't remember how to draw it. When you put in the decrease for the pivot eyelet at the bottom of the V, you have to decide whether it is a left or a right decrease. After examining the photograph, compare it to Chevron 1a in the chevron swatch. Before going any farther, make sure that each eyelet on your chart has a companion decrease and each decrease has an eyelet.

5. You can now put in the chevron of eyelets above the column of bias stitches. There are four eyelets in each arm of the V. Instead of a pivot eyelet, there is a pivot stitch directly above the column of purl stitches. To either side of the pivot stitch, immediately above the columns of decreases, are the first two eyelets at the bottom of the V. Place these two eyelets, then three more in each arm of the chevron, as shown in the chart above right. Note that between the top two eyelets there is a double decrease just like the one in the chevron below. Put it in. In fact, all the decreases are the same as those in the previous chevron except for the absence of the pivot eyelet.

6. You're almost finished. There are two more chevrons of eyelets at both the top and bottom of the pattern, spaced alike. The two lower chevrons are exact duplicates of the one below the eyelet columns that we charted earlier. The two upper chevrons are also like this one, since they include the pivot eyelet that is missing on the chevron we just finished. Filling in the rest of the chart will be easy—just copy the lower chevron.

As for the spacing between each zigzag line of chevrons, we can see that the chevrons aren't adjacent, since that would make them single-stitch chevrons like those in Pattern 17, and obviously they are not. So, for the first time in this exercise we will count stitches. In the photo, the best place to look is in the solid area between two diagonal lines of chevron eyelets, somewhere in the middle section between the pivot eyelets. Look at a row (not a column) of stitches between an eyelet and the decrease for the adjacent line of eyelets. You'll see the eyelet, then one stitch, then the two stitches that make up the decrease for the eyelet in the next line of chevron eyelets. This means

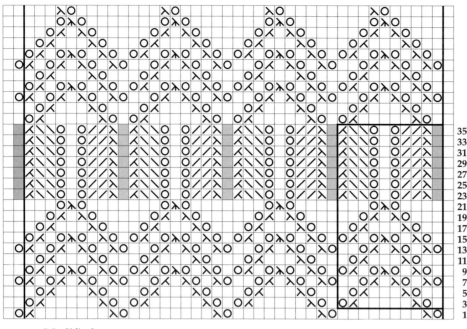

Modified sts

Repeat: 10 sts, 34 Rs.
Add 3 edge sts: 2 at L,
  1 at Rt.
Modified sts at L: Rs 1,
  7, 13.
Even Rs 2 - 22: P all sts.
Even Rs 24 - 36: P, but k
  single st between
  decreases (gray squares).

6. **Chart two more zigzag lines of chevrons. Box one repeat, number the rows and indicate modified stitches.**

that the eyelets of the arms of the chevrons are spaced one stitch and one decrease apart. In that case there is only one way to nest them, shown in the completed chart above. To see for yourself, trace the eyelets and decreases from at least two V's of the lower chevron in Step 5 and move the tracing three squares straight down. You'll see that no other position will produce one plain stitch and one decrease between the eyelets of the arms of the chevrons. If you like, compare this to the charted chevrons of Pattern 13.

Fill in the rest of your chart. Box one repeat. Write on the chart information about the repeat, the edge stitches, the modified stitches and any special instructions. If you need help with these steps, refer to the section on charting a pattern from scratch at the beginning of this chapter.

To complete my chart of Pattern 15, I put an eyelet at the top of the top chevrons, even though it does not appear in the sampler, in order to balance the eyelet at the bottom and complete the pattern so that it can be used as an insertion. To knit the pattern as an allover pattern of horizontal bands, use the repeat box to repeat the lower chevrons and center bias columns again and again. To improve the appearance of the chevrons at the left selvedge I mirrored the decreases for the last eyelets to make the two selvedges symmetrical, and marked this repeat "modified sts."

Other uses for lace knitting charts

Do you practice other needlework techniques? Most charted knitting patterns, and particularly those in this book, can be used as patterns for a variety of other needlework techniques simply by giving the symbols new interpretations. For example, assign various texture stitches to the symbols to create relief patterns for one-color knitting. Or assign a different color to each symbol and knit a multicolored pattern in a plain fabric. The girl's dress project and the two sock projects in Chapter 4 use this technique for the yoke and the decorative bands, respectively.

You needn't restrict yourself to hand knitting either. Some of the other techniques for which these charts would make suitable patterns are machine knitting (multicolored, textured or a combination); crochet; tapestry weaving; macramé; rug hooking and knotting on canvas; fabric appliqué and patchwork; openwork techniques such as filet netting, filet crochet, needle lace, withdrawn or deflected thread (drawn work) and Hardanger; and decorative embroidery techniques such as beading, crewel, cross-stitch, needlepoint, blackwork, Assisi and huck. The photos on the facing page show some swatches worked in other needlework techniques. All are based on Pattern 56 from the sampler.

Blackwork

Crochet

Pattern 56 was used as the pattern for all four of these needlework samples, and the symbols were given both color and texture interpretations, with the textures in each sample suitable for the particular technique. Clockwise from left: The blackwork sample is worked on perforated paper with cotton floss; the needlepoint sample is worked with tapestry wool on canvas; the machine-knitted sample is made in four-color rib jacquard with fine-weight Merino wool; the hand-knitted sample uses a bouncy worsted-weight yarn for its popcorns and twisted stitches; and the crocheted sample is made in fingering-weight sock yarn.

Needlepoint

Machine knitting

Hand knitting

CHAPTER 4

Using Lace Patterns: Four Projects

The sampler is a wonderful learning tool, but it's really just a starting point. Ultimately the goal is to incorporate the patterns and what you have learned from them in your own knitting. The four projects in this chapter use several of the sampler patterns and a variety of yarns to create a lady's pullover sweater, a little girl's dress, two pairs of socks, and a shawl made from leftover mohair yarns. Through these projects you'll discover ways of combining the sampler's patterns to enhance garment shapes.

Instructions are for hand knitting and, where appropriate, for knitting on the machine using hand transfers. The shaping instructions are written out in full, while the lace and other stitch patterns are presented in chart form. Written instructions for the lace patterns can be found with their pattern numbers in Part I.

Explanations for the abbreviations used in the written instructions can be found on pp. 193-198, and instructions on how to read the charts begin on p. 191. An explanation of how to use the sampler charts to knit the patterns on the machine can be found in the Machine Knitters' Glossary on pp. 199-204.

Lady's pullover

For years I have wanted to knit myself an Aran pullover and to sit for hours enjoying a chartful of texture. Well, it has been years and I haven't done it yet, but I satisfied the urge with this sweater, which uses patterns 3, 5, 17, 29 and 62 from the sampler. This is a tightly knitted outdoor sweater made in durable, oiled Shetland wool. It is knitted on small needles, so that I could fit in as much pattern as possible. It is quite windproof—the lace eyelets simply provide ventilation. The shape is loose fitting, with deep armholes and dropped shoulders so you can wear it over other clothes. But it isn't a T-shape. It has an armhole and a shallow sleeve cap to get rid of the underarm bagginess that dropped-shoulder sweaters are prone to have. The blue-gray color with lavender and green overtones is a medium shade that shows off the texture of the cables and eyelets.

You can, of course, knit the sweater in a yarn other than Shetland, and this is probably the best way to alter the size. Using the same type of yarn that I did but with bigger needles will also make a larger size. Since the most important parts of the design are in the middle of the chart, you can also easily shave off or tack on stitches or rows if you need to.

Five lace patterns from the museum sampler are used in this elaborately textured V-neck pullover.

The charts on pp. 176-177 show the right half and center portions of each piece. For the remainder of the left side, mirror the right side of the chart. You can see that the cable turns and the decreases of Pattern 3 in the neck area are mirrored, but that the diamonds of patterns 5 and 17 and the trefoil spot design from Pattern 62 are simply repeated on the left side; their decreases are not mirrored. Pattern 29, in the lower center and also on the sleeve, is already mirrored. Although the back neck is knitted straight across, it scoops because Pattern 3 creates bias in the fabric. At one side of the midline of the back neck, all the decreases are to the left of their eyelets, and on the other side they are to the right.

Only the right-side rows are given on the charts. On the wrong side, knit and purl the stitches as you see them on the needle. The cables are turned at six-row intervals, from the right side, throughout the garment.

Special instructions for the knitting machine are not given with this pullover. The complexity of the lace pattern plus the quantity of purl stitches mixed with cables make this garment easier (and probably faster) to knit by hand. However if you'd like to tackle it, I suggest modifying the purl stitches and changing most of them to knit stitches. The knitting procedures for the shaping of the pieces would be the same as for hand knitters, and you can simply follow the chart.

Schematic for lady's pullover

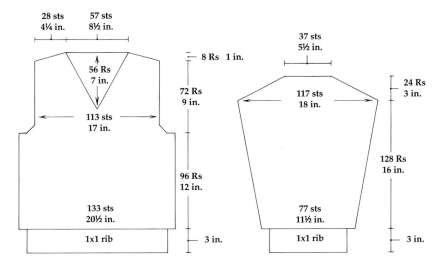

Instructions for lady's pullover

SIZE Medium, to fit a 34-in. to 36-in. bust.

MATERIALS Oiled Shetland-style yarn, 100% wool in fingering/sport-weight size, approximately 21 oz. (595 g). Ndls, size U.S. 4 (3½mm). Smaller ndls for ribs. Short cable ndl.

GAUGE In stockinette st, after washing (see instructions below): 6½ sts, 8 Rs = 1 in.

BACK With smaller ndls, cast on 123 sts and k 3 in. in k1, p1 rib. On the last R (from wrong side), inc 10 sts evenly spaced across R. With larger ndls, start following chart for both shaping and pattern. Shoulders can be shaped either by short Rs or by binding off sts. At end, put back-neck sts on holders.

FRONT K same as back except for neckline. Follow V-shaped outline, as shown on chart. You can make shaping full-fashioned by combining neckline decs with decs along edge of diamond shapes (there are 5 in a diagonal line for each diamond), turning latter decs into double decs. You will still need a single dec on Rs between diamonds (6th R).

SLEEVE With smaller ndls, cast on 67 sts and k 3 in. in k1, p1 rib. On last R (from wrong side), inc 10 sts evenly spaced across R. With larger ndls, start following chart for both shaping and patterning. You can make full-fashioned incs on sides by inc 3 sts in from each edge, as there is no lace pattern

until 4th st from edge. Shape sleeve cap either by short Rs or by binding off sts. At end, put last R of sts on holders or bind them off.

NECKBAND Join one shoulder. With smaller ndls, pick up approximately 140 sts around neck. K 8 Rs in k1, p1 rib. Simultaneously, at point of V, dec 1 st each side of a pivot st every R. Bind off in rib. Join other shoulder and sew neckband seam. Set in sleeves by grafting or backstitch, or by your favorite method. Sew side and underarm seams with mattress st (see p. 116).

WASHING OILED SHETLAND WOOL Use a mild detergent or soap and, for both washing and rinsing, lukewarm water. Dishwashing liquid or hair shampoo works well for the first washing; don't use a wool-wash compound because it will not remove the oil in the wool. Soak the pullover in washing water for a few minutes, then knead it gently, without rubbing or a lot of sudsing up and down. The water will become quite discolored. Rinse several times to get out all the soap. You can add a little fabric softener or hair conditioner to the last rinse if you like. To remove excess water, spin the sweater in the washer or roll it in a towel, then lay it out to dry. After drying, give the sweater a shot of steam where needed. With the oil removed, the yarn will fluff and fill in spaces between stitches. After this first washing, use the type of washing solution you normally do for your best woolens.

Lady's pullover

Front and back

Outline for front V-neck

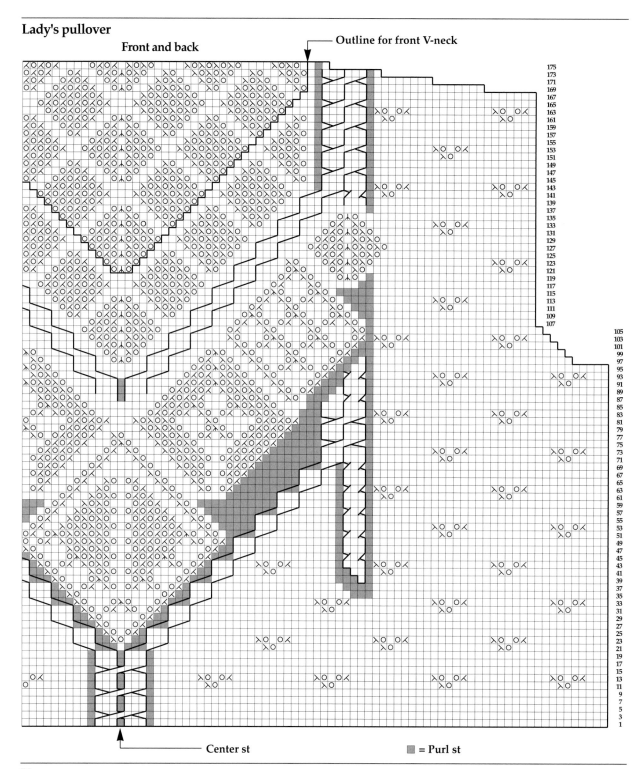

Center st

■ = Purl st

Key

L   Rt

Rt = sl 1 st onto extra ndl and hold in back of work; k next 2 sts, then k held st.
L = sl 2 sts onto extra ndl and hold in front of work; k next st, then k held sts.

Rt

Rt = sl 4 sts onto extra ndl and hold in back of work; k next 3 sts, then p1, k3 off extra ndl.

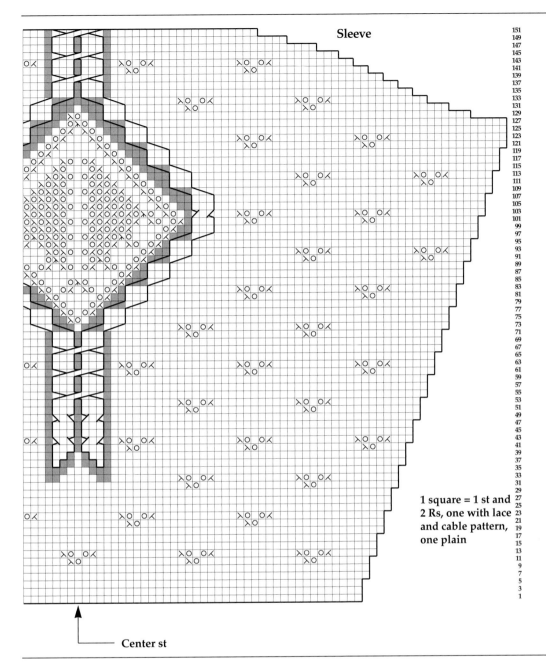

Sleeve

151
149
147
145
143
141
139
137
135
133
131
129
127
125
123
121
119
117
115
113
111
109
107
105
103
101
99
97
95
93
91
89
87
85
83
81
79
77
75
73
71
69
67
65
63
61
59
57
55
53
51
49
47
45
43
41
39
37
35
33
31
29
27
25
23
21
19
17
15
13
11
9
7
5
3
1

1 square = 1 st and
2 Rs, one with lace
and cable pattern,
one plain

Center st

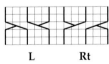

L   Rt

Three-st plain cable (see Symbol 12 in Glossary of Symbols and Techniques on p. 195)

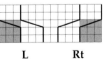

L   Rt

Rt = sl 3 sts onto extra ndl, hold in back of work; k next 3 sts, then k held sts.
L = sl 3 sts onto extra ndl, hold in front of work; k next 3 sts, then k held sts.

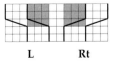

L   Rt

Rt = sl 3 sts onto extra ndl, hold in back of work; k next 3 sts, then p held sts.
L = sl 3 sts onto extra ndl, hold in front of work; p next 3 sts, then k held sts.

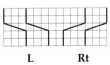

L   Rt

Rt = sl 3 sts onto extra ndl, hold in back of work; k next 3 sts, then k held sts.
L = sl 3 sts onto extra ndl, hold in front of work; k next 3 sts, then k held sts.

Little girl's dress

A pretty dress for a little girl is always appreciated by her mother, even if the child could care less. And mothers like it even better when the dress is sturdy and easy to launder.

I will knit a dress for a quickly growing child only if I think it will be an everyday sort of dress that will get a lot of use. Many people think lace is always dressy, but I don't agree. With careful choice of yarn, color and trims, you can dress it up or down. This dress is knitted in a cabled acrylic yarn that is wonderful for easy-care lace clothing, in a medium shade of jade, trimmed with shades of blue and lavender. The pattern for both the skirt and the yoke is from Pattern 40 of the museum sampler. The yoke is knitted in two-color stranded knitting (fairisle technique on the

machine), with the plain squares on the special chart knitted in aquamarine and the symboled squares in jade. The sleeves and the lower portion of the skirt are knitted in Pattern 8, which is the small diamond-ground pattern that surrounds the polka dots of Pattern 40.

Since the lace patterns are so open, I used quite small needles in order to tighten the stitches and give the fabric some body. This also reduces the possibility of snags in the fabric, so that the active child can do what children do without her mother worrying about damage to the dress.

In the charts for patterns 8 and 40 in Part I, the repeats of the two patterns are offset by one stitch. In the charts given here, Pattern 8's repeat and selvedge stitches have been adjusted so that the transition from one pattern to the other will be smooth.

Schematic for little girl's dress

Skirt and bodice, front and back

21 sts   28 sts   21 sts
3 in.   4 in.   3 in.

-10x1; -11x1 e.o.r.

4 R ½ in.

-2 e.o.r.x3

-16 sts

34 R 4 in.

20 Rs

Two-color pattern

70 sts   Border pattern

¾ in.

-1 e.o.r.x4

-4

94 sts

12 Rs 1½ in.

96 Rs
13 in.

Pattern 40

24 Rs
3¼ in.

Pattern 8

Border pattern

1 in.

110 sts 19¾ in.

Sleeve

-2 e.o.r.x2

38 sts 7 in.

4 Rs ½ in.

-1 e.o.r.x12

28 Rs 3¾ in.

-4

Pattern 8

+2

8 Rs 1 in.

74 sts 13 in.

↓ Border pattern ↓

40 sts

Pattern 8, adjusted

7
5
3
1

Repeat: 6 sts, 8 Rs
Add 4 edge sts: 2
  each side.
Even Rs: P all sts.

Pattern 40, two-color version

12
10
8
6
4
2

11
9
7
5
3
1

Repeat: 18 sts, 12 Rs

■ = MC
□ = CC2

Pattern 40

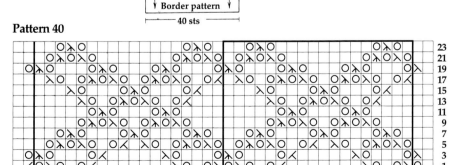

23
21
19
17
15
13
11
9
7
5
3
1

Pattern 40
Repeat: 18 sts, 24 Rs.
Add 4 edge sts: 2 each side.
Even Rs: P all sts.

Instructions for little girl's dress

SIZE   To fit a 24-in. chest. You can easily adjust size by knitting number of sts and Rs given but using larger or smaller ndls (especially for yoke) to achieve a larger or smaller gauge. Measurements for each part of dress are on the diagram on p. 179 in case you want to make other adjustments.

MATERIALS   Coats & Clark "Luster Sheen" (article A.94) 6-ply cabled, 100% Creslan acrylic, in 2-oz. (56.7-g) pull skeins, approx. 173 yd. (158m) per skein. Colors: 5 skeins of MC (#650 jade); 1 skein each of CC1 (#850 blueberry), CC2 (#678 aquamarine), CC3 (#122 light lilac). Any other soft, cabled yarn with a sheen and of comparable weight would be suitable. Four ⅜-in. buttons with shanks. Ndls size U.S. 3 (3.25mm). Crochet hook size 2mm.

FOR MACHINE KNITTING   Standard-gauge machine with fairisle capability for two-color version of Pattern 40 in yoke. Set machine for fairisle technique for this section of knitting. If yours is an electronic machine, you can program the 18-st pattern. If it has a lace-transfer carriage, you can also translate both lace patterns to programs. Otherwise, hand-select and hand-transfer patterns. Refer to your machine's manual for turning sts to make garter-st ridges, or use a garter-bar accessory.

GAUGE   In lace version of Pattern 40, after stretching and *light* steaming: 1 rep of 18 sts, 24 Rs = 3¼ in. sq.; or 5.5 sts, 7.38 Rs = 1 in. In two-color pattern: 7 sts, 8 Rs = 1 in. *Note: Do not use too much heat or steam, as this yarn is acrylic and too much steam can easily damage it. You want only enough to make fabric relax and set sts. After this initial treatment, dress should go through washer and dryer without further attention.*

BORDER PATTERN   The border pattern begins and ends with a specified number of ridges of garter st (1 ridge = 2 Rs).

SIX-ROW BEADING WITHIN THE BORDER
By hand: With CC2 (for skirt) or CC3 (for yoke and sleeve), k 1 R, p 1 R. With CC1, *k1, sl 1 wyib*. On the return R, *p1, sl 1 wyif (sl same st as in previous R)*. With CC2 (for skirt) or CC3 (for yoke and sleeve), k 1 R, p 1 R. **By machine:** With CC2 (for skirt) or CC3 (for yoke and sleeve), k 2 Rs. With CC1, set carr for hold pos, put e.o.n. to h.p., k 2 Rs. Push ndls back so they will be ready to k next R. With CC2 (for skirt) or CC3 (for yoke and sleeve), k 2 Rs.

Note: Special instructions for machine knitters are given in brackets [ ].

SKIRT FRONT AND BACK   K 2 pieces alike. **Lower border:** With CC1, loosely cast on 110 sts and k 3 ridges in garter st, ending on wrong side. With CC2 and CC1, k 6-R beading. With CC1, k 2 ridges in garter st, ending on wrong side. **Main fabric:** With MC, start Pattern 8, knitting 4 reps, 32 Rs. Change to Pattern 40, begin with R 9 on chart, and continue for remainder of skirt, repeating this pattern in its full 24-R rep.

ARMHOLES   After 96 Rs in Pattern 40, bind off 4 sts at beginning of next 2 Rs. Dec 1 st each side e.o.r. until 94 sts remain on ndl. **By hand:** K straight until 11 Rs have been worked from 1st bind-off R, ending on right side. For 12th R (wrong side) dec as follows: *p2tog, p2* across, ending p2tog. You should now have 70 sts. Continue with yoke. **By machine:** Continue straight to the 12th row after initial bind-off. Remove onto waste yarn. To prepare for front yoke, rehang onto 70 ndls as follows: Put *2 sts on one ndl, 1 st on each of next 2 ndls* all across, remove waste yarn. For back yoke, hang only half sts at a time and k each half of yoke separately.

FRONT YOKE   K on 70 sts. With CC2, k 1 ridge of garter st. With CC3 and CC1 k 6-R beading. With CC2, k 1 ridge of garter st. Begin two-color pattern with MC and CC2. K straight in pattern for 20 Rs. **Divide for neck:** You can k 2 sides separately or join separate balls of yarn and k them simultaneously. Put center 16 sts onto a holder [waste yarn]. K 2 Rs in pattern. At neck edge, *dec 2 sts, k 2 Rs in pattern* 3 times. Continue straight until 34 Rs have been worked since start of pattern. **Shoulders:** At shoulder side, bind off or dec 10 sts once, k a R without decreasing, then bind off or put on a holder remaining 11 sts.

BACK YOKE   You can k 2 halves one at a time or simultaneously using 2 sets of yarns. The back opening extends height of entire yoke. On 1st or 2nd R, cast on 1 additional st to each half at point of opening, so that each half has 36 sts. K straight in pattern for 34 Rs. **Shoulders:** At shoulder side, bind off or dec 10 sts once, k a R in pattern, bind off or dec 11 sts once, k a R in pattern, bind off or put on a holder remaining 14 sts for back neck.

SLEEVE   K entirely in Pattern 8. K 2 pieces alike. You can k both sleeves at once using separate balls of yarn, or k them 1 at a time. [On machine, one sleeve requires a total width of 78 ndls.] Cast on 74 sts with an invisible cast on [waste yarn] that can be unraveled to pick up for sleeve band. With MC, k 8 Rs in pattern, at same time inc 1 st each side on the 3rd and 5th Rs. On 9th and 10th Rs, bind off 4 sts once, each side. K 2 Rs in pattern. Beginning with next R, dec 1 st each side e.o.r. 12 times. After 28th R from bind off, dec 2 sts e.o.r. twice, then bind off the remaining 38 sts. Before knitting on border, lay out sleeve, stretching fabric a little to open eyelets, and steam it lightly from wrong side.

BORDER   By hand: Unravel cast on and put 1st R of loops back onto ndl. With right side facing and CC2, k 3 sts, *k2tog* to within last 3 sts, k1 in each of last 3 sts (40 sts on ndl). Complete garter ridge, then k 1 more ridge. With CC3 and CC1, k 6-R beading. With CC2, k 3 ridges of garter st, binding off loosely in k sts on last R. **By machine:** With wrong side facing you, hang loops from 1st R onto 40 ndls, with 2 sts on every 4th ndl. Remove waste yarn. With CC2, k 1 R. Complete garter ridge, then k 1 more ridge. With CC3 and CC1, k 6-R beading. With CC2, k 3 ridges of garter st, binding off loosely in k sts on last R.

FINISHING   Before finishing front and back pieces, lay out skirt sections and steam them lightly from wrong side.

NECKBAND   Join front to back at shoulder seams [join 1 seam]. With CC1, pick up [hang onto ndls] approximately 75 sts from around neck and k in stockinette st for 10 Rs. Bind off all sts. Fold band to inside and sl st in place.

FACING AND BUTTON LOOPS   With CC1, pick up approximately 30 sts, including edge of neckband, along edge of left back yoke. K 4 ridges of garter st, bind off. With CC1, single crochet over selvedge st along edge of Rt back yoke and make 4 button loops as you go, with 1st just under neckband. To set in sleeves, run a gathering thread along top of sleeve cap to adjust gathers, then sew or crochet sleeve in place. Join side seams of skirt with mattress st (see p. 116).

Long and short socks

There are many ways to knit socks. Knitting them flat, the method given here, allows the socks to be knitted either by hand or by machine. Knitting socks flat, however, means that there's more sewing to do to finish them, so hand knitters can knit the leg circularly if they prefer. You can also knit the foot circularly, using the main yarn for the foot and one or two contrast colors for the heel and toe.

I made the heels, toes and soles of the socks shown on p. 182 so that I could disassemble the foot and reknit these parts if they wore a hole—I dislike spending the time to make a nice pair of socks that I can't repair easily. I made these parts in different colors so that I could tell where the shaping for the heel and toe begins and ends.

The heel and toe are made exactly alike, with short-row shaping. This is easy to do on a knitting machine, and I usually use short rows when knitting by hand, too. The shapings are smoother and the heels are not as thick as when they are shaped by other methods, which is an important consideration with a fairly bulky yarn such as this one. To reinforce the heel and toe, I used a fine-weight, transparent monofilament thread sold on a small cone and intended for sergers. It is readily available and does not add bulk. The worn places on your bought socks will probably show this kind of thread holding the web together.

The short socks are knitted from the bottom up since their lace pattern (Pattern 43) is a one-way design that can be knitted only that way. The long socks are knitted from the top down, but since their lace pattern (Pattern 25) can be oriented in either direction, they could also have been knitted from the bottom up. To knit either sock from the other direction, just turn the diagram upside down. The tops of both socks are decorated with color patterns knitted in stranded knitting (fairisle technique on the machine). The designs are derived from the lace pattern charts. Compare the fairisle chart with the lace chart to see how I converted the lace symbols into color symbols.

These playful socks are knitted with four colors of a cotton/acrylic-blend yarn. The short socks are based on Pattern 43, and the long socks are based on Pattern 25.

Instructions for socks

SIZE   Lady's average. Measurements for each part of each sock are marked on the schematics shown on the facing page and on p. 184.

MATERIALS   Pingouin "Corrida No. 3" 4-ply 60/40% cotton/acrylic, in 1¾ oz. (49.6 g) balls, 230 yd. (210m) per ball. Colors: MC (#312 Ecru/off-white), CC1 (#319 Lavande/medium blue), CC2 (#321 Chlorophylle/mint green), CC3 (#323 Capucine/light orange). For short socks, 1 ball each color. For long socks, 2 balls MC, 1 ball other colors. Any other soft, matte-finish cotton or blend of comparable weight would be suitable. Shirring elastic. Monofilament thread. Small crochet hook, about 2mm. Ndls size U.S. 2 (2.75mm). Smaller ndls for ribbing.

FOR MACHINE KNITTING   A standard-gauge machine with fairisle capability for two-color-per-row versions of patterns 43 and 25. Set machine for fairisle technique for this section of knitting. If yours is an electronic machine, you can program the 10-st patterns. If it has a lace-transfer carriage, you can also translate the lace patterns to a program. Otherwise, hand-select and hand-transfer patterns.

GAUGE   In stockinette st, before washing: 7 sts, 9 Rs = 1 in.

TWO-ROW BEADING   **By hand:** With new color, *k1, sl 1 wyib*. On return R, *p1, sl 1 wyif (sl same st as in previous R)*. **By machine:** Set carr for h.p., put e.o.n. to h.p., k 2 Rs with new color. Push ndls back so they will be ready to k next R in instructions.

Short socks

Note: Special instructions for machine knitters are given in brackets [ ].

HEEL (A)   Cast on 31 sts with an invisible cast-on [waste yarn] that can be unraveled for later grafting. With CC1, leave a long tail (for grafting to ankle), k 1 R, p 1 R [k 2 Rs]. Start short Rs in stockinette st, decreasing 1 st at end of each R until

Schematic for short socks

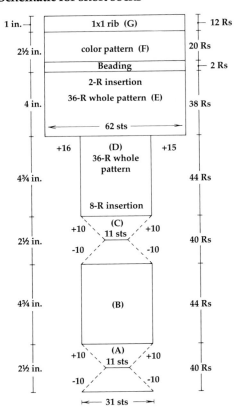

Pattern 43

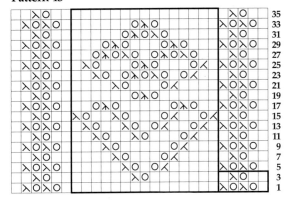

Flower repeat: 15 sts, 36 Rs.
Ground repeat: 5 sts, 4 Rs.
Combined repeat of 1 ground,
1 flower: 20 sts, 36 Rs.
Even Rs: P all sts.

Pattern 43, color version

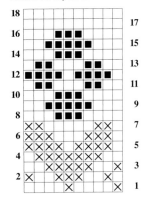

- □ = CC3
- ■ = CC1
- ☒ = CC2

Repeat: 10 sts, 18 Rs.

11 sts are left in middle (remember to "wrap" at end
of each R to prevent holes). Start increasing, 1 st at
end of every R until all sts have been knitted,
ending on wrong side (31 sts).

SOLE (B)   Starting with a right-side R, join CC2
and knit straight in 2-R stockinette stripes of CC2,
then CC1, until there are 11 stripes of each color.
Break off CC1.

TOE (C)   With CC2, follow instructions for heel
(A), starting with "k 1 R, p 1 R [knit 2 Rs]..." and
ending on wrong side (31 sts). Break off CC1.

INSTEP (D): Join MC. Start lace Pattern 43. You will
use 2 reps in width of insertion pattern and
between them, 1 of the flower pattern, for a total of
25 sts. At each selvedge are 3 plain sts for a total of
31 sts. Begin by knitting 2 reps in height (8 Rs) of
insertion, without flower. Then continuing insertion,
k 1 rep of flower (Rs 1-36 on Pattern 43 chart). After
finishing last R, cast on 15 additional sts at yarn
side with invisible cast-on [waste yarn]. This creates
open loops for later grafting to top of heel.

ANKLE (E)   K one more rep of pattern as follows:
At end of 1st R, cast on 16 additional sts with
invisible cast on [waste yarn]. P next R [k 1 R]; you
are ready for R 3 on chart. Incorporate new sts into
pattern, adding a flower plus part of insertion at
each side. Continue to end of rep, ending on
wrong side.

COLOR-PATTERN TOP (F)   Break off MC. With
CC1, make 2 beading Rs. K 2 Rs with CC3, then 18
Rs of color chart, centering a flower above each lace
flower and center eyelet in each insertion. Break all
CC yarns.

RIB (G)   Change to smaller ndls [smaller st size].
Join MC. K 12 Rs in k1, p1 rib. Bind off in rib. Cut
yarn, leaving a long tail for sewing up.

FINISHING Sew center back seam with mattress st (see p. 116). Graft heel and bottom of ankle together. Sew 2 side seams between instep and sole with mattress st. To add elastic, crochet it on inside of rib just below top edge. Use a loose sl st and catch 1 leg of every k st. It will take a little experimenting to find how tight you want it. Machine wash socks in warm water.

Long socks

Note: Special instructions for machine knitters are given in brackets [ ].

RIB (A) With smaller ndls and CC3, cast on 84 sts. K 10 Rs in k1, p1 rib. [Across a width of 84 ndls, use tubular cast-on for 1x1 rib. At smaller st size, k 10 Rs. Transfer sts for stockinette st.]

COLOR-PATTERN TOP (B) Break off CC3. With CC1 and CC2, k 12 Rs in color Pattern 25. Break off CC1 and CC2; join MC. With MC, k 1 R, p 1 R [k 2 Rs]. With CC3, make 2 beading Rs. With MC, k 1 R, p 1 R [k 2 Rs].

KNEE (C) Start lace Pattern 25 and k straight for 2 reps, 24 Rs.

CALF SHAPING (D) Continuing in pattern, at each side dec 1 st on next R, then every following 4th R 3 times; then every 6th R 6 times (9 sts dec each side, 48 Rs).

ANKLE (E) Continuing in pattern, at each side dec 1 more st on next R, then k straight for 15 Rs ending on wrong side. Opposite yarn side, remove 16 sts onto a holder [waste yarn]. K 1 R in pattern. Remove 16 sts at other side same way, p return R [k 1 R, make transfers].

INSTEP (F) K straight in pattern for 44 Rs. Break MC; join CC1.

TOE (G) With CC1, k 1 R, p 1 R [k 2 Rs]. Start short Rs in stockinette st, decreasing 1 st at end of each row until 12 sts are left in middle (remember to "wrap" at end of each R to prevent holes). Start increasing, 1 st at end of every row until all sts have been knitted, ending on wrong side.

SOLE (H) Break CC1; join CC2. K straight in stockinette stitch for 44 Rs. Break CC2; join CC1.

HEEL (I) With CC1, follow instructions for toe, ending on wrong side. Break off CC1, leaving a tail for grafting. Put sts onto a holder [waste yarn].

FINISHING Same as for short sock.

Schematic for long socks

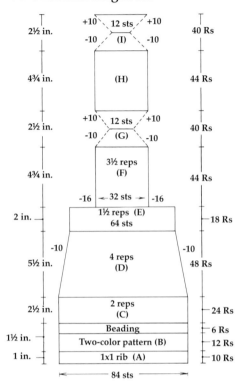

Pattern 25, color version

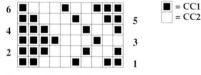

= CC1
= CC2

Repeat: 10 sts, 6 Rs.

Pattern 25

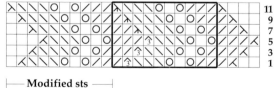

|— Modified sts —|

Repeat: 10 sts, 12 Rs.
Add 4 edge sts at Rt.
Modified st at L, all odd Rs.
Even Rs: P all sts.

This ingeniously constructed shawl uses small amounts of many colors of mohair yarn and is a perfect way to use up leftover balls. It incorporates patterns 13, 15 and 44.

Oddball intarsia shawl

I call this shawl "oddball" because it is knitted of leftover yarn from other projects that has accumulated in my closet. Like knitters everywhere, I regard yarn as a precious commodity and never throw any of it out. When my closet starts to overflow, I make lots of swatches and start designing oddball projects.

This shawl came from my bag of beautiful mohair. Mohair and knitted lace go well together, since the airiness of each is complementary to the other. From my bag I picked out all the balls that had nearly the same content of mohair and found only 12 balls, each a different color. Because of the small amounts of many colors, I designed the color pattern in small panels and stripes so that one ball of a color would last for all four pieces of the shawl. You can use more or fewer colors if you wish. If you don't have mohair, use whatever you do have, but be careful that the fiber content of all the yarns you use is compatible. You don't have to stick to the gauge or needle size given. The shawl can be made bigger with larger needles and bulkier yarn, and smaller with smaller needles and finer yarn.

The shape of the shawl is my favorite because it is so wearable. It drapes over the shoulders and comes together over the chest without bunching up around the neck. I love to wear it over a winter coat. It's knitted upside down in four pieces and uses Pattern 13 in the border, Pattern 15 in the center panels and Pattern 44 in the striped sections. Pieces 1 and 2 in the schematic on p. 186 are triangles that begin with two stitches and increase at each side to 130 stitches. Pieces 3 and 4 are half-size triangles that begin with one stitch and increase on one side only to 65 stitches. When you have finished all four triangles, you join them together in such a way that the join looks like a knitted stitch between a pair of eyelets. Then you knit a border all around in garter stitch, using the yarn that is left from the stripes and panels until it runs out.

Pieces 1 and 2 are knitted following the whole chart on pp. 186-187, but Piece 2 is knitted as a mirror image of Piece 1, with the chart flipped over. Pieces 3 and 4 are knitted using only the right half of the chart, flipping it over for Piece 4. If you have trouble mentally flipping over the chart, you can trace it onto tracing paper with a black-ink pen. Then turn over the tracing paper to view the mirrored design through the back. You can also photocopy it through the back of the tracing paper.

Oddball intarsia shawl

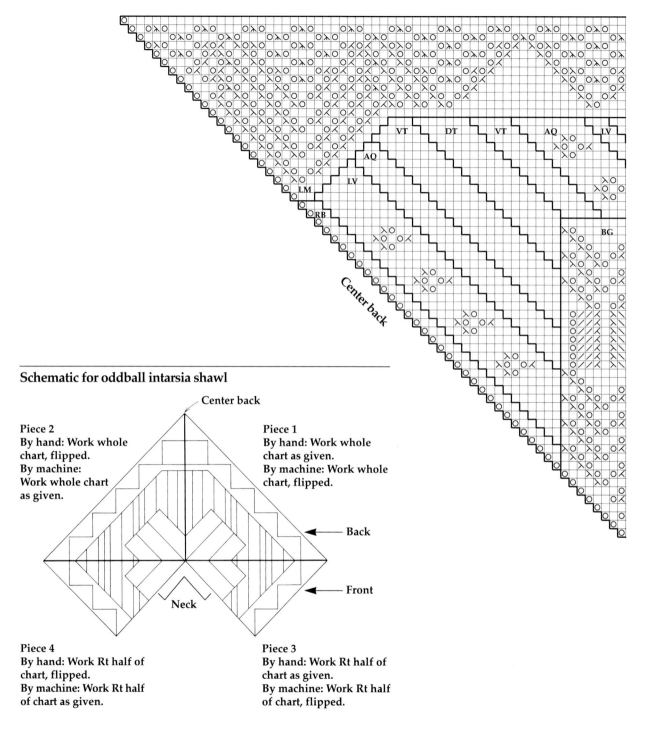

Schematic for oddball intarsia shawl

Center back

Piece 2
By hand: Work whole chart, flipped.
By machine: Work whole chart as given.

Piece 1
By hand: Work whole chart as given.
By machine: Work whole chart, flipped.

← Back

← Front

Neck

Piece 4
By hand: Work Rt half of chart, flipped.
By machine: Work Rt half of chart as given.

Piece 3
By hand: Work Rt half of chart as given.
By machine: Work Rt half of chart, flipped.

Diagram of the four pieces viewed upside down from right side. K the pieces separately in any order.

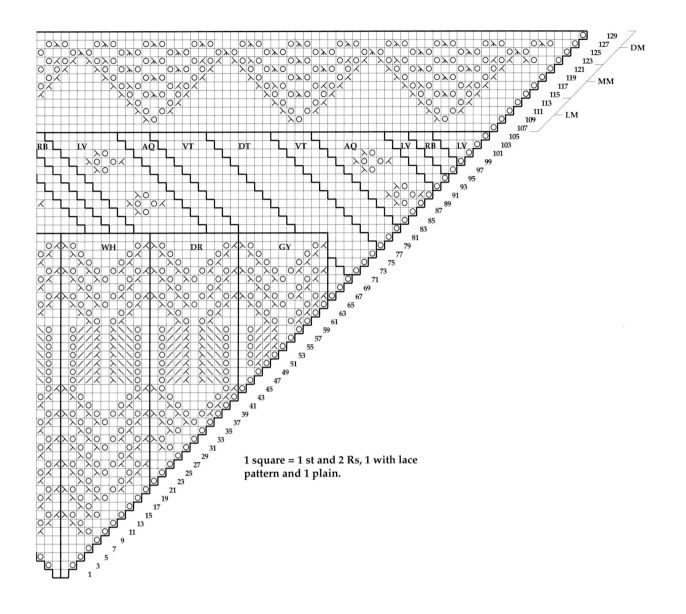

1 square = 1 st and 2 Rs, 1 with lace
pattern and 1 plain.

*Note: See "Materials" on p. 188 for an
explanation of the yarn color
abbreviations used on this chart.*

To have fewer ends to finish, leave a lengthy yarn tail at the selvedge side when you start and end every color that touches the selvedge. You can then use these to join the pieces.

Instructions for oddball shawl

SIZE After blocking, the shawl is 33 in. down center back from neck edge to point, including border.

MATERIALS 1¾-oz. (49.6-g) balls of mohair yarn with at least 75% mohair content, 1 ball each of 12 different colors. For 4 vertical panels at start of knitting, I used off-white (WH), light blue-gray (BG), light dusty rose (DR) and light gray (GY). For stripes, I used royal blue (RB), deep teal (DT), violet (VT), lavender (LV) and aquamarine (AQ). For wide border across top of knitting, I used three shades of magenta: the point and first 4 grid Rs across are in lightest shade (LM); then there are 4 grid Rs each in medium (MM) and darker (DM) shades. Ndls size U.S. 10 (6mm). Circular ndl approximately 29 in. to 32 in. long of same ndl size as for main knitting. Crochet hook or latch hook big enough to hold yarn comfortably.

FOR MACHINE KNITTING A large-gauge (bulky) machine with intarsia capability and as many ndls as possible. If you have a Passap Vario Big or one of Bond models with extension plates, you can k up to 130 ndls. Otherwise, take work off machine and onto hand-knitting ndls when you run out of machine ndls and finish knitting it by hand. Pieces 3 and 4 require only 65 ndls.

GAUGE Not of great importance. Mine is 3½ sts, 5 Rs = 1 in. in stockinette st. If you have more sts and Rs per in., your shawl will be smaller; if fewer, it will be larger.

Note: Special instructions for machine knitters are given in brackets [ ].

PROCEDURE **By hand:** Piece 1: Work chart as given.

Rows 1 and 2: On R ndl, make a sl knot in WH, then a sl knot in BG. Turn, p in each st using same colors as established, twisting yarns at color change to hold join tog. **Row 3:** With WH, yo, k1; with BG, k1. **Row 4:** With BG, yo, p1; with WH, p2. **Row 5:** With WH, yo, k2; with BG, k2. **Row 6:** With BG, yo, p2; with WH, p3.

Continue as established, beginning each R with a yo to make loops up sides. The first lace pattern begins on R 11. From that point make all odd-numbered (right-side) Rs in pattern, and p all even-numbered (wrong-side) Rs. You can make color changes on either right-side or wrong-side Rs, whichever is more convenient. When you get to end (after R 130), put all sts on a holder or piece of yarn.

Piece 2: K with whole chart flipped over to mirror pattern.

Piece 3: Use only Rt half of original chart, making 1 straight edge and 1 increased edge.

Piece 4: Use only Rt half of chart, but flip it over to mirror pattern.

By machine: Piece 2: Work whole chart as given.

Rows 1 and 2: On 2 center ndls, hang a sl knot of WH on Rt ndl and a sl knot of BG on L ndl. By hand, make a st on BG ndl; bring WH up under BG (to twist yarns) and lay in its hook from L-Rt, make a st on WH ndl. Set RC to 002, carr at Rt side. Set cam for intarsia if your carr requires it. **Row 3:** At Rt, bring 1 new ndl to w.p. Lay WH across new ndl and center ndl, bring BG yarn up from under WH (to twist) and lay in its hook. K 3rd R from Rt-L. **Row 4:** At L, bring 1 new ndl to w.p. Lay BG across new ndl and center ndl, bring WH yarn up from under BG (to twist) and lay across its 2 ndls. K 4th R from L-Rt.

Continue in this way, always adding a new needle at the carr side, every R, to make loops up sides. At RC 12, make first transfers for lace pattern. For each horizontal R on grid, you will first k 2 Rs in colors given for squares, then make indicated transfers. When you get to end (after R 130), remove sts onto waste yarn.

Piece 1: K with whole chart flipped over to mirror pattern.

Piece 4: Use only Rt half of chart, making 1 straight edge and 1 increased edge.

Piece 3: Use only Rt half of chart, but flip it over to mirror pattern.

FINISHING When all 4 pieces are done, weave and trim yarn ends except for selvedge tails.

JOINING   Lay out pieces in correct orientation with their right sides up. Start all joins at neck edge. Joining yarn always stays underneath work, with hook above work. With a separate yarn of same color as at edge (or an attached yarn tail) and a crochet hook or latch tool, poke hook down through first loop at left-hand [right-hand] side and bring up a loop of yarn on hook. Poke hook down through first loop at right-hand [left-hand] side and bring up a loop of yarn, pulling it through loop already on hook (1 sl st made). Poke hook down through second loop at left-hand [right-hand] side and bring up a loop of yarn, pulling it through loop already on hook (next sl st made). Poke hook down through second loop at right-hand [left-hand] side and bring up a loop of yarn, pulling it through loop already on hook (next sl st made). Continue this way, from side to side, always pulling up yarn of same color as loop you are poking into. When you reach end, put a safety pin in last loop, which will be picked up into border. Join should look like a plain st between two eyelets. Finish off all remaining yarn ends.

BORDER   Use whatever colors you have left. (I used one ridge each of LG, AQ, VT, then 2 ridges RB.) With circular ndl, R side facing and starting at center neck, pick up and k approximately 98 sts down one edge of front. Go around corner, making 3 sts into corner st, then k into each open loop, removing waste yarn or holding thread as you go. Make 3 sts into each joining loop that is waiting on the safety pin and 3 sts into the second corner st. Pick up about 98 sts along remaining front edge. Turn and k all the way back again, one st into each st. Turn, 1 ridge made. Make as many border ridges as you want; on right-side Rs only, inc 1 st each side of central corner sts, and dec 1 st at neck edge at beginning and ending of R. When you get to last ridge, k right-side R, then bind off in k sts on wrong-side R. With yarn end, sew 2 sides of neck edge tog.

BLOCKING   If necessary, brush shawl lightly to bring up nap. Wash in cold-water wool wash, then spin in washing machine to damp dry. Lay out a sheet on a bed or carpet and stretch out shawl. Don't pin it, just measure with a yardstick to be sure it's symmetrical and even all around.

ABBREVIATIONS USED IN THIS BOOK

B	Back.
dec(s)	Decrease(s). Subtract a stitch or stitches from a row.
e.o.r.	Every other row.
F	Front.
g	Gram(s).
in.	Inch(es).
inc(s)	Increase(s). Add a new stitch or stitches to a row.
K, k	Knit.
kwise	Knitwise. Insert the needle into a stitch as if to knit it.
L	Left.
mm	Millimeter(s).
Ndl, ndl(s)	Needle(s).
oz.	Ounce(s).
P, p	Purl.
pnso	Pass next stitch over another stitch or stitches.
psso	Pass a slipped stitch over another stitch or stitches.
p2sso	Pass 2 slipped stitches over another stitch or stitches.
pwise	Purlwise. Insert the needle into a stitch as if to purl it.
Rep, rep	Repeat.
Rt	Right.
R(s)	Row(s).
Sl, sl	Slip. Move a stitch from one needle to the other without knitting or purling it.
sl 1-k2tog-psso	Slip 1, knit 2 together, pass the slipped stitch over the knitted stitch. A double decrease that slants left. (See Symbol 26 in the Glossary of Symbols and Techniques.)
ssk	Slip, slip, knit. A single decrease that slants left. (See Symbol 21 in the Glossary of Symbols and Techniques.)
st(s)	Stitch(es).
tog	Together.
wyib	With yarn in back.
wyif	With yarn in front.
yd.	Yard(s).
yo	Yarn over. An open, or eyelet, increase.

{. . . .}	Repeat the instructions within the parentheses the number of times stated immediately following the parentheses.
. . . .	Repeat the instructions within the asterisks continuously for the pattern repeat. Instructions before and after the asterisks are for the left and right selvedges.

Additional abbreviations for machine knitters

C	Center.
carr	Carriage.
e.o.n.	Every other needle.
h.p.	Holding position.
n.w.p.	Nonworking position.
pos	Position.
RC	Row count.
w.p.	Working position.

HOW TO READ THE CHARTS

If you are experienced at reading and knitting from charts, you can skip to "Getting started" on p. 192. Machine knitters should read up to "Getting started," then move on to the Machine Knitters' Glossary starting on p. 199.

General instructions

The chart is a representation of the fabric, including selvedge stitches, as seen from the right side. One square on the chart represents one stitch in the knitting. One horizontal row of squares on the chart represents one row or round of knitting.

The odd-numbered rows are right-side rows. These are read square by square (stitch by stitch) from right to left and are knitted with the right side of the work facing the knitter. If the knitting is worked on two needles, as was the case with this sampler, the even-numbered rows are wrong-side rows. They are read square by square (stitch by stitch) from left to right and are knitted with the wrong side of the work facing the knitter. If the knitting is worked circularly, the even-numbered rows, like the odd-numbered rows, are right-side rows and are likewise read from right to left.

Each symbol represents a specific knitting operation that will produce the stitch as it appears from the front of the fabric. A complete explanation of the symbols and their actions can be found in the Glossary of Symbols and Techniques, starting on p. 193; instructions for working these stitches on a knitting machine using hand-transfer methods can be found in the Machine Knitters' Glossary on p. 199.

Specific instructions for the charts in this book

All stitches, increases, decreases and so on that are knit stitches as viewed from the right side are in white squares. Thus the knitting maneuver represented by any symbol within a white square is to be worked so as to form a knit stitch on the right side of the fabric. All stitches, increases, decreases and so on that are purl stitches as viewed from the right side are in gray squares. The maneuver represented by any symbol in a gray square is to be worked so as to create a purl stitch on the right side of the fabric. Since this sampler

is knitted mainly in stockinette stitch, the right-side rows are mostly knit stitches. Squares without symbols represent plain stitches.

Solid black squares indicate that the number of stitches per row varies from one row to another in the repeat. Since the chart must accommodate the row with the greatest number of stitches, the rows with fewer stitches have extra squares that are blacked out. Simply skip over the black squares when reading the chart.

Many of the charts do not include the even-numbered, wrong-side rows. The reason is that in these patterns, as in many lace patterns, the wrong-side rows are purled plain with no patterning. Leaving out these plain rows simplifies the chart and makes the knitted design more apparent at a glance. There is always an explanatory note to this effect with these charts.

The glossaries contain all the necessary information for making decreases and other stitches from both the right and wrong sides of the fabric. The procedure to make a particular stitch or decrease from the wrong side is usually different from the procedure to make the same stitch or decrease from the right side, but the results on the right side of the fabric will be the same.

Most charts contain at least two repeats of the pattern both vertically and horizontally. The stitches and rows in one complete repeat are outlined with a box in the lower right corner of the chart, and the number of stitches and rows in the repeat is also written with the chart. The additional repeats in the chart illustrate the overall effect of the pattern when it is repeated vertically and horizontally. Note that the number of repeats in the chart is not necessarily the same as in the sampler.

Some of the patterns have been corrected or improved from the way they were worked in the sampler. Where the patterning is incomplete in the sampler, as in patterns 3 and 30, for example, it has been completed in the chart. In several patterns, including patterns 2, 24, 49, 51, 52 and 61, the direction or pairing of decreases is inconsistent. In the charts I have usually given one or two repeats with one decrease style and one or two repeats with the other. Use whichever style you prefer.

In the charts for patterns 33, 47, 64, 75 and 90 the number of stitches and/or rows has been modified from the original sampler pattern for various reasons.

In order to make straight, even selvedges that look the same on both edges, it is sometimes necessary either to add a few extra stitches to one or both edges of the knitting, or to modify the first or last stitch or two within the repeat. Where stitches have been added, they are shown between the edge of the chart and a heavy vertical line running the height of the chart. A note accompanying the chart also indicates the number of edge stitches. Edge stitches must be added to your calculations for casting on. Where selvedge stitches within the repeat have been modified, the whole repeat is marked with "Modified st" or "Modified sts" below the chart. The charts in this book have been designed so that modified stitches nearly always occur at the end of the last repeat (at the left side of the chart) and are knitted at the end of the last right-side repeat.

Several of the sampler patterns consist of two different patterns arranged in vertical panels. In such cases, the chart identifies the repeat for each separate pattern as well as the repeat for the combined patterns.

There are a few solid, texture patterns in the sampler, as well as some patterns with small cables and crossed or twisted stitches. These patterns have special symbols, which are included in the Glossary of Symbols and Techniques with complete instructions for their interpretation.

Getting started

Two-needle knitting—The number of stitches to cast on for each horizontal repeat is the same as the number of squares in Row 1 of the repeat box, unless a note below the box indicates otherwise. Multiply the number of squares in Row 1 of the repeat box by the number of repeats to be made, then add any edge stitches. Begin Row 1 by knitting any edge stitches on the right side of the chart, then knit all the pattern repeats, modifying stitches if indicated in the last repeat. Complete the row by knitting any edge stitches at the left edge of the chart. Turn the work. Begin Row 2 from the left side of the chart and proceed in reverse order across the charted row. Work all stitches on the return row following the instructions for making the stitch from the wrong side, so that the stitches look as they should on the right side. If even-numbered rows are not given on the chart, purl these rows plain or follow the special instructions.

Circular knitting—Edge stitches and modified selvedge stitches are not necessary in circular knitting. Thus, cast on and knit only a multiple of the stitches and rows contained in the pattern repeat box, disregarding edge stitches and modified stitches.

Read the odd-numbered rows as for two-needle knitting, from right to left. But because in circular knitting all rows are worked in rounds with the right side of the fabric facing the knitter, read the even-numbered rows from right to left as well, working the stitches the same as on the odd-numbered rows. If the instructions say to purl the even-numbered rows, knit them instead.

Wherever the written instructions for a sampler pattern contain a lengthy maneuver, as in Pattern 2, for example, I have substituted the chart symbol in place of the written instruction. The chart symbol and its explanation are given at the beginning of the instructions. For a more complete explanation of the special instruction, find the symbol and its explanation in the Glossary of Symbols and Techniques.

GLOSSARY OF SYMBOLS AND TECHNIQUES

This glossary explains what each symbol used in the charts in this book represents and how to work the stitches by hand. (For information on working the patterns by machine, see the Machine Knitters' Glossary on p. 199.) The instructions assume that you know the fundamentals of knitting; if you need additional help, consult one of the knitting-technique books listed in the Bibliography on p. 205.

All the symbols in the charts are representations of the stitches as they look on the front of the work, but since you must sometimes work the stitches from the back, explanations of how to do this are included wherever appropriate. The pattern numbers in parentheses following a stitch explanation refer to the patterns in the sampler where the less common symbols are used.

A few of the decreases do not occur in the sampler patterns at all, but I have included their instructions to provide a complete glossary of lace-knitting decreases should you wish to make a substitution.

The glossaries here include only the symbols used in lace knitting and in the charts in this book. The Japanese Symbolcraft notation, from which the symbols used here derive, includes many more symbols, but they relate to other kinds of knitting. The Bibliography lists further information on the subject.

Keep a photocopy of this glossary by you as you work. You'll soon memorize the meaning of the symbols because they depict the action of the stitches or the appearance of the stitches after the action is completed.

Symbols for hand knitting

1. ☐ Knit stitch
Made from right side: Knit this stitch.
Made from wrong side: Purl this stitch.

---

2. ▨ Purl stitch
Made from right side: Purl this stitch.
Made from wrong side: Knit this stitch.
A vertical column of gray squares alternating with a vertical column of white squares indicates that pattern contains ribbing, as in Pattern 14. A horizontal row of gray squares alternating with a horizontal row of white squares indicates that pattern contains garter stitch, as in Pattern 16. Blocks of gray squares indicate that pattern has knit-purl embossing within its repeat, as in Pattern 57.

---

3. ■ Skip this space when reading chart
Black squares indicate that rows within repeat have various numbers of stitches. Since chart must be drawn to accommodate row with greatest number of stitches, rows with fewer stitches have extra squares blacked out. Placement of black squares is not significant to pattern; they have been positioned to delineate visually the pattern's elements.

---

4. ◲ ◱ Bias, or slanted, stitch
L R

A knitted or purled stitch that slants because it lies between an eyelet and its decrease. It can slant left or right. In hand knitting, a bias stitch does not require any special operation (although it does in machine knitting), but it helps the knitter visualize the design and enhances chart's information.

---

5. ☑ Slip stitch with float in back
Made from right side: With yarn in back, slip 1 stitch purlwise. (Patterns 79 and 84)
Made from wrong side: With yarn in front, slip 1 stitch purlwise. (Patterns 84 and 86)

6. ☑ Slip stitch with float in front

Made from right side: With yarn in front, slip 1 stitch purlwise. (Pattern 86)

Made from wrong side: With yarn in back, slip 1 stitch purlwise. (Patterns 72 and 79)

7. ☑ Twisted slip stitch

Made from wrong side: With yarn in front, slip 1 stitch knitwise. (Pattern 82)

8. ⌒ Bind off

Made from wrong side: Purl first stitch. *Purl next stitch. Slip first stitch over second stitch and off needle.* Continue from * to * until number of stitches necessary is bound off. There will be one stitch, already purled, remaining on right needle, which is first stitch beyond bind-off on chart. (Pattern 11; Edging 2, p. 158)

9. ▤ Wrapped stitches

Made from right side: Knit (as shown at right) 3 stitches onto an extra needle. Wrap yarn counterclockwise around the 3 stitches at least 3 times, ending on wrong side of work. Slip the 3 stitches onto right needle and continue. (Patterns 70 and 71)

Made from wrong side: Purl 3 stitches onto an extra needle. Wrap yarn counterclockwise around the 3 stitches

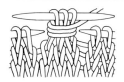

at least 3 times, ending on wrong side of work. Slip the 3 stitches onto right needle and continue. (Pattern 70)

Twisted and crossed stitches

10. ⧖ ⧗ Plain, two-stitch twist
L   R

Right twist, made from right side: As shown at right, knit second stitch from front (1), knit first stitch from front (2), then drop both from left needle together (3). Second stitch crosses to right in front of first stitch. (Pattern 84)

Alternate method: Knit first two stitches together and leave on left needle. Insert right needle between two stitches just knitted and knit first stitch again. Drop both stitches from left needle.

Left twist, made from right side: As shown at far right, reach behind first stitch and knit second stitch through its back loop (1), then knit first stitch from front as usual (2) and drop both from left needle together (3). First stitch crosses to left in front of second stitch.

Alternate method: Reach behind first stitch and knit second stitch through its back loop. Still from behind, insert right needle from right to left through back loops of both stitches together, knit them together, and drop both from left needle.

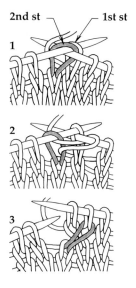

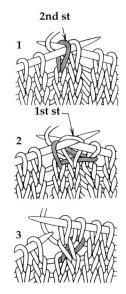

11. ⧖ ⧗ Decreased twist
L   R

Right twist, made from right side: Knit third and second stitches together from front, then knit first stitch from front and drop all from left needle together. This makes a single decrease as well as a right twist. (Pattern 85)

Left twist, made from right side: Knit second and third stitches together through their back loops, then knit first stitch through its front loop and drop all from left needle together. This makes a single decrease as well as a left twist.

12. 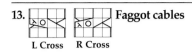 **Plain cables**

Made from right side: Slip 2 (or 3) stitches onto an extra needle and hold in back of work for a right cross or in front of work for a left cross. Knit next 2 (or 3) stitches, then knit held stitches. (Patterns 22 and 87)

13.  **Faggot cables**

Made from right side: Slip 2 stitches onto an extra needle and hold in back of work for a right cross or in front of work for a left cross. Knit next 2 stitches, yarn over, slip-slip-knit (ssk) the 2 stitches off extra needle. (Patterns 24 and 37)

Single increases: One stitch increased

14. ☐ **Yarn over**
Made from right or wrong side: Wrap yarn around needle once so that there is one new loop over top of needle. Direction of wrap depends on whether preceding and following stitches are knit or purl stitches. On next row, one stitch is knitted or purled into the new loop.
Knit, yarn over, knit or purl: If a stitch has been knitted, yarn is in back. To work yarn over, pass yarn under needle to front, then over needle to back. Yarn is in position to knit next stitch (shown at top left). If next stitch is to be purled instead, bring yarn, after passing it over needle, back under needle to front again. You can now purl next stitch (top right).
Purl, yarn over, knit or purl: If a stitch has been purled, yarn is in front. Pass yarn over needle to back. This makes yarn over, with yarn in position to knit next stitch (bottom left). If next stitch is to be purled instead, bring yarn, after passing it over needle, back under needle to front again. You can now purl next stitch (bottom right).

K, YO, K   yarn over

K, YO P   yarn over

P, YO, K   yarn over

P, YO, P   yarn over

15. ⬇ **Two-stitch increase**
Made from right side: Purl 1, knit 1 into stitch; or knit 1, purl 1 into stitch (shown at right). If you pair increases, make one of each. (Pattern 68; Medallion, p. 161)
Made from wrong side: Purl 1, knit 1 into stitch; or knit 1, purl 1 into stitch. If you pair increases, make one of each. (Pattern 68)

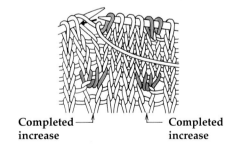

Completed —⌐   ⌐— Completed
increase   increase

16. ⊤ ⊦ Left, right increase
L   R

Increase one stitch to left, on right side: Knit into next stitch on needle, then knit into stitch in row below needle (shown at right). (Medallion, p. 161; Pattern 63 mirrored, p. 145)

Increase one stitch to right, on right side: Knit into next stitch in row below needle (shown at far right) then knit into next stitch on the needle. (Medallion, p.161; Pattern 63 mirrored, p. 145)

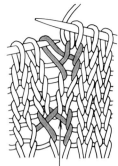

Left increase

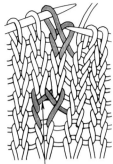

Right increase

Completed increase   Completed increase

Double increases: Two stitches increased

17. ◯◯ ◇◇ Yarn over twice

Made from right or wrong side: Wrap yarn around needle twice so that there are two new loops over top of needle. Direction of wraps depends on whether preceding and following stitches are knitted or purled.

Follow instructions for yarn over (Symbol 14), but wrap yarn twice around. On next row, knit into one loop, purl into other, unless instructed otherwise. (Patterns 11, 23, 83, 88, 89; Edging 1, p. 157, Edging 3, p. 159)

18. ⬇ Three-stitch increase

Made from right side: Knit 1, purl 1, knit 1 into same stitch, into front, back, front of stitch. (Pattern 80; Medallion, p. 161)

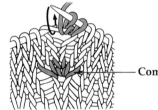

Completed increase

Single decreases: One stitch decreased

19. ⟋ Knitted, slants to right

Left stitch lies on top of right stitch. Left stitch slants to right only if yarn over is to its left; the left stitch is vertical if yarn over is to its right.

Made from right side: Knit 2 together.
Made from wrong side: Purl 2 together.

20. ⟋ Purled, slants to right

Left stitch lies on top of right stitch. Left stitch slants to right only if yarn over is to its left; left stitch is vertical if yarn over is to its right.

Made from right side: Purl 2 together. (Patterns 51, 57, 61, 64)
Made from wrong side: Knit 2 together. (Patterns 79, 81, 86; Edging 2, p. 158, Faggot 2b, p. 146)

21. ⧅ Knitted, slants to left

Right stitch lies on top of left stitch. Right stitch slants to left only if yarn over is to its right; right stitch is vertical if yarn over is to its left.

Made from right side: Slip 1 stitch knitwise, knit next stitch; then pass slipped stitch over knitted stitch (sl 1-k1-psso), as shown at right.

Alternate method: Slip 1 stitch knitwise 2 times, insert left needle into fronts of the 2 stitches from left and knit off together (ssk), as shown at far right.

Made from wrong side: Purl 1 stitch, slip 1 stitch knitwise, return both stitches to left needle. Pass slipped stitch over purled stitch, return purled stitch to right needle.

Alternate method: Slip 1 stitch knitwise 2 times, return turned stitches to left needle. Insert right needle

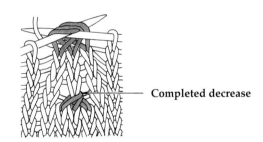

SL 1-K1-PSSO   **SSK**

Knit 1   Slip 1

Completed decrease

through back loops of the 2 stitches from left to right and purl them together (p2tog back). (Patterns 2, 11, 24, 52, 54, 55, 66, 68, 70, 73, 74, 75, 77, 89, 90)

22. ⧄ Purled, slants to left

Right stitch lies on top of left stitch. Right stitch slants to left only if yarn over is to its right; right stitch is vertical if yarn over is to its left.

Made from right side: Purl 1 stitch, slip 1 stitch knitwise, return both stitches to left needle. Pass slipped stitch over purled stitch, return purled stitch to right needle (p1-sl 1-psso).

Alternate method: Slip 1 stitch knitwise 2 times, return stitches to left needle. Insert right needle from left to

right through back loops of the 2 stitches and purl them together (p2tog back). (Patterns 57 and 64)

Made from wrong side: Slip 1 stitch knitwise, knit next stitch, pass slipped stitch over knitted stitch (sl 1-k1-psso).

Alternate method: Slip 1 stitch knitwise 2 times, insert left needle from left to right into fronts of the 2 stitches and knit off together (ssk). (Pattern 26)

23. ⧄ Twisted, slants to left

This is a special decrease, used in Tunisian knitting.

Made from right side: Insert needle from right to left

through back loops of next 2 stitches, and knit them together (k2tog back). (Pattern 82)

Double decreases: Two stitches decreased

24. ⇑ Knitted, three-stitch cluster decrease

Three stitches are turned sideways in a row. Depending on angle of stitches around this decrease, three stitches are sometimes layered with left stitch on top, slanting to the right, making it a popular substitute for Symbol 28 made from right side.

Made from right side: Knit 3 stitches together through fronts of stitches, as shown at right. (Patterns 25, 51, 68)

Made from wrong side: Purl 3 stitches together through fronts of stitches. (Patterns 2, 51, 68)

Completed decrease

25. ⬆ Purled, three-stitch cluster decrease

Made from right side: Purl 3 stitches together through fronts of stitches. (Edging 1, p. 157)

Made from wrong side: Knit 3 stitches together through fronts of stitches.

26. ⧅ Knitted, slants to left

Right stitch is on top, left stitch in middle, center stitch on bottom.

Made from right side: Slip 1 stitch knitwise, knit next 2 stitches together; then pass slipped stitch over knitted stitch (sl 1-k2tog-psso).

Made from wrong side: Purl 2 stitches together, then slip next stitch knitwise. Return both stitches to left needle, pass slipped stitch over purled stitch and return to right needle. (Patterns 11, 66, 69, 70, 73)

27. ⊠ **Purled, slants to left**

Made from right side: Purl 1, then slip 2 stitches together knitwise. Return all 3 stitches to left needle, pass 2 slipped stitches over purled stitch and return to right needle. (Pattern 57)

Made from wrong side: Slip 2 stitches together knitwise, knit next stitch, pass 2 slipped stitches over knitted stitch. (Pattern 89)

---

28. ⊠ **Knitted, slants to right**

Left stitch is on top, right stitch in middle, center stitch on bottom.

Made from right side: Slip 1, knit 1, pass slipped stitch over knitted stitch (sl 1-k1-psso), or slip one stitch knitwise separately 2 times, insert left needle from left to right into fronts of the 2 stitches and knit off together (ssk). Return stitch to left needle, pass next stitch over knitted stitch as shown and return to right needle. (Patterns 22, 48, 49, 50, 51, 61; Edging 1, p. 157; Edging 3, p. 159; Medallion, p. 161; Pattern 63, mirrored, p. 145)

Made from wrong side: Slip 1 stitch purlwise, purl 2 together back (see Stitch 21, wrong side), pass slipped stitch over purled stitch. (Pattern 2)

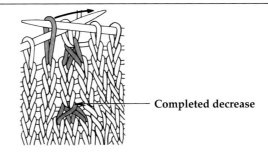

— Completed decrease

---

29. ⊠ **Purled, slants to right**

Made from right side: Slip 1 stitch knitwise 2 times, return both stitches to left needle, insert right needle into back of both stitches together and slip to right needle, purl next stitch, pass 2 slipped stitches over purled stitch.

Made from wrong side: Knit 1, slip 1 stitch knitwise 2 times, return both slipped stitches to left needle, insert right needle into back of both stitches together and slip to right needle. Move all 3 stitches to left needle, pass 2 slipped stitches over knitted stitch, return knitted stitch to right needle.

---

30. ⊠ **Knitted, vertical decrease**

Center stitch is on top, left stitch in middle, right stitch on bottom.

Made from right side: Slip 2 stitches together knitwise, knit next stitch; then pass 2 slipped stitches over knitted stitch, as shown. (Faggot 3d, p. 147)

Made from wrong side: Slip 1 stitch knitwise 2 times, return both stitches to left needle, insert right needle into back of both stitches together and slip to right needle, purl next stitch, pass 2 slipped stitches over purled stitch.

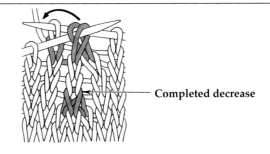

— Completed decrease

---

31. ⊠ **Purled, vertical decrease**

Made from right side: Purl 2 together, then slip 1 stitch knitwise. Return both stitches to left needle, pass slipped stitch over purled stitch, return to right needle. (Pattern 45; Pattern 92; Edging 1, p. 157; Medallion, p. 161)

Made from wrong side: Slip 1 stitch knitwise, knit next 2 stitches together, pass slipped stitch over knitted stitch (sl 1-k2tog-psso). (Pattern 80)

This section is a general explanation of the most important points about using hand-knitting lace patterns with a knitting machine. As with this book's approach for hand knitters, these instructions assume that you know the basic procedures for knitting and patterning on your machine. If you also have some knowledge of hand knitting, you will find that knitting the patterns on the machine increases your understanding of both kinds of knitting, since knitting, after all, is knitting.

The symbols used in the charts are ones commonly used for lace knitting on the machine. However, the principal concept to understand when using hand-knitting lace charts with a knitting machine is that, when making decreases, you must reverse the layering of the stitches from what is shown in the chart. That is because hand-knitting charts are drawn to show the front side of the fabric, whereas machine-knitting charts are drawn to show the back of the fabric, since this is the side the machine knitter sees as he or she knits. To help you "convert" the charts for knitting on the machine, I've provided instructions for all the decrease symbols in the Machine Knitters' Glossary that will correctly layer the stitches for the charts in this book. Many of the decreases involve more than one step and thus are time-consuming. But since these decreases make possible the entire spectrum of hand-knitted effects, the time spent is worthwhile. If you use these decreases and transfers, you can pretty much duplicate the sampler patterns on the machine.

In the section called "Streamlined decreases" (p. 204), all the decreases and transfer procedures have been defined as though the hand-knitting charts were really intended for knitting on the machine. The various styles of decrease in the full vocabulary have been consolidated so there is only one left decrease, one right decrease and one double decrease. These are the decreases that require the fewest steps or that are possible to do with the kind of automated transfer equipment in use today. They are the decreases most commonly seen in machine-knitting literature. If you want your knitting to grow faster, with fewer transfer movements for each decrease, or if you want to automate the pattern for your lace carriage, use the stitch-transfer instructions in this part of the Glossary. The finished design will look different, though not necessarily better or worse, because many of the

decreases will be layered differently than they are in the sampler, resulting in a different look to the linear parts of the design.

The knitted swatch on p. 200 shows how Pattern 33 looks when knitted on the machine using both the full vocabulary of decreases and streamlined decreases. The two pattern repeats at the bottom of the swatch were made with the hand transfers described in "Full vocabulary of decreases" (p. 202). The pattern is the same as if it were hand-knitted except that the single and double decreases in Row 7 of the diamond are transposed. When a pattern is knitted on the machine, asymmetrical elements such as these will be in a reversed position on the right side of the fabric. The top half of the swatch was knitted with streamlined decreases. You can see the differences between the decreases in the center of the triangles, the top edges of the diamond and the lower edges around the opening of the diamond.

To make it easier to use the streamlined decreases, photocopy or redraw the chart you plan to knit and change the decrease symbols to those used in streamlining or to whatever you are accustomed to. You can also combine the convenience of automated needle selection and transfers with hand transfers to gain some of the special effects of hand-knitted lace patterning not otherwise possible on the machine. A thorough explanation of converting the sampler patterns to punchcard or electronic program is beyond the scope of this book, but the sidebar on p. 201 shows an example.

The patterns that are most suitable for knitting on the machine are those that have the same number of stitches in every row of the repeat (i.e., charts without black squares) and in which the even-numbered rows are purled plain, such as patterns 4, 5 and 6. Patterns where all the rows are patterned, such as 54 and 55, are also possible. The next most suitable patterns are those that have columns of purl stitches, which periodically must be dropped and latched up to look like knit stitches as the work faces you on the machine (for example, patterns 60 and 61).

In the Classification of the Sampler Patterns on pp. 206-208, you'll find the sampler patterns grouped according to the criteria mentioned above. Using these listings you can select a pattern according to the

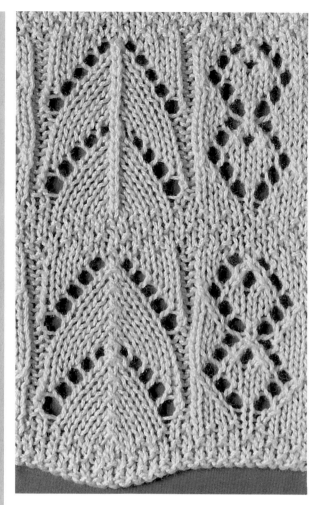

The bottom half of this swatch of Pattern 33 was knitted on a machine using hand transfers; the top half was knitted using streamlined decreases. To work the chart below, knit two rows between each row of transfers. After every 18 rows or so, drop and unravel the two columns of stitches (the gray squares) between the motifs, one column at a time, and latch up the stitches as knit stitches.

amount of automation or hand transferring you'd like to do. The patterns can be knitted manually with hand-held transfer tools on any single-bed machine, a process I term "hand-knitting on the machine," or they can be converted to punchcard or electronic program for machines equipped with lace transfer carriages.

Notes

For charts with row numbers at the right side (odd-numbered rows) only, each row on the chart means two knitted rows, with the transfers made on the second of the two rows. Every other row is missing from the chart because it is a plain row with no transfers. If there are gray squares for purl stitches in these rows, they apply to both the rows, as indicated in a note accompanying the chart. Knit two rows, then make any transfers and turn the knit stitches into purl stitches.

For charts with row numbers at both sides, each row on the chart means one knitted row. Knit one row, then make any transfers and turn knit stitches into purl stitches. If you plan to automate the pattern and therefore must make two passes with the carriage before starting the transfer sequence, you can knit the stitches with the first pass, then set the carriage to free-pass back again. Hold the resulting float of yarn out of the way during the transfers. For the next row on the chart, free-pass first, then knit the row on the return pass. Alternate these two procedures.

Cables, twisted stitches, slipped stitches and increasing a stitch by hanging a purl loop on an empty needle are standard knitting-machine symbols and patterning methods. They are not covered in this glossary.

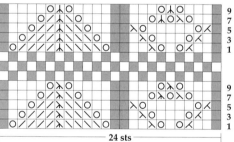

— 24 sts —

Translating patterns to punchcard or electronic program

Here is an example, using Pattern 33, of a chart for a punchcard or electronic program for automatically transferring stitches using a transfer carriage. The finished fabric will look like the top half of the swatch on the facing page. On each row, the carriage transfers the stitch from the needle that corresponds to the black square to the adjacent needle in the direction that the carriage is traveling. The first 11 rows on the card are for just the first row of pattern. This chart is suitable for the transfer carriages on Brother, Knitking and Toyota knitting machines.

To translate a pattern, transfer the stitch movements onto the card starting with the decrease itself, followed by any intervening stitches between the decrease and the eyelet. In the diagram at right, each marked square represents a selected needle that will lose its stitch to the adjacent needle in the direction the transfer carriage is moving. Compare the diagram to the chart for the pattern shown on the facing page square by square for each pattern row. In the triangle shape, each bias stitch has to be moved one at a time as the lace carriage cannot transfer two or more adjacent stitches at once. The sequences pertaining to each row of pattern are marked by brackets on the right side of the diagram.

To begin, cast on and knit two rows with the main carriage, ending at the right side. Now start the transfer carriage from the left side. At the next "2" marker, stop and knit two rows with the main carriage before starting the transfer carriage again.

Pattern 33 for punchcard or electronic program

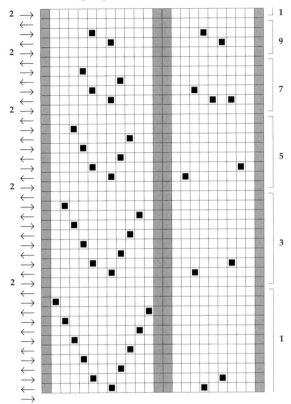

■ = Punched hole on card or black square on program grid.

▓ = Needle positions corresponding to purl stitches. At the end of each repeat, drop them one at a time and latch them up to look like knit stitches from the wrong side (purl stitches from the right side).

→ = Direction of lace carriage and stitch
← transfer. If you want these markings on your card, move them (and the "2" markers) up the appropriate number of rows for your machine.

Symbols for machine knitting

1. ☐ **Knit stitch**
A purl stitch as viewed on machine.

2. ▨ **Purl stitch**
A knit stitch as viewed on machine. After knitting row with carriage, drop stitch off needle and reknit it with latch tool to turn it around, then hang it back on needle. If there are several purl stitches in a column, wait until you come to topmost one, then drop and unravel column to row with first purl stitch and latch them up again as knit stitches. You can also use a second bed of needles or a garter-carriage accessory to make knit stitches.

3. ■ **A nonexistent stitch**
Most patterns with black squares have varying numbers of stitches in rows within repeat. Usually, work must be removed and rehung each time stitch count changes, or stitches moved inward and outward with transfer tools. If stitch count is reduced by only one stitch within repeat, you can sometimes put empty needle out of work on those rows without moving other stitches.

4. ◺ ◹ **Bias, or slanted, stitch**
◺ ◹ This stitch slants to left or right because it
L R lies between a decrease and its accompanying eyelet. You must move stitch to next needle in direction indicated when making transfer for decrease. (See "Full vocabulary of decreases" below.)

5. ⊙ **An empty needle in working position**
An empty needle in working position creates an eyelet when next row is knitted. (See "Full vocabulary of decreases," below.)

6. ⊙⊙ **Two adjacent empty needles in working position**
Leaving two empty needles in working position creates a double or very large eyelet. To neaten eyelet after making transfers, put one of empty needles out of work and knit next row. Put empty needle back in work and knit second row. Pick up loose lower thread from first row and hang it on an adjacent needle, as shown. Continue with knitting.

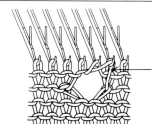
— **Loose thread from first row**

7. ◹ **Bind off**
Bind off this stitch as you would for a buttonhole if symbol is in middle of pattern; bind it off as for an armhole if symbol is on a selvedge. If it is a buttonhole bind-off to make a large eyelet, on next two rows you can cast on again using every other needle, using same procedure as for double eyelet (see Symbol 6).

Full vocabulary of decreases

The symbol O (Symbol 14 in the Glossary of Symbols and Techniques) is an empty needle when a transfer is completed. It remains in working position and will create the eyelet when the next row is knitted.

Bias stitches, indicated in the charts by the symbols / / / or \ \ \ (Symbol 4 in the Glossary of Symbols and Techniques), must be moved over by one needle toward the decrease. The number of bias stitches between a decrease and its eyelet varies from pattern to pattern and often within a pattern; in this Glossary three stitches are shown. Use a single-decker transfer tool and move the stitches one at a time, or a multiple-decker transfer tool and move them all together. Always transfer the stitches that make up the decrease first, then transfer the intervening stitches until the needle for the eyelet is empty. This procedure is also followed when automating a pattern.

If you're confused about which eyelet belongs to which decrease on a chart, start reading the chart row from either edge and circle the first eyelet and its decrease (or the first two eyelets and a double decrease) to indicate that they are paired. Work across the row until each eyelet is matched with its companion decrease.

Pairing eyelets and decreases

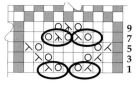

Starting at one edge, circle the first eyelet/decrease pair, then continue across row.

Single decreases: One eyelet is paired with each decrease

8. ☐◻◸
L R

Transfer right stitch to left needle, then both stitches to right needle.

L R

Completed transfer

9. ☐◻◿◿◿◸
1 2 3 L R

Transfer right stitch to left needle, then both stitches to right needle; move stitches 1, 2, 3 to right by 1 needle.

1 2 3 L R

Completed transfer

10. ◺◻◻
L R

Transfer right stitch to left needle.

L R

Completed transfer

11. ◺◿◿◿◻
L R 1 2 3

Transfer right stitch to left needle; move stitches 1, 2, 3 to left by 1 needle.

L R 1 2 3

Completed transfer

12. ◹◻
L R

Transfer left stitch to right needle, then both stitches to left needle.

L R

Completed transfer

13. ◹◿◿◿◻
L R 1 2 3

Transfer left stitch to right needle, then both stitches to left needle; move stitches 1, 2, 3 to left by 1 needle.

L R 1 2 3

Completed transfer

14. ☐◻◹
L R

Transfer left stitch to right needle.

L R

Completed transfer

15. ☐◻◿◿◿◹
1 2 3 L R

Transfer left stitch to right needle; move stitches 1, 2, 3 to right by 1 needle.

1 2 3 L R

Completed transfer
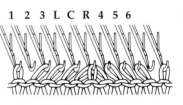

Double decreases: Two eyelets are paired with each decrease

16. ☐◻◬◻
L C R

Transfer center stitch to right needle, both stitches to left needle, then all 3 stitches to center needle.

L C R

Completed transfer

17. ☐◻◿◿◿◸◻◻◻◻
1 2 3 L C R 4 5 6

Transfer center stitch to right needle, both stitches to left needle, then all 3 stitches to center needle; move stitches 1, 2, 3 to right by 1 needle and stitches 4, 5, 6 to left by 1 needle.

1 2 3 L C R 4 5 6

Completed transfer

18. ◸◻◻◻◻☐◻
L C R 1 2 3 4

Transfer center stitch to left needle, both stitches to right needle, then all three stitches to left needle; move stitches 1, 2, 3 to left by 2 needles; move stitch 4 to left by 1 needle.

L C R 1 2 3 4

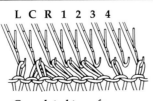

Completed transfer

19. ☐◻◬◻
L C R

Transfer center stitch to left needle, both stitches to right needle, then all 3 stitches to center needle.

L C R

Completed transfer

20.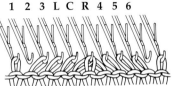
123LCR456

Transfer center stitch to left needle, both stitches to right needle, then all 3 stitches to center needle; move stitches 1, 2, 3 to right by 1 needle and stitches 4, 5, 6 to left by 1 needle.

1 2 3 L C R 4 5 6

Completed transfer

21.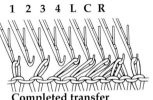
1 2 3 4 L C R

Transfer center stitch to right needle, both stitches to left needle, then all three stitches to right needle; move stitches 4, 3, 2 to right by 2 needles; move stitch 1 to right by 1 needle.

1 2 3 4 L C R

Completed transfer

22.
L C R

Transfer left stitch to center needle and right stitch to center needle.

L C R

Completed transfer

23.
1 2 3 L C R 4 5 6

Transfer left stitch to center needle and right stitch to center needle; move stitches 1, 2, 3 to right by 1 needle and stitches 4, 5, 6 to left by 1 needle.

1 2 3 L C R 4 5 6

Completed transfer

24. ☐○⇑○☐
L C R

Transfer left stitch to center needle, both stitches to right needle, then all 3 stitches to center needle.

L C R

Completed transfer

25.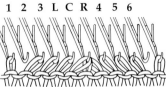
1 2 3 L C R 4 5 6

Transfer left stitch to center needle, both stitches to right needle, then all 3 stitches to center needle; move stitches 1, 2, 3 to right by 1 needle and stitches 4, 5, 6 to left by 1 needle.

1 2 3 L C R 4 5 6

Completed transfer

Streamlined decreases

Streamlined decreases are the simplest transfers to accomplish on the machine. There is one right single decrease, one left single decrease and one double decrease, all shown for single transfers as well as multiple transfers with intervening bias stitches. All the decreases from the "Full vocabulary of decreases" are consolidated under these transfers. You can substitute these transfers in any of the patterns, but remember that the lines of decreases will have a different appearance, although the eyelets and bias stitches will be unchanged. If you plan to translate a pattern for your transfer carriage, use these decreases, since these are the ones that the lace carriage is able to accomplish automatically. The sidebar on p. 201 shows an example of Pattern 33 translated for transfer carriage.

26. ☐○╱☐   Transfer left stitch to right needle. (See
   L R   Symbol 14 in the Machine Knitters' Glossary.)
☐○╲☐
   L R

27. ☐○╱╱╱╱☐   Transfer left stitch to right needle;
  1 2 3 L R   move stitches 1, 2, 3 to right by 1
☐○╱╱╱╲☐   needle. (See Symbol 15 in Machine
  1 2 3 L R   Knitters' Glossary.)

28. ☐╲○☐   Transfer right stitch to left needle. (See
  L R   Symbol 10 in the Machine Knitters' Glossary.)
☐╱○☐
  L R

29. ☐╲╲╲╲○☐   Transfer right stitch to left needle;
 L R 1 2 3   move stitches 1, 2, 3 to left by 1
☐╱╲╲╲○☐   needle. (See Symbol 11 in Machine
 L R 1 2 3   Knitters' Glossary.)

30. `O⊼O`
L C R
`O⋏O`
L C R
`O⋏O`
L C R
`O⇕O`
L C R
Transfer left stitch to center needle and right stitch to center needle. (See Symbol 22 in Machine Knitters' Glossary.)

31. `O╱╱╱⊼╲╲╲O`
1 2 3 L C R 4 5 6
`O╱╱╱⋏╲╲╲O`
1 2 3 L C R 4 5 6
`O╱╱╱⋏╲╲╲O`
1 2 3 L C R 4 5 6
`O╱╱╱⇕╲╲╲O`
1 2 3 L C R 4 5 6
Transfer left stitch to center needle and right stitch to center needle; move stitches 1, 2, 3 to right by 1 needle and stitches 4, 5, 6 to left by 1 needle. (See Symbol 23 in Machine Knitter's Glossary.)

32. `⊼╲╲╲O╲O`
1 2 3 4 5 6 7
`O╱O╱╱╱⊼`
7 6 5 4 3 2 1
Transfer stitch 2 to needle 1, then stitch 3 to needle 1; move stitches 4, 5, 6 to needles 2, 3, 4; move stitch 7 to needle 6.

BIBLIOGRAPHY

General knitting techniques

Compton, Rae. *The Illustrated Dictionary of Knitting.* Loveland, Colo.: Interweave Press, 1989.

Hiatt, June H. *The Principles of Knitting.* New York: Simon and Schuster, 1989.

Mountford, Debra, ed. *Harmony Guide to Knitting Techniques and Stitches.* New York: Lyric Books Ltd., 1992.

Righetti, Maggie. *Knitting in Plain English.* New York: St. Martin's Press, 1986.

Stanley, Montse. *The Handknitter's Handbook.* London: David & Charles, 1986

Thomas, Mary. *Mary Thomas's Knitting Book.* London: Hodder and Stoughton Ltd., 1938. Reprint. New York: Dover Publications, 1972.

Editors of *Vogue Knitting* magazine. *Vogue Knitting.* New York: Pantheon Books, 1989.

Zimmermann, Elizabeth. *Knitting Without Tears.* New York: Charles Scribner's Sons, 1971.

—. *Knitting Workshop.* Pittsville, Wis.: Schoolhouse Press, 1981

Lace knitting patterns and techniques

Don, Sarah. *The Art of Shetland Lace.* London: Bell & Hyman Ltd., 1981. Reprint. Berkeley, Calif.: Lacis, 1991.

Eichenseer, Erika. *Strickmuster für Mode & Tracht.* Rosenheim, Germany: Rosenheimer Verlagshaus, 1991.

Fanderl, Lisl. *Bauerliches Stricken.* Rosenheim, Germany: Rosenheimer Verlagshaus, 1975.

—. *Bauerliches Stricken 3.* Rosenheim, Germany: Rosenheimer Verlagshaus, 1983.

Goldberg, Rhoda. *New Knitting Dictionary.* New York: Crown, 1984.

Hewitt, Furze. *Knit One, Make One.* Kenthurst, Australia: Kangaroo Press, 1990.

—. and Billie Daley. *Classic Knitted Cotton Edgings.* Kenthurst, Australia: Kangaroo Press, 1987.

—. *Motifs, Borders and Trims.* Kenhurst, Australia: Kangaroo Press, 1988.

Kinzel, Marianne. *First Book of Modern Lace Knitting.* England: Artistic Needlework Publications, 1954. Reprint. New York: Dover Publications, 1972.

—. *Second Book of Modern Lace Knitting.* London: Mills & Boon Ltd., 1961. Reprint. New York: Dover Publications, 1972.

Lorant, Tessa. *Hand and Machine Knitted Laces.* London: B.T. Batsford Ltd., 1982.

—. *Knitted Lace Collars*. Somerset, United Kingdom: Thorn Press, 1983.

—. *Knitted Shawls and Wraps*. Somerset, United Kingdom: Thorn Press, 1984.

—. *Knitted Quilts & Flounces*. Somerset, United Kingdom: Thorn Press, 1982.

—. *Collection of Knitted Lace Edgings*. Somerset, United Kingdom: Thorn Press, 1981.

Phillips, Mary Walker. *Creative Knitting: A New Art Form*. New York: Van Nostrand Reinhold, 1971. Reprint. St. Paul, Minn.: Dos Tejedoras, 1986.

Thomas, Mary. *Mary Thomas's Book of Knitting Patterns*. London: Hodder and Stoughton Ltd., 1943. Reprint. New York: Dover Publications, 1972.

Walker, Barbara G. *A Treasury of Knitting Patterns*. New York: Charles Scribner's Sons, 1982.

—. *A Second Treasury of Knitting Patterns*. New York: Charles Scribner's Sons, 1985.

—. *Charted Knitting Designs*. New York: Charles Scribner's Sons 1982.

Machine-knitting techniques and lace patterning

Gartshore, Linda. *The Machine Knitter's Dictionary*. London: B.T. Batsford Ltd., 1983.

Guagliumi, Susan. *Hand-Manipulated Stitches for Machine Knitters*. Newtown, Conn.: The Taunton Press, 1990.

Kinder, Kathleen. *Techniques in Machine Knitting*. London, B.T. Batsford Ltd., 1983.

—. *Machine Knitting: The Technique of Lace*. London: B.T. Batsford Ltd., 1992.

Lewis, Susanna and Julia Weissman. *A Machine Knitter's Guide to Creating Fabrics*. Asheville, N.C.: Lark Books, 1986. Reprint. New York: Sterling Press, 1987. Reprint. Poole, Cheshire, United Kingdom: Metropolitan Publishers, 1992.

Nabney, Janet. *An Illustrated Handbook of Machine Knitting*. London: B.T. Batsford Ltd., 1987.

Pattern arrangement

Stevens, Peter S. *Handbook of Regular Patterns*. Cambridge, Mass.: The MIT Press, 1981.

Washburn, Dorothy K., and Donald W. Crowe. *Symmetries of Culture*. Seattle: University of Washington Press, 1988.

Japanese publishers of knitting books using Symbolcraft

Kodansha
Nihon Vogue
Ondori

Nearly all the books and periodicals from these publishers have titles and brief text in Japanese, with many photos, diagrams and Symbolcraft notation for the patterns. You can find them in Japanese bookstores throughout the country and often in the needlecraft section of other bookstores. Information and a catalog of current Nihon Vogue books and magazines can be obtained by sending a self-addressed, large envelope with first-class postage for 3 oz. to Yo's Needlecraft, 940 East Dominguez, Suite P., Carson, CA 90746 (310) 515-6473.

CLASSIFICATION OF THE SAMPLER PATTERNS

The sampler patterns are classified here according to the many different subjects discussed in the text, so that it's easy to find all the patterns in the sampler that share a given characteristic. For example, you can locate all the patterns that have motifs of vertical zigzags or all those arranged as stacked triangles. At the end of this section are further classifications pertaining to knitting the pattern on a knitting machine.

Pattern arrangements

All-over arrangements
Alternating adjacent motifs (tessellated patterns): 4, 9, 11, 12, 26, 29, 36, 38, 45, 46, 59, 68, 70, 78, 91
Alternating inverted triangles: 13, 15, 35
Alternating lopped triangles: 16, 56, 57
Alternating spaced motifs: 3, 20, 40, 42, 53, 76, 89
Alternating stacked motifs: 7, 17

Half-dropped motifs: 25, 32, 51, 60, 77
Stacked diamonds: 5, 10, 18, 44, 48, 49, 63, 73
Stacked lopped triangles: 58
Stacked triangles: 14, 24, 33, 34, 61, 69
Staggered lopped triangles: 65
Diagonal stripes or panels: 1, 19, 21, 47, 62, 75, 85
Horizontal stripes or panels: 2, 13, 15, 23, 31, 35, 73, 90
Vertical stripes, panels or columns: 6, 10, 22, 24, 25, 27, 28, 32, 33, 37, 41, 43, 44, 50, 51, 52, 55, 58, 60, 61, 63, 64, 65, 67, 69, 77, 87, 88

Motifs

Fan: 2, 52
Fancy grouped diamonds (medallions): 5, 7, 17, 29, 48, 74
Fern: 24, 51, 61
Flower: 43
Horseshoe: 32, 33, 34, 69
Large boxy shapes: 14, 18, 38, 63, 66, 73, 74, 75, 91
Leaf: 50
Leaves from diamonds and triangles: 12, 36, 38, 45, 46, 47, 64, 65, 78, 89, 90
Zigzags, horizontal: 13, 15, 17, 35, 74, 90
Zigzags, vertical: 6, 16, 25, 52, 54, 56, 57, 60, 65, 77, 87

Ground patterns

Diamonds: 4, 5, 7, 8, 19, 22, 30, 33, 34, 40, 42, 43, 47, 57, 58, 59, 64, 90
Eyelet meshes: 21, 23, 31, 39, 83, 88, 89
Faggots: 14, 24, 27, 28, 37, 41, 50, 51, 53, 55, 61, 63, 67, 69, 76, 81
One-stitch diagonal stripes: 1, 3, 10, 20, 43, 46, 47, 49, 55, 66, 73, 91
    Horizontal zigzags: 17, 35
    Mirrored: 12, 29, 48
    Vertical zigzags: 65
Spot patterns: 44, 35, 62, 76

Knit-purl textures

Garter stitch and variants: 16, 18, 21, 22, 23, 31, 59, 72, 80, 81, 83, 88, 89
Narrow ribs: 14, 36, 37, 41, 44, 63
Purl stitches as accents or outlines: 2, 15, 24, 28, 33, 38, 45, 50, 51, 61, 87
Small areas of purl stitches: 26, 56, 57, 58, 64
Wide ribs: 60, 67

Other texture patterns

Brioche patterns
    Faggot pattern: 81
    Fisherman rib: 79
    Honeycomb pattern: 86
    Tunisian: 82
Crosses, twists and textures
    Blackberry: 80
    Cables: 22, 24, 37, 87
    One-step crosses or twists: 84, 85
    Wrapped stitches: 70, 71
Slip-stitch patterns: 72, 84

Chevrons

Chevron eyelets with adjacent decreases
    Diagonal outlines: 5, 9, 11, 18, 26, 36, 43, 66, 68, 70, 73, 75
    Diagonal lines in one direction: 1, 3, 21, 39, 55, 62, 75
    Diagonal lines in mirror image: 29, 48, 66
    Fillers of one-stitch diagonal stripes: 10, 12, 46, 49
    Lattices: 20-91
    Zigzags, horizontal: 13, 15, 17, 35, 74
    Zigzags, vertical: 65, 77, 87
Chevron eyelets with adjacent decreases crossing over the eyelets: 25, 39, 90
Chevron eyelets with combined vertical and diagonal decreases: 56
Chevron eyelets with decreases separated and parallel: 25, 56, 57, 58, 60, 65
Chevron eyelets with decreases in vertical columns: 16, 32, 34, 38, 45, 46, 47, 54, 59, 69, 88, 89
Chevrons patterned every row: 66, 69, 73, 74, 75
Elongated chevrons: 26, 56
Faggoted chevrons: 24, 54
Two-eyelet chevrons: 25, 51, 61, 78

Bias effects

Eyelets and decreases, separated and parallel, moving diagonally
    Balanced on horizontal axis: 25, 56, 57, 60
    Balanced on vertical axis: 56, 57, 58, 65
Eyelets with adjacent decreases
    Balanced on horizontal axis: 66, 77
    Unbalanced: 1, 3, 21, 31, 39, 55, 62, 75
Eyelets and decreases separated and in vertical columns
    Balanced on horizontal axis: 52
    Balanced on vertical axis: 15, 38
    Unbalanced: 64
Patterns with black squares: 2, 46, 50, 52, 58, 59, 64, 65, 83, 88, 89

INDEX OF TECHNIQUES

Editor: Mary Galpin Barnes
Senior editor: Christine Timmons
Designer/layout artist: Catherine Cassidy
Copy/production editor: Pam Purrone
Illustrator: Lee Hov
Charts: Jeanne Criscola, Andie DiFranza
Photographer: Susan Kahn, p. 118, 122, 129, 130, 132-134,
136-138, 144-147, 150, 157-160, 171, 172, 174, 178, 182, 185, 200

Typeface: Palatino
Paper: Warren Patina Matte, 70 lb., neutral pH